PROFOUND RETARDATION AND MULTIPLE IMPAIRMENT

Volume 1: Development and Learning

PROFOUND RETARDATION AND MULTIPLE
IMPAIRMENT

Volume 1: Development and Learning
Volume 2: Education and Therapy

Profound Retardation and Multiple Impairment
Volume 1: Development and Learning

JAMES HOGG, Ph.D. and JUDY SEBBA, Ph.D,
Hester Adrian Research Centre, University of Manchester

AN ASPEN PUBLICATION
Aspen Publishers, Inc.
Rockville, Maryland
1987

Library of Congress Cataloging in Publication Data

Hogg, J. (James)
  Profound Retardation and Multiple Impairment

  An Aspen Publication.
  Contents: V. 1. Development and Learning — V. 2.
Education and Therapy.
  Includes Index.
  1. Mentally Handicapped — Diseases. 2. Vision Disorders
3. Hearing Disorders. 4. Physically Handicapped.
5. Developmental Psychobiology. 6. Handicapped — Functional
Assessment. 7. Mentally Handicapped — Education. I. Sebba,
Judy. II. Title. (DNLM: 1. Handicapped. 2. Mental
Retardation. WM 300 H716P)
RC570.7.H64   1986   371.92'8   86-20670

CONTENTS

*To our parents
for their support and interest
over the years*

ACKNOWLEDGEMENTS

We would like to thank several people for their detailed reading of individual chapters in these volumes, particularly Judith Coupe, Alison Frankenberg, Chris Kiernan, Elena Lieven, Peter Mittler, Ivan Tucker and David Wood. The chapters are undoubtedly improved as a result of their constructive and critical comments, though the shortcomings remain the writers' responsibility.

We are also grateful to those who have allowed us to use their assessment and curriculum material, notably Judy Bell, Christine Gunstone, Rebecca Fewell, John Presland, Gerry Simon, Jenny Warner and Chris Williams.

Many ideas have been derived from comments and discussions from participants and tutors involved in BIMH Workshops on 'The Education of People with Profound and Multiple Handicap', and from Colin Robson who has been engaged in evaluating this course.

Thanks, too, must be given to those people with whom we have worked over the years who are profoundly retarded and multiply handicapped and to their parents. It is encounters with them that have challenged our ideas and raised new questions to be addressed.

We are particularly indebted to Christine Houghton and Nicky Stoddart for typing the full manuscript of this volume and dealing with our continual and often disorganised requests for further changes.

Finally, we would like to express our gratitude to our families for their support over the years in which we have written these volumes.

PREFACE

This is the first of two volumes concerned with the development and education of people with profound retardation and multiple impairments. While we deal in some detail in the first chapter of this volume with the choice of this terminology and the definition we have employed, it is worthwhile here to comment briefly on our choice of terms. Until the quite recent past, the term 'idiot' was acceptable in describing individuals who, relative to their age, showed the *most* limited mental development of those considered 'mentally handicapped'. Indeed, some of the papers cited in this volume will be seen to have the term 'idiot' in their titles, employing the word in a neutral and scientific fashion. While the pejorative connotation of this word led to its being dropped from the vocabulary of the field, the original meaning of the Greek term 'idiotes' was 'a private person', one who was, in fact, 'unfathomable'.

It is this meaning that is conveyed in our own chosen term, 'profound'. Such individuals are indeed unfathomable in the sense that it is only with extreme difficulty that we can understand what they experience and their capacity for relating to and influencing the world around them. Much of the research reported in this volume can be seen as an attempt more fully to understand the abilities of people with profound retardation in these respects. In addition to this sense of 'profound', there is also the use of the term to define a sub-group of individuals who are mentally handicapped in terms of formal classification systems. Thus, in using 'profound retardation' we are able to give a fairly exact set of criteria in relation to intelligence and adaptive behaviour that can be recognised by others. Use of such criteria also ensure that we do really focus on the group with which we are concerned and do not drift upwards with respect to ability, as has so often occurred in the past in similar discussions.

It has not proved possible to be quite so exact with respect to our choice of the term 'multiple impairments'. While published work often does specify an Intelligence Quotient for the individuals studied, exact assessment data on vision, hearing and physical impairments are rarely given. However, we make the assumption that if such impairments are reported in people also assessed as profoundly retarded, then the detrimental effects of such impairments on the individual's adaptive functioning is sufficiently in evidence for us to consider them within our overall definition.

To both research workers and those providing services, people with profound retardation and multiple impairments have constituted a major challenge with respect to understanding their functioning and delivering appropriate programmes. Work in both respects has tended to lag behind that with more able people with retardation, though as these two volumes bear testimony, there is now a considerable body of literature and practice with which those concerned with such people should be familiar. While care and nurturing of people with profound retardation are essential elements of provision, it is also crucial that we fully appreciate and analyse their psychological and behavioural functioning as well. There is no easy way to approach this task. Those working with this group must have a background that enables them to understand not only the nature of the disabilities, but also what to do with this knowledge.

In this volume we present this essential background, a background that goes some way beyond a specific concern with profound retardation and multiple impairment in their own right. Later in the volume we show the extent to which progress has been made in our understanding of people with profound retardation through analysis of their behaviour in a developmental framework. In order to make this information accessible, we summarise much of the relevant information on developmental theory and experiment in Chapter 3. The choice of material for inclusion here has been determined by its relevance to the work on profound retardation discussed subsequently rather than any attempt to be comprehensive in coverage.

There is a second area of developmental research that is equally relevant to those concerned with profound retardation, though somewhat less accessible. This is the effect of specific sensory and physical impairments on early development. In Chapters 4, 5 and 6 we bring together this information with reference, respectively, to visual, hearing and physical impairment. Again, we believe that knowledge of such impairments on development is essential if we are to understand and improve our provision for people with profound retardation and multiple impairments. The way in which we use such information is still open to much discussion, however. Do additional impairments simply add together or do they interact and compound each other? We set the scene for Chapters 3 to 6 in Chapter 2, where briefly we discuss this issue. Perhaps most progress will be made in understanding the effects of additional impairments on the development of people who are profoundly retarded through carefully monitored intervention programmes by those dealing with this group on a day to day basis. Certainly at present the available information from research is limited.

Again, pursuing the issue of background knowledge, we turn in Chapter 7 to recent advances in developmental assessment that have proved of value in beginning to understand people with profound retardation. In Chapter 8, the actual studies that have been undertaken are drawn together, and it is at this point that we are able to begin a synthesis of the various strands that have been previously laid down in the book. In Chapter 9 we turn to the relation between learning and development, an important bridge if we are to utilise our knowledge of development in behavioural programmes that derives from the field of learning studies. It is here, too, that we describe the nature of learning in people with profound retardation.

It is our hope that this wide-ranging background will lead to a fuller understanding of people with profound retardation and multiple impairments. Certainly we can anticipate that as developmental theory advances, so will our understanding of this group. This will be further enhanced by advances in technology, particularly with respect to microelectronics, which increase the range of behaviours the individual can engage in and which we in turn can observe. In addition, progress is already being made in the use of physiological measures to determine what is being perceived and understood in people for whom overt behavioural indications are not possible.

The value of the background presented in Volume 1 ultimately depends on how far it enables those working with people with profound retardation and multiple impairments to enhance development and adaptive functioning through intervention. In Volume 2, subtitled *Education and Therapy*, we consider the other streams that must also be channelled into this activity. In the first chapter of that volume we go beyond developmental assessment to consider a range of other instruments that contribute to the development of suitable programmes. These include measures of adaptive functioning as well as sensory and physical abilities. In Chapter 2, the elements of assessment are brought together in a wider account of a curriculum model that provides the overall framework for intervention with both children and adults. Succeeding chapters then deal with broad areas of the curriculum, notably, the development of cognition (Chapter 3), of communication (Chapter 4), of motor development and competence (Chapter 5) and of self-help skills (Chapter 6). In these chapters, much of the intervention work described draws heavily on the developmental background presented in Volume 1. In Chapter 7 we discuss behaviour problems in this population and some of the main techniques that have been employed in dealing with them. Specifically we focus on self-injurious and stereotyped behaviour, though the techniques described are generalisable to other forms of behaviour disorder.

While much of the material we have drawn on is concerned with behavioural methods, we also offer accounts and where possible studies of other forms of therapy and intervention relevant to this group. In some instances, for example, physiotherapy, the main responsibility for such work will rest with a qualified professional. However, these activities cannot be exclusively restricted to such professionals, and we provide some background on the possible roles of teachers and trainers in these areas.

In order to ensure that these volumes were ever completed, some decisions had to be taken on what to omit from them. Above we commented that issues of care are not the whole story with respect to this group. While this is certainly the case, care activities and medical provision are essential elements in any service for people with profound retardation and multiple impairments. Issues of health care, use of drugs, control of epilepsy and so on have all been omitted. We hope to remedy this situation in a third, edited, volume to which specialists will contribute accessible accounts on a range of relevant issues. Similarly, we virtually excluded reference to the family needs of those with a son or daughter with profound retardation and multiple impairment. At present we are engaged in an extensive survey on this issue and hope that in due course this will be made available to the interested reader.

It is our hope that these volumes, whatever their imperfections, will focus attention on this group of people; that they will encourage those working in the field to acknowledge the complexity of their task and the extent of the information they are obliged to draw on, if they are to fulfil this task effectively. We hope, too, that the books will stimulate more systematic studies of the understanding and abilities of people with profound retardation and multiple impairments, in order that the task of fathoming the unfathomable can be realised.

1 DEFINITIONS AND PREVALENCE

This chapter defines the population with which this book is concerned. We recognise the need for classification systems both for research and for administrative purposes of resource allocation. However, we are also aware of the danger of classification being used to deny people the right of access to services. The text which follows is restricted to discussion of a relatively well defined group although many aspects of the development, assessments and techniques we describe are applicable to others as well.

Uses and Limitations of Definitions

In order to define our population, various terms are available in current usage such as 'profoundly mentally handicapped', 'profoundly multiply handicapped', 'special care', 'profoundly retarded' and 'special needs'. Some definitions are based on performance on normative assessment tests, others refer to the functional skills of the child such as dressing and continence and still others may depend on the services received by the individual, such as whether he or she is in a particular class of a special school or special needs unit of a daycare facility. The choice of definition for a particular individual is partly determined by the purpose for which it is required. Those in daily contact with the individual with responsibility for developing educational or training programmes, might be more interested in a definition based on functional skills, than in one based on a numerical score.

We have chosen to use the term 'retardation' rather than 'mental handicap' because it is still the term used in the major classification systems such as that provided by the American Association on Mental Deficiency and described later in this chapter. In addition, we prefer the use of 'retardation' as it avoids the necessity to include the term 'mental' which seems to have been the root of historical confusions between retardation and psychiatric disorders. The term 'impairment' is used to describe a sensory or physical system which is severely dysfunctional. This dysfunction can have handicapping consequences, though through education, therapy or changes in the environment some consequences can be reduced or eliminated.

Distinction between Aetiology and Diagnosis

MacKay (1976) has clarified the distinction between aetiology, or cause of retardation, and diagnostic label. The example he chooses is 'microcephaly' which is frequently given as an aetiology but which is really a descriptive term based on the measurement of the person's relative head circumference. It does not provide an explanation of why the retardation occurred. For example, Down's Syndrome is frequently given as an aetiology when it is really a descriptive term associated with a particular chromosome abnormality and does not actually indicate the factors which might have caused it to occur. This confusion pervades studies of the causes of retardation.

Distinction between Incidence and Prevalence

Marozas, May and Lehman (1980) have highlighted the confusion which exists between the use of the terms 'incidence' and 'prevalence' and have shown that in many texts they are used interchangeably. They suggest the universal adoption of Morton and Hebel's (1978) definitions of incidence as the number of new cases of a condition identified in a population over a period of time and prevalence as the number of people in a population who have the condition at a given point in time.

In keeping with this distinction, it is prevalence rates rather than incidence rates which are reported, unless otherwise specified. The distinction between prevalence and incidence is important because the prevalence of severe retardation has increased in recent years due to reduced infant mortality rates but the trends in incidence are not yet clear (Alberman 1984). Both these rates are further affected by changes in definition and assessment procedures.

The Definition of Multiple Impairment

This book is concerned with people who are profoundly retarded and multiply impaired. Thus, the person must be not only profoundly retarded but will have one or more additional impairments to physical, auditory or visual function or some combination of such impairments. This chapter reviews definitions of profound retardation and these impairments and prevalence of each of them in turn. There are likely to be some people who are multiply impaired who are not retarded including many of those who have physical or sensory impairments.

Definitions and Prevalence of Profound Retardation

Definitions of Profound Retardation

The most commonly used classification system is based on psychometric assessment of intelligence and distinguishes between profound and other degrees of retardation. This is provided by the American Association on Mental Deficiency (Grossman 1983) and is based on obtained intelligence quotients (IQs) from tests such as the Stanford-Binet Intelligence Scale or the Cattell Infant Intelligence Scale. There are as follows:

Category	*IQ Range*
Mild	50–55 to approx. 70
Moderate	35–40 to 50–55
Severe	20–25 to 35–40
Profound	Below 20 or 25

(Adapted from Grossman 1983 p.13)

This system classifies according to IQ scores and provides a definition of profound retardation based on normative assessment tests. IQ scores are used because intelligence tests have been standardised on sufficiently large populations to give a figure for an average intelligence of 100 with a standard deviation of 15 IQ points. The rest of the population are distributed evenly either side of this figure with people described as profoundly retarded deviating 5 standard deviations from this average point. We recognise the shortcomings of measuring and using IQ scores but they are used to enable us to relate the performance of an individual to that of his or her peers (Berger and Yule 1986). An alternative definition of profound retardation based on normative assessments, derived from developmental scales rather than IQ scores, is suggested by Hogg, Foxen and McBrien (1981) in which the term 'profound retardation' is applied to children whose Mental Age is less than or equal to one quarter of their Chronological Age.

Limitations of using normative assessments with people who are profoundly retarded are discussed in Chapter 1 of Volume 2 and have led to definitions of profound retardation based on a description of the person's functional skills or lack of them. Thus, Presland (1982), who describes 'special care' children as profoundly mentally handicapped or functioning as though they were, suggests they have virtually no language, are barely ambulant and have difficulty manipulating objects as well as being unable to feed, dress or toilet themselves. A further functional definition comes from Sontag, Burke and York (1973) who describe them as children who are usually not toilet trained, display severe behaviour problems, are nonverbal, delayed in self-help, social and motor skill development and may suffer from severe physical or sensory impairments. Staff interviewed in a survey of profoundly mentally handicapped children in Scotland (Browning, Bailey and Clark 1981) listed similar characteristics to those mentioned in these functional definitions.

The National Development Team (NDT) set up by the British Government as an independent body to offer practical advice and guidance to authorities providing services for people who are mentally handicapped has classified mentally handicapped people according to their level of dependency (National Development Team 1985), the highest level of dependency constituting Group IV who are characterised as severely handicapped, doubly incontinent with multiple physical handicaps, severe epilepsy, extreme hyperkinetic behaviour and aggressive to self and others. This offers a further functional definition but like some of the others given above, suffers from grouping so many imprecise characteristics together. It is unlikely that any individual within the category will have all the characteristics attributed to it. The NDT Group IV category can therefore only be seen as approximating the population we have described as profoundly retarded and multiply impaired.

A further way of defining profound retardation is based on the services received by them. The National Development Team identified the service needs of their Group IV residents as mostly requiring some form of long-term residential care with higher staffing ratios than are required by less dependent groups. Prior to 1975, profound retardation was defined in Scotland in terms of exclusion from educational services because these individuals were considered to be suffering from a disability of such a nature as to make them unsuitable for education or training (Browning, Bailey and Clark 1981). Prior to the 1970 Education Act in England and Wales, children with moderate, profound and severe retardation were considered ineducable, in that they were not the responsibility of the education authorities.

In one of the functional definitions given above, profoundly retarded people were described as 'special care'. This term originated in the designating of certain classes in schools for Educationally Subnormal (Severe) children (ESNS), as 'special care' classes or more recently 'special needs' classes. However, a survey of ESNS schools in the North-west of England (Preddy and Mittler 1981) suggests that only 10 per cent of the children in special care classes had an IQ of less than 25 or had been labelled untestable. This figure may have been depressed by the lack of information on the intellectual status of the children, but somewhat surprisingly over two-thirds of the children with an IQ of less than 25 or labelled untestable were not in the special care classes. It appears that profound retardation alone is less likely to be synonymous with 'special care' than severe retardation (on the previous definitions given) with additional impairments. The high proportion of children with multiple impairments in special care classes will become evident later in this chapter.

Fryers (1984) has pointed out that functional definitions which describe the current skills of the individual may reflect lack of educational opportunity rather than potential. The detailed specifications of services required cannot therefore rely on such imprecise definitions. He points out that a functional definition would need to be standardised and reproducible, in order to make estimates of prevalence, to which we now turn, possible.

Prevalence of Profound Retardation

The prevalence of profound retardation is difficult to establish, figures varying with the type of definition adopted. Bernsen (1981) concluded that 42 per cent of 154 people with severe retardation (defined as IQ < 50 aged 4–22 years) in Denmark were profoundly retarded, whereas Fryers (1984) noted that the proportion of 5–9 year olds with severe retardation (also defined as IQ < 50) who were profoundly retarded varied from 50 per cent to 20 per cent from 1961 to 1980. The proportion of children receiving 'special care' has clearly increased during this time period, but as noted above 'profound retardation' and 'special care' are not synonymous. Fryers offers several possible explanations for this apparent decrease. These include increasing longevity due to better medical care not really having affected those who were mostly profoundly retarded. Another explanation concerns greater degrees of early stimulation and less illness resulting in higher functioning for some of this group. Dupont (1981) also in Denmark reports that 2.5 per cent of retarded people living in the community were profoundly retarded compared to 20.4 per cent of those living in institutions. Linna, Koivisto and Herva (1981) report that 13.5 per cent of 1,000 retarded people they surveyed in Finland were profoundly retarded. Considering residents of long-stay hospitals (mostly adult) with retardation assessed as part of the work of the National Development Team (1985), 43 per cent were defined as Group IV dependency.

The proportion of populations with retardation which is defined as profoundly retarded varies according to the age group concerned as shown by figures from Jacobson, Sutton and Janicki (1985) in Table 1.1.

Table 1.1: Proportion of People with Profound Retardation in Each
Age Group of Persons with All Levels of Retardation

Age group of persons with retardation	*Proportion with profound retardation as a percentage*
40–59 years	50
60–79 years	40
80+ years	20

Source: Figures from Jacobson, Sutton and Janicki (1985).

The authors make the point that the increasing life expectancy has not
been as great for the population with profound retardation as for people
who are less retarded.

The North-west survey (Preddy and Mittler 1981) found 19 per cent
of all children in ESNS schools in special care classes, whereas 27.5
per cent of the ESNS school population were reported to be in special
care classes in a survey of the West Midlands (Taylor, Crawford and
Thobroe 1981). On the basis of these surveys we can estimate that approximately 8,000 children are in special care classes of the total number
of just over 32,000 that are in ESNS schools in England and Wales
(Department of Health and Social Security 1980). However, the North-
west survey figures might suggest that most of these children could not
be classified as profoundly retarded on the basis of IQ scores and that
most children who were profoundly retarded will be found in other classes
in the schools. In Scotland 71 per cent of those attending special schools
for children who are severely and profoundly retarded were labelled by
staff as being profoundly retarded (IQ < 35) (Browning *et al.* 1981).

Fryers concludes from his own Salford study and from others he cites
that the prevalence rate of profound retardation is a little less than 1 per
1,000 with little difference between the 5–9 year old and 10–14 year
old groups distinguished in his study.

Definitions and Prevalence of Physical Impairment with Profound Retardation

We have defined our population as those people with profound retardation and multiple impairments and we are therefore restricting our
discussion of physical impairment here to its occurrence with profound
retardation. There are some individuals whose diagnostic label immediately implies a physical impairment, such as cerebral palsy and spina
bifida.

Definitions of Physical Impairment

Functional definitions of the physical disabilities displayed by individuals who are profoundly retarded include references to their mobility such as 'walk only when assisted' and 'unable to walk' (Preddy and Mittler 1981 p. 103). In the West Midlands survey, teachers were asked to indicate the number of children in special care classes who were 'physically handicapped to such an extent that it seriously influences their day-to-day life' (Taylor *et al.* 1981 p. 79). Difficulties with fine motor skills such as limited use of hands or arms would also be likely to lead to the child being labelled physically impaired.

Prevalence of Physical Impairment with Profound Retardation

Studies which combine individuals with profound retardation and those with severe retardation under the general classification of 'severe' retardation have in one case reported 17 per cent of these people having cerebral palsy (Dupont 1981) and 18 per cent in another (Gustavson 1981). However, when we consider populations in special care classes the percentage increases, 24 per cent with cerebral palsy in Browning *et al.*'s (1981) study, with a slightly higher figure of 29 per cent in Preddy and Mittler's (1981) survey. Jacobson and Janicki (1983) have shown that the prevalence of cerebral palsy and epilepsy increases with more marked intellectual impairment. When functional definitions of physical impairment are considered the percentage of individuals who are profoundly retarded or in special care classes and who have physical impairments are as reported from various studies in Table 1.2.

Table 1.2: The Percentage of Individuals with Profound Retardation or in Special Care Classes who are Unable to Walk

Study	Definition of population	Percentage unable to walk
Browning *et al.* (1981)	profound retardation	35
Preddy and Mittler (1981)	special care	50
Wald and Zdzienicka (1981)	profound retardation	50

Whether the individual was ambulant was the characteristic identified by Browning *et al.* to be the most likely to differ between the children resident in hospital and those living at home, 32 per cent of those living at home being nonambulant compared to 46 per cent of those living in hospital.

Definitions and Prevalence of Auditory Impairment with Profound Retardation

Definitions of Auditory Impairment

Definitions of hearing impairment vary considerably from source to source. Hearing impairment has been defined as a generic term indicating loss of hearing from mild to profound as indicated by examination of the ear, formal tests and functional use of hearing. The term generally inclues the sub-classifications of deaf and hard of hearing (Healey 1975). The degree of hearing loss is not directly related to the classification of the child for educational purposes. Hearing loss tends to be defined in terms of the amount of sound not being perceived whereas the assessment of educational needs may consider additional variables such as the child's ability to use hearing aids successfully.

One classification system of degree of hearing loss is provided by the National Executive Committee of the British Association of the Teachers of the Deaf (1981 p. 83) and is as follows:

Hearing Impairment	Level of Loss
Slight	Not more than 40 dB
Moderate	41–70 dB
Severe	71–95 dB (and those with a greater loss acquired after 18 months)
Profound	96 dB or over (acquired before 18 months)

Categories of hearing impairment, as with categories of retardation should be used cautiously, but are helpful when comparing relatively large numbers of people.

Prevalence of Auditory Impairment with Profound Retardation

The use of classification systems of hearing loss such as the one described above relies on some method of 'objective' testing of hearing. In Volume 2 Chapter 1, on assessment, various methods of assessing hearing impairment in people who are profoundly retarded are discussed but much of the information on the prevalence of hearing losses in this population relies on staff reports rather than formal testing and precise levels cannot be identified. Furthermore, the prevalence of hearing loss reported is likely to under-estimate the 'true' prevalence since a high proportion of people who are profoundly retarded have not had any formal assessment. Kropka (1980) found that 75 per cent of people classified as NDT Group IV in a mental handicap hospital who had a hearing loss had not received a formal audiological assessment. Furthermore, hearing losses fluctuate (Nolan, McCartney, McArthur and Rowson 1980), making reliable figures even more difficult to establish. There are some aetiologies, for example rubella, which may be associated with both retardation and hearing impairment. There may be a danger of people with hearing impairments being classified as retarded or as more retarded than they are (Kropka 1980).

Because of these factors, the prevalence of reported hearing loss in the retarded population varies considerably. Gustavson (1981) found that 5 per cent of children with severe retardation had a hearing impairment but Lloyd (1970) reviewed studies of hearing loss in this population and reported figures ranging from 20 to 30 per cent. However, these studies also include people with mild and moderate retardation.

Nolan *et al.* (1980) found that 47 per cent of people with retardation in an Adult Training Centre (ATC) had hearing losses, but that when those with and without Down's Syndrome were sub-divided, the incidence of hearing loss in the Down's Syndrome group was 69 per cent compared to 40 per cent in the non-Down's group. Cunningham and McArthur (1981) provided further support for the high incidence of hearing loss associated with Down's Syndrome. In their sample of 24 infants with Down's Syndrome, all were found to have a hearing loss though half of them had passed the local authority hearing tests. Although Down's Syndrome people do not constitute a large proportion of the profoundly retarded population, 10 per cent of this population identified in the Scottish survey (Browning *et al.* 1981) were Down's Syndrome, the high prevalence of hearing loss in this sub-group might well be significant.

The surveys relying on staff reports give figures which are assumed to be under-estimates due to lack of availability of audiological assessment. Kropka (1983) found that 10.6 per cent of the hospitalised retarded population surveyed were reported to having a hearing loss. The Northwest survey of ESNS schools (Preddy and Mittler 1981) reported 2.8 per cent of all pupils in these schools as having a hearing loss and the West Midlands surveys (Taylor *et al.* 1981) reported 2 per cent of children in special care classes and 2 per cent of adults attending special care units at ATCs (Crawford, Taylor and Thobroe 1984) as being deaf or partially hearing to such an extent that this impairment seriously influenced their day to day life. The Scottish survey (Browning *et al.* 1981) reports slightly higher levels among children who are profoundly retarded, 3 per cent being reported deaf and a further 5 per cent partially hearing.

A relation between the degree of retardation and the prevalence of hearing loss was suggested by Hutton, Talkington and Altman (1973) who noted that with increasing levels of retardation there is an increasing incidence of sensory impairment. This is supported by Keiser, Montague, Wold, Maune and Pattison (1981) who found that among adults with Down's Syndrome, the lower the Mental Age the higher the prevalence of hearing losses. Furthermore, Kropka (1983) reported that the lower the IQ levels, the greater the prevalence of deafness and partial hearing. She also found evidence that once residents who were profoundly retarded had been formally assessed, they were just as likely as those who were less severely retarded to be issued with hearing aids but less likely to use them. Hence, the level of hearing functioning among the profoundly retarded population may be even lower than necessary.

Definitions and Prevalence of Visual Impairment with Profound Retardation

Definitions of Visual Impairment

The definitions of visual impairment vary from study to study, as do those of auditory impairment. Blindness and partial sightedness are occupationally defined for registration purposes, blindness implying inability to perform any work for which eyesight is essential. The usual operational definition involves a visual acuity of less than 3/60 on the Snellen Charts, which means that the person can only see an image at less than three metres that a normally sighted person sees at 60 metres. Partial sightedness involves substantially defective vision but persons categorised as blind usually have light perception, the prevalence of those without any light perception being only 5 per cent of those registered blind (Ellis 1979).

A variety of terms are used in studies of prevalence, including 'visual handicap', 'visual impairment', 'blindness', 'partial sight', 'visual acuity' and many more. Functional definitions are used by most of the surveys of schools or residential facilities. The North-west survey (Preddy and Mittler 1981), for example, used a definition requiring that the child was reported to have some difficulty in seeing with glasses as prescribed, or great difficulty in seeing without glasses.

Prevalence of Visual Impairment with Profound Retardation

The prevalence of visual impairments among people with retardation varies considerably between studies as with audition, due to differences in definitions used, whether formal assessment has been made or not and difficulties in using standard visual assessments with people who are most profoundly retarded. Grunewald (1975), in a national study in Sweden, found 2.7 per cent of people who were institutionalised and retarded were visually impaired, 15 times the prevalence of such impairment in the general population. Gustavson (1981), also in Sweden, reported that 10 per cent of children with severe retardation had impairments of vision. Table 1.3 indicates percentages of people classified blind and partially sighted in populations who are retarded from various studies.

Table 1.3: Percentage of People Classified as Blind or Partially Sighted in Populations who are Retarded

Study	Definition of population	Percentage blind	Percentage partially sighted
Browning *et al.* (1981)	profound retardation	9.0	12.0
Ellis (1982)	retarded hospital residents	3.6	4.4
Kropka and Williams (1980)	retarded hospital residents	6.0	7.9
National Development Team (1985)	retarded hospital residents	5.2	no figures given
Warburg (1970)	retarded hospital residents	5.0	7.0–8.0

As we have seen above, the terms 'visual impairment', 'blind' and 'partially sighted' have all been used in surveys. In addition, some studies have reported on percentages of visual defects. Woods (1979) found that 42 per cent of children classified as ESNS had visual defects compared to the 7.4 per cent identified in the North-west survey (Preddy and Mittler 1981). This much higher rate reflects both the wideness of the term 'visual defect' and the fact that the individuals in Wood's sample were referred to a child development centre and all received formal assessment of their vision.

Specific impairments are linked to specific types of visual problems. Myopia and strabismus (squints) occur in higher rates among people with Down's Syndrome (Gardiner 1967) and Black (1980) found visual abnormalities among 78 per cent of children with cerebral palsy who were severely retarded. This high rate may again reflect the formal assessments that were made in this study and as the author points out, a high proportion of the children had never been examined by an ophthalmologist before. Van Dijk (1982) also shows the high frequency of bi-lateral cataracts in rubella-damaged children.

Studies differentiating between rates of visual impairment among people who are profoundly retarded and other levels of mental handicap are rare. Iivanainen (1974) found a prevalence of 12 per cent optic atrophy among people who are profoundly retarded. In the West Midlands survey (Taylor *et al.* 1981) 3 per cent of children in special care classes of ESNS schools and 5 per cent of people in Adult Training Centre special care units (Crawford *et al.* 1984) were reported by staff as being blind or partially sighted. This is considerably lower than Browning *et al.*'s (1981) figures from Scotland of 9 per cent of children with profound retardation being blind and 12 per cent partially sighted. These last figures may be higher through inclusion of children with profound retardation but who are not in special care classes.

Kropka and Williams (1980) noted that visual handicaps were more prevalent among residents who were mildly retarded than among those with severe retardation, although elsewhere it has been suggested that the more severe the degree of retardation, the more frequent and more severe are the additional impairments (Dupont 1981). What is clear is that people who are retarded are especially susceptible to eye problems (Ellis 1979) and that the more profoundly retarded they are, the more difficulties are associated with the assessment of their vision. Ellis (1986) provides a comprehensive discussion of the prevalence and assessment of visual problems in people with retardation. These problems are discussed fully in Chapter 1 of Volume 2.

The Definitions and Prevalence of Behaviour Problems with Profound Retardation

Though we have chosen not to include behaviour problems as an additional impairment, many authors report on the frequency of these problems. Chapter 8 of this volume considers why they develop in people with profound retardation and multiple impairment and Chapter 7 in Volume 2 deals in detail with their definition and treatment.

Definitions of Behaviour Problems

A wide variation exists in the number and type of behaviours exhibited that staff may report as 'behaviour problems'. Many factors will influence whether a particular behaviour is regarded as a problem or not. First, social and cultural variables will influence the definition and parameters of 'acceptable' and 'unacceptable' behaviour. What is acceptable in one culture, or indeed sub-culture, may be unacceptable in another. Second, the intensity, duration or frequency of the behaviour may affect whether or not it is regarded as a problem. Hence, every individual is expected to scream on occasion, but continual screaming all day would be regarded as a behaviour problem. Third, the setting (time, place or circumstances) in which the behaviour occurs may determine its appropriateness or otherwise. Hence a behaviour such as urinating is regarded as normal in the lavatory but is clearly a problem if done in the dining room. For a full discussion of situational aspects of defining behaviour problems see Leudar and Fraser (1986).

Finally, the age of the individual child may influence whether the behaviour is considered a problem. For example, headbanging and rocking may be apparent in the normal development of babies (Stainback and Stainback 1980) and other apparently purposeless and bizarre behaviours such as hand watching might be understandable in terms of Piagetian sensorimotor development (Kahn 1984). The persistence of these behaviours, however, beyond 5 years of age would be regarded by most as a problem. Kahn makes the point that whether an individual who is profoundly retarded displays these behaviours, is performing a normal behaviour or merely a repetitive meaningless behaviour, depends upon his or her stage of cognitive functioning.

There are no widely accepted standardised measures of behaviour problems (though see Leudar and Fraser 1986), and a variety of terms can be found in the literature such as emotionally handicapped/disturbed, behaviourally disturbed/disabled, maladjusted, delinquent, autistic and psychotic. Classification systems exist, one of which has been proposed by the American Psychiatric Association (1979) and represents a psychiatric, descriptive approach. Mental disorders are classified into 'mental retardation', 'attention deficit', 'conduct disorders', 'anxiety disorders', 'eating disorders', 'stereotyped movement disorders', 'pervasive development disorders', 'specific development disorders' and 'other disorders'. A more educational orientation is proposed by Quay (1972) whose factor analytic approach classifies deviant behaviour into 'conduct disorders', 'personality disorders', 'inadequate and immature behaviours' and 'socialised delinquency'. Neither of these systems provide information for treatment or programming and both, as in any such system, may result in the classification being retained regardless of behaviour change. A fuller discussion of these two systems and a review of the literature on more specific terms such as autism, psychosis and schizophrenia can be found in Stainback and Stainback (1980).

The Prevalence of Behaviour Problems with Profound Retardation

Given the difficulties and variation discussed in the definitions of behaviour problems, the prevalence figures vary considerably. Clearly figures relying on staff reports will tend to reflect behaviour problems which interfere with the individual's learning or social functioning and the degree of difficulty experienced in reducing such problems. Further-more, figures vary according to whether a distinction is drawn between mild and severe behaviour problems and it is generally reported that mild problems are far more prevalent. An additional source of variation stems from whether the individuals identified are those who, at one time or another, display behaviour problems or those who show persistent problems.

Hence, Stainback and Stainback (1980) review studies in which the percentages of the general school population with behaviour problems ranges from between 2 and 59 per cent although the rates for severe problems alone are much lower. Variations in rates appear to occur according to sex (more prevalent in males than females), socioeconomic class (more prevalent among lower socioeconomic classes) and age (more prevalent among adolescents). They also noted that the prevalence was much higher among children labelled with any handicapping condition, including retardation, visual, hearing and physical impairments.

As many as 40 per cent of children with severe retardation under 16 have been reported to have stereotyped behaviours (Corbett 1977). Self-injurious behaviours were found in 13 per cent of these children, a similar rate to those reported by Tierney, Fraser, McGuire and Walton (1982) and by Schroeder, Mulick and Rojahn (1980) among people with retard-ation in residential settings. These last authors also review studies reporting prevalence among normal babies in the range 7 to 17 per cent, but noted that these behaviours usually develop at 7–8 months and dis-appear by 5 years of age (Kravitz and Boehm 1971 cited in Schroeder *et al.* 1980). Hence, these behaviours can be seen as a part of 'normal development' which only becomes a 'problem' when they persist beyond the stage at which they usually disappear. Headbanging was reported by Schroeder *et al.* (1980) to be the most common self-injurious behaviour among people with retardation, usually in combination with biting, scratching, gouging and hair-pulling.

Level of retardation has been linked to the prevalence of behaviour problems, Schroeder *et al.* (1980) and Eyman and Call (1977) noting that self-injurious behaviours were more prevalent among people who were severely and profoundly retarded than among those who were mildly and moderately retarded. Eyman, Borthwick and Miller (1981) found that age of clients was an important factor with people who were pro-foundly retarded and over 13 years showing a higher prevalence of maladaptive behaviour than younger people. Ross (1972) noted that the lower the level of retardation, the more frequent and severe the self-injurious behaviour is likely to be. Taylor *et al.* (1981) found that 26 per cent of children in special care classes had mild behaviour problems and a further 19 per cent had severe problems, the percentage in the Adult Training Centre special care units (Crawford *et al.* 1984) being slightly higher. These figures are comparable to the rates reported by Browning *et al.* (1981) among children who were profoundly retarded. Taylor *et al.* noted that nearly half of the children who were in special care classes, but had no physical or sensory impairments showed behaviour problems. It is suggested that these children's behaviour problems may contribute to their placement in special care classes, a point also made by Preddy and Mittler (1981) in the North-west survey.

Further discussion of behaviour problems may be found in Chapters 4, 5, 6, and 8 of this volume and in Chapter 7 of Volume 2.

The Prevalence of Multiple Impairments

Multiple impairment was defined above as retardation with one or more additional impairments which might include any combination of physical, auditory or visual impairment. In Bernsen's (1981) sample of children who were retarded, 82 per cent had an additional impairment, just less than half of these having one additional impairment and 5 per cent having four additional impairments (in this case epilepsy was included). Nearly half of these children were classified as profoundly retarded which may have contributed to this high prevalence of additional impairments since, as has been mentioned, the more severe the degree of retardation, the more frequent and the more severe are the additional impairments (Dupont 1981). Gustavson (1981) found that 48 per cent of the children with severe retardation in the Swedish sample had one or more additional central nervous system impairments.

In the Kropka (1983) survey of residents in mental handicap hospitals, 36 per cent of those who were reported deaf and 44 per cent of those reported partially hearing were also said to have limited vision. Ellis (1979) reviews studies suggesting an increased prevalence of behaviour problems, particularly stereotyped and self-stimulatory behaviours among people who are retarded and visually impaired. (See Chapters 4 and 8 in this volume and Chapter 7 in Volume 2.)

In the West Midlands survey (Taylor *et al.* 1981), 3 per cent of children in special care classes were found to have both visual and auditory handicap in addition to their retardation and a further 8 per cent had visual, hearing and physical impairments. In the North-west survey

(Preddy and Mittler 1981) the figures are much higher, as shown in Table 1.4.

Table 1.4: Percentage of Multiple Impairments Reported in Preddy and Mittler (1981) among Children who were Profoundly Retarded

Percentage of children with profound retardation	Number of impairments
37	1
47	2
13	3
3	4

It has to be noted that by definition all these children were multiply impaired and unlike the West Midlands survey many of them were not in the special care classes. In Jacobson and Janicki's (1983) survey they noted that half the population classified as profoundly retarded had additional impairments.

Summary and Conclusions

In this chapter, an attempt has been made to review some of the literature on the definitions and prevalence of profound retardation and multiple impairment of a physical, auditory or visual nature. What appears to emerge are not clear definitions with precise figures agreeing on the prevalence of each condition, but a varied picture influenced by many factors such as country of origin, definition, placement, identification and date of study. However, there is some indication that for the population with which this book is concerned, i.e. people who are the most profoundly retarded, a high prevalence of additional impairments exists. This suggests the need for interdisciplinary approaches to the assessment and educational programming of these individuals, with recognition of the difficulties of identifying their additional impairments and their exact levels of intellectual functioning. In order to set such assessment and intervention in a wider framework, in the next chapter we will proceed to describe a developmental context in which the effects of both specific impairments and their consequences for people who are profoundly retarded can be considered.

References

Alberman, E. (1984) 'Epidemiological Aspects of Severe Mental Retardation' in J. Dobbing (ed.), *Scientific Studies in Mental Retardation*, Royal Society of Medicine, London, Macmillan, Basingstoke

American Psychiatric Association (1979) *Diagnostic and Statistical Manual of Mental Disorders* 3rd edn, American Psychiatric Association, Washington, D.C.

Berger, J. and Yule, W. (1986) 'Psychometric Assessment' in J. Hogg and N.V. Raynes (eds.), *Assessment in Mental Handicap: A Guide to Tests, Batteries and Checklists*, Croom Helm, London

Bernsen, A.H. (1981) 'Severe Mental Retardation Among Children in a Danish Urban Area: Assessment and Etiology' in P. Mittler (ed.), *Frontiers of Knowledge in Mental Retardation: Vol. II: Proceedings of the Fifth Congress of the IASSMD*, University Park Press, Baltimore

Black, P.D. (1980) 'Ocular Defects in Children with Cerebral Palsy', *British Medical Journal, 281*, 487–8

Browning, M.M., Bailey, I.J. and Clark, O. (1981) *Schools and Units for Profoundly Mentally Handicapped Children in the Strathclyde Region of Scotland*, Jordanhill College of Education, Glasgow

Corbett, J. (1977) 'Mental Retardation Psychiatric Aspects' in M. Rutter and L. Hersov (eds.), *Child Psychiatry, Modern Approaches*, Blackwell Scientific, London

Crawford, N., Taylor, P. and Thobroe, E. (1984) 'Special Care in 19 Adult Training Centres', *Mental Handicap, 12*, 54–6

Cunningham, C. and McArthur, K. (1981) 'Hearing Loss and Treatment in Young Down's Syndrome Children', *Child: Care, Health and Development, 7*, 357–74

Department of Health and Social Security (1980) *Mental Handicap: Progress Problems and Priorities*, HMSO, London

Dupont, A. (1981) 'Epidemiological Studies in Mental Retardation: Methodology and Results', *International Journal of Mental Health, 10*, 56–63

Ellis, D. (1979) 'Visual Handicaps of Mentally Handicapped People', *American Journal of Mental Deficiency, 83*, 497–511

Ellis, D. (1982) 'Visually and Mentally Handicapped People in Institutions: Part 1: Their Numbers and Needs', *Mental Handicap, 10*, 135–7

Ellis, D. (1986) *Sensory Impairments in Mentally Handicapped People*, Croom Helm, London/College Hill Press, San Diego

Eyman, R.K., Borthwick, S.A. and Miller, C. (1981) 'Trends in Maladaptive Behavior of Mentally Retarded Persons Placed in Community and Institutional Settings', *American Journal of Mental Deficiency, 85*, 473–7

Eyman, R.K. and Call, T. (1977) 'Maladaptive Behavior and Community Placement of Mentally Retarded Persons', *American Journal of Mental Deficiency, 82*, 137–44

Fryers, T. (1984) *The Epidemiology of Severe Intellectual Impairment: The Dynamics of Prevalance*, Academic Press, London

Gardiner, P.A. (1967) 'Visual Defects in Cases of Down's Syndrome and in Other Mentally Handicapped Children', *British Journal of Ophthalmology, 51*, 469–74

Grossman, H.J. (ed.) (1983) *Classification in Mental Retardation*, American Association on Mental Deficiency, Washington, D.C.

Grunewald, K. (1975) 'Blind, Deaf and Physically Handicapped Mentally Retarded: An Epidemiological Study as a Base for Action', *Proceedings of the 3rd Congress of the International Association for the Scientific Study of Mental Deficiency, 1*, 349–52

Gustavson, K.H. (1981) 'The Epidemiology of Severe Mental Retardation in Sweden', *International Journal of Mental Health, 10*, 37–46

Healey, W. (ed.), (1975) *The Hearing Impaired Mentally Retarded*, American Speech and Hearing Association, Washington, D.C.

Hogg, J., Foxen, T. and McBrien, J. (1981) 'Issues in the Training and Evaluation of Behaviour Modification Skills for Staff Working with Profoundly Retarded Multiply Handicapped Children', *Behavioural Psychotherapy, 9*, 345–57

Hutton, W.O., Talkington, L.W. and Altman, R. (1973) 'Concomitants of Multiple Sensory Deficit', *Perceptual and Motor Skills, 37*, 740–2

Iivanainen, N.B. (1974) *A Study of the Origins of Mental Retardation: Clinics in Developmental Medicine (No. 51)*, Heinemann, London

Jacobson, J.W. and Janicki, M.P. (1983) 'Observed Prevalence of Multiple Developmental Disabilities', *Mental Retardation, 21*, 87–94

Jacobson, J.W., Sutton, M.S. and Janicki, M.P. (1985) 'Demography and Characteristics of Aging and Aged Mentally Retarded Persons' in M.P. Janicki and H.M. Wisniewski (eds.), *Aging and Developmental Disabilities*, Brookes, Baltimore

Kahn, J.V. (1984) 'Cognitive Training and its Relationship to the Language of Profoundly Retarded Children' in J.M. Berg (ed.), *Perspectives and Progress in Mental Retardation: Vol. II: Biomedical Aspects*, University Park Press, Baltimore

Keiser, H., Montague, J., Wold, D., Maune, S. and Pattison, D. (1981) 'Hearing Loss of Down's Syndrome Adults', *American Journal of Mental Deficiency, 85*, 467–72

Kravitz, H. and Boehm, J. (1971) 'Rhythmic Habit Patterns in Infancy: Their Sequence, Age of Onset and Frequency', *Child Development, 42*, 399–413

Kropka, B. (1980) 'A Study of the Deaf and Partially Hearing Population in the Mental Handicap Hospitals of Devon', unpublished manuscript, Royal Western Counties Hospital, Devon

Kropka, B. (1983) 'A Summary of the Results of the Questionnaire into Hearing Impairment and the Mentally Handicapped in N.H.S. Hospitals and Hostels in England and Wales', unpublished report, British Institute of Mental Handicap, South West Division, Exeter

Kropka, B. and Williams, C. (1980) 'A Survey of Blind and Partially Sighted Residents in the Mental Handicap Hospitals of Devon', *Apex, 8*, 43–4

Leudar, I. and Fraser, W. (1986) 'Behaviour Disturbance and Its Assessment' in J. Hogg and N.V. Raynes (eds), *Assessment in Mental Handicap: A Guide to Tests, Batteries and Checklists*, Croom Helm, London

Linna, S.L., Koivisto, M. and Herva, R. (1981) 'Chromosomal Etiology of Mental Retardation: A Survey of 1000 Mentally Retarded Patients' in P. Mittler (ed.), *Frontiers of Knowledge in Mental Retardation: Vol. II: Proceedings of the Fifth Congress of the IASSMD*, University Park Press, Baltimore

LLoyd, L.L. (1970) 'Audiologic Aspects of Mental Retardation' in N.R. Ellis (ed.), *International Review of Research in Mental Retardation: Vol. 4*, Academic Press, London

MacKay, R.I. (1976) *Mental Handicap in Child Health Practice*, Butterworth, London

Marozas, D.S., May, D.C. and Lehman, L.C. (1980) 'Incidence and Prevalence: Confusion in Need of Clarification', *Mental Retardation, 18,* 229–30

Morton, R.F. and Hebel, J.R. (1978) *A Study Guide to Epidemiology and Biostatistics,* University Park Press, Baltimore

National Development Team for Mentally Handicapped People (1985) *Fourth Report 1981–1984*, HMSO, London

National Executive Committee, British Association of Teachers of the Deaf (1981) 'Audiological Definitions and Forms of Recording Audiometric Information', *Journal of the British Association of the Teachers of the Deaf, 5,* 83–7

Nolan, M., McCartney, E., McArthur, K. and Rowson, V.J. (1980) 'A Study of the Hearing and Receptive Vocabulary of the Trainees of an Adult Training Centre', *Journal of Mental Deficiency Research, 24,* 271–86

Preddy, D. and Mittler, P. (1981) 'Children with Severe Learning Difficulties: A Survey in North West England', Final report to the Department of Education and Science, University of Manchester, Manchester

Presland, J.L. (1982) *Paths to Mobility in 'Special Care'*, British Institute of Mental Handicap, Kidderminster

Quay, H.C. (1972) 'Patterns of Aggression, Withdrawal and Immaturity' in H.C. Quay and J.S. Werry (eds.), *Psychopathological Disorders of Childhood,* Wiley, New York

Ross, R.T. (1972) 'Behavioral Correlates of Levels of Intelligence', *American Journal of Mental Deficiency, 76,* 545–9

Schroeder, S.R., Mulick, J.A. and Rojahn, J. (1980) 'The Definition, Taxonomy, Epidemiology and Ecology of Self-Injurious Behaviour', *Journal of Autism and Developmental Disorders, 10,* 417–32

Sontag, E., Burke, P. and York, K.R. (1973) 'Consideration for Serving the Severely Handicapped in the Public School', *Education and Training of the Mentally Retarded, 8,* 20–6

Stainback, S. and Stainback, W. (1980) *Educating Children with Severe Maladaptive Behaviours,* Grune and Stratton, New York

Taylor, P., Crawford, N. and Thobroe, E. (1981) ' "Special Care" in 44 Schools for the Mentally Handicapped', *Apex, 9,* 79–81

Tierney, I.R., Fraser, W.I., McGuire, R.J. and Walton, H.J. (1982) 'Stereotyped Behaviours—Prevalence, Function and Management in Mental Deficiency Hospitals', *Health Bulletin, 39,* 320–7

Van Dijk, J. (1982) *Rubella Handicapped Children. The Effects of Bilateral Cataract and/or Hearing Impairment on Behaviour and Learning,* Swets and Zeitlinger, Lisse

Wald, I. and Zdzienicka, E. (1981) 'Simple Neurological and Clinical Means of Diagnosing Severe Mental Retardation: Studies in Poland', *International Journal of Mental Health, 10,* 47–55

Warburg, M. (1970) 'Tracing and Training of Blind and Partially Sighted Patients in Institutions for the Mentally Retarded', *Danish Medical Bulletin, 17,* 148–52

Woods, G.E. (1979) 'Visual Problems in the Handicapped Child', *Child: Care, Health and Development, 5,* 303–22

2 DEVELOPMENT AND MULTIPLE IMPAIRMENT

In the preceding chapter we described the ranges and degrees of impairment found among people who are profoundly retarded and multiply impaired. To the teacher, trainer or parent concerned with the overall development and well-being of such people, the most persistent difficulty voiced is 'Where do I start?' Given the slowness of developmental advance, the obvious inhibiting influences of physical and sensory impairment and frequent attendant behaviour problems, the task can appear overwhelming. This difficulty reflects the fact that in contrast to many other areas of therapy and education, there is as yet no well-defined theoretical or procedural framework in which to analyse and intervene with such people. While it would be naïve to think that those dealing with able-bodied children in the ordinary sector of education, or even those dealing with children with specific sensory or physical impairments, have a fully worked out theory of education and the means for realising aims in unproblematical fashion, it is certainly the case that the framework in which they operate is well enough defined to offer some reassurance about their activities. This is not the case for those working in 'special care' or 'special needs' units, and our hope is that in a modest way this book will begin to show how educationalists, psychologists and other therapists can contribute to the development of such a framework.

The problems that we are confronting have not until recently been in any way alleviated by research undertaken by psychologists concerned with child development and learning processes in childhood. During the last 25 years there has been a burgeoning of work in the field of development and learning in the area of retardation. Most of this has focused on people in the severe to moderate range of ability, and a substantial part of that work has dealt with readily identifiable, but none-the-less important, aetiological groups, notably that of Down's Syndrome. From the point of view of the behavioural scientist, there are good reasons why research should have taken this course. Primarily, of course, study of people in the severe-moderate range is called for in order to improve our understanding of retardation in its own right, and to provide information that will enable us to improve education and training for them. It must also be acknowledged, however, that those in this range offer attractions with respect to the design of research that are often lacking when we consider work with people who are profoundly retarded. The former can be placed in experimental groups on the basis of the same aetiology and matched to other groups with regard to their general level of mental development or even some specific aspect of development such as language level. These groups can be sufficiently large to permit statistical treatment and hopefully some degree of generalisation of findings to the whole population of retarded people with those characteristics.

This is not so with children and adults who are profoundly retarded. The patterns of impairment, nature of brain damage and the difficulties of intuitively placing them in any kind of meaningful framework with respect to general development has precluded studies of the sort that have readily been undertaken with their more able peers. In a sense, the scientific problems of studying such people have tended to lead to their neglect and hence valuable information of the sort we now have for those who are severely and moderately retarded has not emerged at the accelerating rate that has typified retardation studies generally.

Nevertheless, within this general upward sweep of research, increasing attention has been devoted to people who are profoundly retarded. From a small number of classic studies undertaken in the late 1940s and 1950s, to be described later in the course of this book, an increasing number of studies have been undertaken. Many of these have been made possible by an acceptance of what Baumeister (1967) described as 'the study of retarded individuals in their own right', i.e. we do not need to make comparisons between carefully matched groups of retarded and non-retarded people in order to glean valuable information on their functioning and development. However, few of us would now follow Baumeister in his second assertion that in considering retardation: 'The study of normal behavior is quite irrelevant to this purpose' (p. 875). While Baumeister's plea stemmed essentially from exasperation with technical difficulties in achieving matching between groups, his suggestion was totally applicable to studies of people who are profoundly retarded for whom most formal matching procedures are inherently untenable. But in undertaking such studies, what can our point of departure be if we are not matching to groups of contrasted or matched ability? Increasingly we have turned, as have those studying severe and moderate retardation, to the framework of child development that has advanced rapidly during the period in which mental retardation studies have blossomed, and to the massive body of literature on learning processes that is now available.

Much of this book reflects this mapping of our observations on profound and multiple impairment onto developmental information and our understanding of learning processes. Our consideration of this map and the way we have begun to sketch it has raised important questions, some of which have received little attention elsewhere, and others of which need a dusting off and reconsideration. First, we have already emphasised the difficulty we encounter in placing people with profound retardation and multiple impairments in any kind of informative framework. If this is really so, are we justified in relating our observations of them to the development of able-bodied children? If, as we shall show in Chapter 7, it is possible to establish such a connection, what are the limits to relating the two sets of objectives? Are we saying simply that the development of people with profound impairments is just slow, or differs in respects that make the link between change in their behaviour and typical development too tenuous to be useful? Some will recognise lurking in these complicated questions an issue which has bedevilled the study of profound, severe and moderate retardation for some time, and which tends now to recur in almost any general discussion about development in retarded people. Indeed, the 'Developmental vs Difference' controversy has duly reoccurred here, and we will devote a little attention to the question raised by the controversy in order to place the above questions on a more explicit footing.

The origin of the 'Developmental vs Difference' debate stemmed from the writings of Zigler (1969). Zigler's interest was exclusively in retarded children who were delayed either due to social factors, or who were simply dull because of below-average inherited intelligence, or as a result of some combination of these two factors. He argued that the development of such children was essentially normal with respect to sequences, stages and the processes underlying their cognitive growth. They were, in effect, simply slower in development but not different in these respects. Central to Zigler's argument was the assumption that such children did not have damaged or abnormal brains. Since large sections of the retarded population in the profound to moderate range do exhibit organic factors of this sort, Zigler did not suggest or claim that his developmental hypothesis was applicable here. On the contrary, such people may show normal patterns and processes of development—or these may differ, but Zigler was adamant in indicating that his theory was *not* being applied by him to them.

Nevertheless, the issue of development vs difference was shifted downwards in the ability range as if it were a meaningful issue to resolve in one direction or the other with the variety of aetiological groups that make up the profound to moderate population. We would like to suggest here that this downward extension and the attempt to pose the question as to which is 'correct' has little meaning for several reasons. First, the extent to which children are similar in their pattern of development is dependent in part on the level of analysis employed. A comparison between sighted and partially sighted children on a standard developmental test involving a single measure such as Mental Age will show broadly similar *trends* in the acquisition of overall competence though at different *rates*. Inspection of sub-scales on such a test my reveal differences in patterns of acquisition against this background of 'normal' but slow development. Even closer inspection, for example, of language development, will reveal important idiosyncracies, e.g. in the speech by which the child refers to him or herself. Thus, while the normal developmental course can be broadly established, though occurring at a slower rate (the developmental position), highly significant deviances *do* exist, i.e. the difference position. Second, in addition to the level of our observations affecting our judgements regarding development and difference, this balance may vary within different areas of development at different times. Third, we do not know enough about individual differences in development in the able-bodied population, though we are fully aware of their existence, to draw hard and fast lines on when deviation becomes difference.

We can return to the question we posed regarding the relation of developmental theory to our understanding of people who are profoundly impaired: 'Are we really justified in relating our observations of them to the development of able-bodied children?' If we accept that there is no answer to the question in terms of *either* a developmental explanation *or* a difference explanation, then the issue becomes one of studying development in a given group of people with respect to: (i) differing levels of analysis, from general tests of development through to experimental explorations; (ii) within different areas of development; and (iii) within different stages of a given area. What is emerging from such an analysis is a far richer account of deviance and normality in development than any simplistic opposition between these concepts. The answer to our question must therefore be 'yes', not because of an assumption of slow but normal development in people who are profoundly retarded, but because that framework offers us a context in which to observe and question, a framework which would otherwise be lacking, and a context in which the presence or absence of deviancy can be considered.

If our consideration of this debate seems in any way remote from the reality of working with children, then we would suggest that judgement is suspended until Chapters 4, 5 and 6 have been read. In these we set available information on early development in impaired children against the account of development in nonimpaired children presented in Chapter 3. These reviews of work with visually, auditorily and physically impaired children provide a very real indication of all the points noted above. In these chapters it is possible to see how different areas of development are affected by the impairment at different times in the child's life, and often how by quite atypical means the child overcomes a delay and achieves a given milestone or acquires a developmentally important ability.

Our reason for including chapters on the developmental effect of impairment on children who might otherwise not have been disabled, i.e. children who are not at risk for severe or profound mental retardation, is not simply to illustrate the fluctuating and complex effects of impairment on child development. More importantly, we present this information to show what effects many of the impairments exhibited by people who are profoundly retarded themselves may have on selected areas of their development.

This decision raised two further fundamental questions which have received little attention. The first is: Is the overall effect of multiple impairments simply the sum of their individual consequences? Or, as much of the literature on multiple handicap asserts, rather than demonstrates, do multiple handicaps together lead to distinctively new and different problems emerging? The second question is: Against a background of profound retardation, do findings on visual, auditory and physical impairment have implications for understanding the development of people who are profoundly retarded? Both these questions will only receive full answers when careful research has been undertaken to answer them. At present, the best we can do is to clarify the questions that need answering and the issues involved, and point to why it seems to us inappropriate to neglect such information on specific impairments at this stage of our attempt to understand the disabilities of people who are profoundly retarded and multiply impaired.

In discussing the way impairments might sum and interact, we introduce two words to characterise the two extreme possibilities. These were 'sum' and 'emerging'. This question of 'additive' or 'emergent' consequences may have a familiar ring since it is the central issue of the old psychological question as to whether the sum is equal to, or greater than, its parts. Gestalt psychologists argued strongly for the sum being greater than its parts, an argument which if correct would indicate only limited value in considering here specific impairing consequences. However, the Gestalt psychologists' argument can be countered: the parts of any system work together according to certain laws. In studying a system, in this case a system of developing behaviour, we need to understand these laws if we are to determine how individual parts of the system work and interact. Not understanding these laws at present does not mean that the system is inherently unpredictable, only that as yet we do not fully understand it. In the present situation, this means that though additional impairments may not simply add their effects, they may prove to be predictable when a more adequate theory of development and impairment has been evolved. Alternatively, in the present instance, we might consider this whole issue in terms of the *subtractive* effect of additional impairments. Frankenberg (1983) points out that her own preference in working with visually impaired children is to view impairments as subtracting from the available channels of communication and learning.

In the area with which we are concerned, the study of people with profound retardation and multiple impairments may enhance our understanding of these emergent effects, possibly by a careful consideration of their interaction in individuals. Again, these effects will undoubtedly be complex and will depend on the relative severity of the impairments and will have to be considered in relation to specific phases of development. It may well be that only by a judicious combination of developmental assessment (Chapter 7) and functional analysis (Chapter 8) will we be able to uncover their influences in the case of individuals.

What then of the influence of specific impairments in people who are described as 'profoundly retarded'? To answer this question, at least in principle, we must return briefly to our discussion of the development vs difference controversy. Here we concluded that any 'answer' to this issue would depend on the nature of a child's development in any given area. The direct relevance of information from blind, but not mentally retarded, children to an individual who is profoundly retarded will depend on the rate and nature of that child's development. In our chapter on visual impairment we note that blind children do not become mobile until they have learnt to reach for an object on the basis of sound, though they are neuromuscularly equipped to move about several months before this. For the person who is potentially mobile, blind and profoundly retarded, the significance of reaching for an object on the basis of sound can become a critical objective linked to teaching mobility and one informed directly by our knowledge of development in blind children. However, we do not think it likely that general prescriptions can be arrived at on the basis of Chapters 4–6. Rather the effects of impairments on mother-child interactions, communication, sensorimotor development, motor development and behaviour disorders will have to be considered in relation to our comprehensive assessment of an individual person and our specific objectives for him or her.

In the preceding paragraph we have made a simplifying assumption, namely that children with visual, auditory and physical impairments are invariably able-bodied with respect to other functions. This can be the case, of course. Such impairments can exist independently of extensive brain damage either because impairment is peripheral, i.e. to the sense organs or muscular system, or because the damage to the central nervous system (CNS) is highly localised. In many instances visual, auditory and physical damage and mental retardation are in varying degrees and combinations associated. The word 'associated' is an interesting one in this context. While those of us taking *intellectual* retardation as our starting point might see other impairments as additional or secondary, it is sobering to have approached the question through the literature on specific impairments and found that the 'additional' handicap in many cases is 'mental retardation', the primary concern being, for example, deafness or blindness. This is, of course, nothing more than a matter of focus and convenience in writing on the topic of multiple handicap. Ideally, however, we would be advised to think in terms of the *association of impairments* (including intellectual impairment) as a configuration of conditions to be given equal weight in our considerations rather than to be arbitrarily designated as 'primary', or 'secondary', or 'additional'. In the succeeding four chapters we will emphasise the totality of development and show how any given area will interact with others to condition the pattern and course of development. This totality must also reflect the full span of impairments if we are ever to establish their effect on overall development.

It is, then, highly likely that a pattern of associated impairments will result from extensive damage to the CNS. The nature of this damage and its behavioural consequences is progressively being explored in relation to a variety of impairments. With respect to hearing impairment, for example, Vernon (1969a) discusses interrelations between organic and psychological factors in the development and modification of human behaviour: 'The hypothesis is that many of the secondary disabilities—such as expressive and receptive communication disorders, mental deficiency, markedly atypical behavior, and learning disabilities—which characterize many multiply handicapped deaf children are caused by brain damage resulting from the same condition that led to deafness' (p. 2). He goes on to consider the consequences of differing causes of hearing impairment and their relation to a variety of 'secondary' conditions, and also attempts some account of the specific forms of brain damage with which they are associated. The association of impairments that can result from a given cause can also be considered with respect to specific syndromes. Vernon (1969b) describes Usher's Syndrome, a genetic condition resulting in the double handicaps of congenital deafness and a progressive blindness known as retinitis pigmentosa. The condition is also associated with mental retardation and other neurophysiological pathology. Vernon comments that case studies suggest that Usher's Syndrome cannot be viewed as simply the amalgam of visual and auditory impairment but reflects diffuse injury to the nervous system. The neurological basis of the multiple impairments in cerebral palsy will also reflect such impairments arising from extensive damage.

Both our developmental information and that derived from specific impairments must be taken in conjunction with this general state of affairs. Neurophysiological assessments of the people with whom we are concerned will obviously throw some light on their general state and the nature of the damage. Any full account of people with profound retardation and multiple impairment will eventually have to come to terms with the nature and extent of CNS damage. Though this is something we will from time to time touch on, a full treatment is not possible within the present book. Instead we will make our main touchstones developmental and learning processes as investigated in psychological studies, and it is to the first of these that we now turn. In the following chapter we present a general developmental framework which provides an important background to the studies of profound retardation and impairments described in this volume, as well as to the curriculum and intervention issues described in Volume 2.

References

Baumeister, A.A. (1967) 'Problems in Comparative Studies of Mental Retardates and Normals', *American Journal of Mental Deficiency*, *71*, 869–75

Frankenberg, A. (1983) personal communication

Vernon, M. (1969a) *Multiply Handicapped Deaf Children: Medical, Education and Psychological Considerations*, Council for Exceptional Children Research Monograph, Washington, D.C.

Vernon, M. (1969b) 'Usher's Syndrome — Deafness and Progressive Blindness', *Journal of Chronic Diseases*, *22*, 133–51

Zigler, E. (1969) 'Developmental versus Difference Theories of Mental Retardation and the Problem of Motivation', *American Journal of Mental Deficiency*, *73*, 536–56

3 A FRAMEWORK FOR CONSIDERING EARLY DEVELOPMENT

Introduction

Those working with people who are profoundly retarded and multiply impaired have increasingly turned towards information derived from developmental psychology to both increase their understanding of the person's behaviour and determine directions in which they might develop curriculum aims. At the simplest level this may take the form of utilising developmental checklists reflecting major milestones in child development. Beyond this, some attempt may be made to recreate the conditions through which developmental processes are expected to evolve. These approaches by teachers and other therapists are paralleled by research workers who have examined the nature of development in people who are profoundly retarded from a developmental perspective.

In this chapter, we propose to review relevant work in the field of child development. Our criterion of relevance is an extremely practical one. If a teacher, for example, were to be presented with the various psychological studies of people who are profoundly retarded reviewed in Chapter 7, what would he or she need to know about theories of child development to understand the studies? In other words, the particular theories and points of view considered in this chapter have been selected to reflect the main concepts of Chapter 7, and to some extent Chapters 4–6 in which the impact of specific impairments is considered. Thus, this chapter does not pretend to be a comprehensive account of child development, though it does cover important elements of early development such as cognitive, communicative and motor progress. Nor, because the studies described later are diverse, does it adopt a single theoretical perspective. Indeed, there is no *single* theory of child development that embraces *all* aspects of a child's development in such a way that we can hitch our educational wagon to it and proceed securely on our way. Child development theories tend to focus selectively on particular aspects of development. Accounts of some aspects of development do not readily fall within any given theory, but are based on a number of related studies often carried out by different investigators. This is particularly apparent in the area of language and communication. Here we now have a host of studies and hypotheses about language acquisition, but no single unified theory on which there is general agreement. A similar situation holds for the development of manipulative skills, though here the studies are few and far between compared with language research. In contrast, Piaget has offered a highly influential theory of how the child interacts with his or her world from early infancy, building up knowledge of the world from these interactions, and how, from this knowledge, language develops.

While an understanding of these diverse psychological processes underlying development is necessary for any full theory of child development, it must be emphasised that a variety of maturational processes are also taking place in the developing child. These processes are occurring in both the central nervous system and the musculature and are essential prerequisites for the changes in behaviour that we associate with the young developing child. That these processes are occurring more slowly, or are defective, in many people with profound retardation is certainly the case, and that behaviour and physical maturation interact and influence each other is well established.

In the 1930s, however, the maturational aspect of child development was given greater weight by developmental psychologists, and the prevalent view was that development would tend to proceed at its own rate with little possibility of its being positively influenced by environmental factors. When transposed to a consideration of people with mental handicap, such a view is obviously a pessimistic one. If such people are maturing relatively slowly, the argument would go, then little can be done to enhance or accelerate development. Where there is also evidence for identifiable immaturity or abnormality of neuromuscular development, then the position is even more pessimistic.

But our view of the nature of development has changed since that time and this change fits well with the more positive attitudes towards the education of people with mental handicap that have evolved. At the heart of these changes is the view that development occurs through the way in which the individual interacts with his or her social and physical environment. Not only does the environment influence the child, but the child's behaviour alters the environment, which in turn further influences the child. The key word here is *interdependence*. The child and the environment mutually affect each other, for better or worse, as we shall see, and each in different ways adapts to the other. This view of the developing child as part of a complete system of interdependent people and objects is very similar to the way in which we have come to view systems in nature. We are all aware of the way in which natural systems are influenced by changes in a single component. The disappearance of one species can break a whole chain of naturally occurring relationships because a predator on that species has to find an alternative source of food, or decline. This in turn will affect other species and the balance of nature will change. We are familiar with the description of this state of affairs as 'ecological'. By this, we mean that animals and plants in nature form an interdependent system in which change in one part of the system will alter a whole series of relations. This ecological view has been increasingly applied to our study of child development and Bronfenbrenner (1979) has used the term 'the ecology of human development' to reflect the child-environment interdependence to which we referred above. We believe that this way of approaching development is of great importance in its own right and is also of relevance to work with people who are severely and profoundly retarded. What we hope to show is, that by considering their development from an ecological perspective, we not only come to understand them in their own right, but can better establish ways in which to intervene in order to enhance their development.

A further important aspect of this interdependence is the way in which apparently distinct areas of development influence *each other*. However useful it is for purposes of discussion and curriculum development to distinguish between 'motor development', 'cognitive development' and 'language', for example, we shall see how interdependent such functions are, and how impairment in one area can have far-reaching consequences for others. This is amply illustrated in Chapters 4–6 on specific impairments, and must be assumed to be particularly influential in impairing the development of individuals who are profoundly retarded and multiply impaired.

How far, for our present purpose, we should pursue child development through the years of growth is not a simple question. We must clearly consider the first years of life from, say, 0 to 24 months. It is during this period that the foundations of more advanced behaviour are laid down as the child becomes more competent in dealing with his or her world. By the end of this period language is likely to be developing apace, and will continue to do so for several years to come. In our review we follow development for a few years past the age of 2. It is convenient, if somewhat arbitrary, to think in terms of an upper limit of a nonhandicapped 4 year old level of development. The degree of competence exhibited by such children reflects a remarkable achievement when we consider the developments that have taken place in a mere 48 months of life. Indeed, for people who are profoundly retarded and multiply impaired, such an achievement would represent massive motor, cognitive and communicative gains and would more than adequately define a set of long-term aims to be realised step by step through the achievement of more limited objectives over several years.

Though in many ways controversial despite its apparent general acceptance, we take as our starting point a brief account of Piaget's theory of early cognitive development. There are several highly practical reasons why we should set the scene in this way in addition to the value of the theory itself. First, to understand many of the recent developments that have occurred in the study of language acquisition by children, we need to be familiar with some of the basic cognitive concepts employed by Piaget. Similarly, the development of skilled action can also take as its starting point the organisation of sensorimotor behaviour as he described and accounted for it. Secondly, if we are to review developmental studies of people who are profoundly retarded and multiply impaired as we do in Chapter 8, then we must again have some knowledge of Piaget's account of development which has informed the vast majority of such studies. Thirdly, and in parallel, the attempt to overcome the problem of the so-called untestability of such people has led many workers into the use of developmental tests that reflect Piaget's own account of development (see Hogg 1986). In Chapter 7, therefore, we will draw upon the summary presented here in order to describe further such assessment instruments. Fourthly, and closely related to the issue of assessment, the development of curricula for such people has been increasingly informed by Piagetian observations on the key behaviours that reflect cognitive development. Where necessary, to complement the Piagetian account, we will draw upon other theoretical positions that we believe are of value to understanding development, especially in the area of language and manipulative skill. Taken together, these influences point not to the proven truth of Piaget's theory, but to its utility. Bates (1976) has commented on 'heuristics from Piaget's theory' and it is very much as a result of the heuristic value of the theory that those working with and studying people who are profoundly retarded have turned to it.

Early Cognitive Development

The period of early childhood is characterised by remarkable and rapid changes in the way in which the infants and toddlers come to cope with the objects and people that make up their world. From the point of view of this book, it is first necessary to understand what the main areas of development are in which these changes occur. Secondly, we need to follow the course of these developments at different times through the early years and the manner in which the changes come about. Closely linked to these last two considerations is a third, namely, what are the actual processes that underlie, or make possible, such developmental changes? In the literature on cognitive developmental psychology, these four considerations are approached by considering *domains* of development, *stages* in the changes in these domains and the *transitions* between stages, and the psychological *mechanisms* underlying change within and between stages. Before considering each of these in turn a general comment on the approach we have adopted to these issues is in order.

Piaget and His Influence

In considering the early development of children's understanding of the world, nearly all accounts lead to the writings of the Swiss psychologist-philosopher, Jean Piaget. In several key books of great influence (Piaget, 1951, 1953 and 1955) he has described the domains, stages, transitions and mechanisms involved in these developments. Philips (1981) in his primer on Piaget points out that Piaget's theory is cognitive in nature and is concerned with how the mind works and understands, rather than with the control and prediction of behaviour. Indeed, Piaget's account of development has been heavily criticised for being too abstract, and too little concerned with concrete reality. It has been left to other developmental psychologists to begin to relate Piaget's account to more carefully controlled observations of children's behaviour and what children actually do in real situations.

Given our concern with practical intervention with people whose development is markedly delayed, these studies are of special importance, and though at this stage of the book we are mainly concerned to give an account of early development, at various points later we will return to the practical implications of some of these investigations.

Nevertheless, the studies to which we are referring have all quite explicitly taken as their starting point the writings of Piaget, and the way in which they *describe* development is through the vocabulary developed by Piaget. One important aspect of Piaget's terminology that is invariably used is that employed to describe the stages and periods of development. The two periods with which we are concerned *here* are referred to by him as the 'Sensorimotor period', which roughly covers the first 24 months of the nonhandicapped child's development, and the 'Preoperational period'. Though the latter covers roughly the age range 2–7 years, in this book we shall focus on developments up to about 4 years of age, the period of 2–4 years sometimes being referred to as the 'preconceptual' or 'symbolic' sub-stage.

From birth, in the earliest phase of sensorimotor period, Piaget considers that the child is actively engaged in constructing an understanding of the world. This development of understanding is achieved through active intellectual construction, not at this time through language, but through perception of the world and physical movement directed to it. It is this basis of intelligence in perception and movement that is conveyed in the term 'sensorimotor' (Uzgiris 1976).

At the end of this period, too, children have developed means-end behaviour, in which a particular outcome can be achieved without recourse to trial and error by mental representation of the action. The manipulative behaviour that this development permits will become increasingly complex during the next five years that constitute, roughly, the preoperational period. Similarly, the mental imagery that has begun to develop at the end of the sensorimotor will also be elaborated and the preoperational period is marked by the increasing complexity of language and the child's ability to represent the world through signs. We will return later in this chapter to both language and manipulative development in this period (pp. 50–63 and pp. 63–74).

Despite the marked gains shown by children over this period, there are certain important limitations as well. First, the mental representations underlying both manipulative and action sequences tend to reflect actions and events as already experienced by the child. Such thinking is referred to by Piaget as 'figurative'. The child can organise and manipulate the schemes that represent his or her world. Nevertheless, these manipulations do not lead to changes in the way the child thinks about reality. Thinking that leads to such transformations requires 'operative' knowledge that leads to the modifications of thought and goes beyond simply representing reality.

This absence of operative thinking is reflected in some important characteristics of the young child in the preoperational period. The child is regarded as egocentric conceiving the world from his or her own viewpoint. The norms of social exchange that eventually prevail have not yet been achieved. As yet, it is suggested, the child cannot adopt another's point of view whether in terms of language (what information does the other person need to understand me?) or perceptually (how does that look from her point of view?). Second, figurative thinking with its close tie between experience and thought, does not permit important aspects of logical thought. Inhelder (1968) points out that the preoperative child is incapable of formal thought, of deduction, of synthesis, is insensitive to contradictions, impermeable to experience and rarely conscious of his or her own processes.

It is towards the end of this period that operative thinking begins to emerge, characterised by all the opposites to Inhelder's description. The child can break with thoughts that are dependent upon the immediate sequences and forms of reality and begin to transform them through operative thinking. A full account of this change would take us far beyond the scope of this book and a familiar example will suffice. The preoperational child when shown a ball of plasticine broken into two balls will judge this as a change of quantity, often considering that more plasticine exists in the two-ball than in the one-ball situation. The child cannot mentally represent this situation by reversing the event and mentally recombining the two balls in order to conclude that the quantity actually has remained the same despite being divided into two. This example could be proliferated with respect to many other aspects of reality that involve not only material changes, but organisation involving classification and seriation and the organisation of time and space. A specific example, e.g. that with plasticine balls, is not of central importance in itself, but indicative that a certain type of operative thinking has emerged.

It should be clear now why the term 'preoperational' is applied to this period. It precedes the concrete and formal operation stages that ensue, but which take us far beyond the abilities of people classified as profoundly retarded. As will be apparent, developmental changes do occur with symbolic function advancing during the first, preconceptual, sub-stage, and towards the end of the intuitive sub-stage examples of egocentrism being abandoned can be seen and some operative thought will occur. These events have a long way to go before true operational thought occurs and hence the sub-stage is known as 'intuitive'.

Sensorimotor Development

Piaget argues that the child is not born with an adult understanding of the world of objects. The nature of objects and their properties and relations between objects has to be constructed by children in interaction with their environment. We will come shortly to some of the suggested mechanisms by which Piaget proposed that this understanding is achieved. First, however, the nature of the achievement will be described. In discussion of the *domains* of development that occur in young children, as distinct from the *stages* of development, six major domains typically figure:

Object Permanence. Philips (1981) notes that on the basis of a variety of actions the child learns to construct the special configuration of experiences that is typical of that particular object i.e. the permanence of the object. By 'a scheme' we are referring to actions which are often repeated and are directed to a variety of objects, i.e. are generalisable. Examples of such schemes are seeing, reaching and grasping, and we will have more to say on these behaviours in our subsequent section on manipulative development. Object permanence is reflected in search for an object that has disappeared, but the full *object concept* takes longer to develop. For example, if an object is hidden at one place, then rehidden, the child will initially search at the first place for the object. Next, the child will follow such displacements if they can be seen, but not if they are executed with the object not visible, when again the child will look in the first place. Finally the child searches first at the last place where the object might have been hidden: 'The object concept now remains stable in the face of the momentary changes in the sensory field (seeing an object from various angles and distances, seeing it disappear behind a screen, and so on)' (Philips 1981 p. 53).

Spatial Understanding. This is clearly related to the development of the object concept and must be seen as an essential aspect of the full development of the concept of the object. The understanding of spatial relations is progressively developed, according to Piaget, not given at birth. This development is again dependent upon actions directed towards objects in the environment and the outcome of those actions. As Philips (1981) noted, 'When there are no objects, there is no space and vice versa' (p. 53). Again, schemes of looking, reaching, grasping and manipulating lead not only to consistent dealing with stable objects but to knowledge regarding the effect of these actions on the position of an object in relation to the child, and of objects in relation to each other. Much discussion of spatial development has focused on Piaget's Stage IV and the kind of errors made by the infant in manually reaching for an object hidden beneath a screen, e.g. under screen A to the child's left-hand side, which is then moved beneath screen B to the child's right side. Here the 8 to 11 month infant continues to reach to A even when the object is seen to be moved to B. Piaget and Inhelder (1956) suggest that this perseveration comes about because for the infant the object only exists in the space defined by the infant's manual act of gaining the object by reaching for it.

One consequence of this is that if the child is moved in relation to the screens (A and B), then he or she will still reach to the same side to retrieve the objects. For example, if A is to the child's left and B to the right, the infant will successfully reach to the left screen if the object is placed beneath it. If he or she is then moved through 180° then

A will be to the right. However, the child will still reach left to the location at which B now is. This has been referred to as 'spatial egocentrism'. (See Chapter 3, Volume 2.)

Piaget and Inhelder's view in this as in other domains is that the infant progressively constructs the object through circular reactions of reaching. An alternative account of the development of spatial understanding is that it does not involve such active construction, but is perceived directly by the infant. Certainly recent studies of infants do show that infants can utilise information on the colour of the screens and the background colour of the surface on which they are placed and are certainly not purely egocentric in their spatial understanding at sensorimotor IV (Butterworth, Jarrett and Hicks 1982). We will comment again on these alternative views when we discuss spatial development and intervention in Volume 2, Chapter 3.

Time. In addition to the permanence of objects and their relations in space, time is a further important dimension to be understood. The rudimentary conception of time emerges essentially from activities involved in the search for objects described above. Initially the child loses interest in a disappeared object, later persisting in following it through a series of displacements. Thus, present actions towards objects become linked in time to past actions and a basic understanding of the temporal dimension begins to emerge.

Intentional Behaviour and Means-End Relations. We can only infer intention from observing behaviour. An essential element of intentional behaviour is seen by Piaget as the ability to achieve a specific goal by separating the means of attainment from the end itself. The most familiar example of such a separation is when towards the end of the first year of life the child removes some obstacle to reach and grasp an object behind it. In addition, such intentional behaviour will be adaptive, i.e. it will show systematic changes in response to alterations in the nature of the means-ends behaviour. Two important stages of this area of development occur in the second year of life. In the first half of this year the child is able to discover the means to achieve intended goals through active experimentation. Piaget (1953) describes in detail such experimentation with special reference to the use of supports, sticks and strings to retrieve an otherwise unobtainable distant object. This does not occur as sometimes happens in the later part of the first year by accident, but involves intended *co-ordination* of schemes that even then were available. In the second half of the year, however, the child moves from the use of existing schemas in an experimental fashion to the invention of means to an end through mental combination of schemes that can involve quite new, invented ways of achieving an intended goal.

Causality. In the early stages of object concept development, children's actions have been directed in a relatively simple way to the environment and to their own bodies and clothing. In this situation the child has no conception of him or herself as a cause of a particular event. Towards the end of the first year the distinction between him or herself as cause and other people or events as causes becomes clearer. Thus, the child learns that an adult can be caused to effect a particular outcome. Such an understanding clearly has important implications for the development of causality and communication, and we will return to this point in our later discussion of language development (pp. 56–9).

Imitation. Imitation by children of events in their world is a familiar occurrence. From Piaget's perspective, imitation proceeds through several phases during the sensorimotor period and provides the basis for important developments in the preoperational period. Before imitation proper occurs, children exhibit 'pseudoimitation', i.e. they will imitate an imitation of their own behaviour. The first true imitation will still only be of actions in the child's own repertoire and in addition the action to be performed must be visible to the child, i.e. a hand gesture rather than a facial expression. At the point at which children achieve the concept of permanent objects as entirely distinct from themselves, towards the end of the first year, they can view another's actions as realities in their own right, i.e. novel, distinct actions or imitable events. In the next phase, three further important developments take place in the nature of imitation. First, children can directly imitate novel and complicated events without the need for practice; second, imitation of actions and events by nonhuman or nonliving objects occurs; third, imitation of absent objects is observed.

Certain aspects of these developments in imitation are seen by Piaget as being fundamental to the development of the representation of language as it evolves in the preoperational period. Before elaborating on this point, however, some further general observations need to be made on these developments during the sensorimotor period.

First, we have offered in the foregoing only the briefest description of the achievements of children during the sensorimotor period. Obviously the fullest source will be found in the writings of Piaget himself. From the point of view of the teacher of the person who is profoundly retarded, however, it is more likely that this fuller picture will be derived from the various items in Piagetian developmental scales that have been evolved specifically to reflect the steps towards these achievements. For example, Uzgiris and Hunt's (1975) innovatory scales of development based on Piagetian theory offer such a source and will be discussed with other scales more fully later (Chapter 7).

Second, the magnitude of these achievements which have typically been gained by 2 years of age should be noted. These have led one writer to raise the possibility that not only is sensorimotor development *necessary* for subsequent development, but is actually *sufficient* for it to take place (Bower 1979). He goes on to qualify this by saying that: 'Even if we cannot accept this extreme claim, we are still forced to accept the strong probability that development in the sensorimotor period contains, in kernel form, the ground plan of a great deal of subsequent development, even if it does not specify the whole of subsequent development' (Bower 1979 p. 141). To those dealing with people who are profoundly developmentally delayed, the importance of this possibility cannot be overemphasised. If Bower is even partially correct, then the encouragement of the developments occurring in the sensorimotor period constitute a central task of those working with such children, and, what is more, a task that *must* be successfully accomplished if further progress is to be made. If Bower's first suggestion is in fact the case, then we might even be justified is arguing that the primary goal of education with people who are profoundly retarded is to assist them to construct reality as we see this achieved by nonimpaired or less impaired children during the first two years of life.

Third, we have already indicated that the developmental domains described under separate headings above are actually closely related. Uzgiris (1976) has suggested that Piaget himself claimed that the various domains will be related. As she indicates, however, there is a lack of evidence as to what *does* constitute a developmental domain during this period. From the practitioner's point of view, some of the evidence she reviews provides helpful pointers as to how we might define specific curriculum areas with regard to sensorimotor domains. Uzgiris suggests, for example, that the domains of object permanence and spatial relations tend to consolidate first in the child's development. Other areas follow, but in ways that vary across children. She suggests that in general, imitation, understanding of causality and the development of means-end behaviour follow in that order of consolidation. Her observation of individual differences is an important one since it points away from the simple and unthinking use of sequential checklists towards a more comprehensive view of children's development. Certainly, in children with impairments we would expect even greater individual variation than in the nonimpaired population, and sensitivity to such variation will be important.

Preoperational Period

By the end of the sensorimotor period the child has constructed an understanding of reality which is relatively stable and in which much is understood about the nature and properties of objects and relations between them. In the preoperational period, the child begins to develop the means of representing through play and language this understanding. To understand this development more fully, we need to appreciate the way in which a real object is related to something that represents it. Piaget (1951) gives the example of an 8 or 9 month old child finding a toy beneath a blanket because the outline of the toy can be seen. The shape, an attribute of the object, is an index of the object and a mental represent-atation is not required to anticipate the toy. The symbols that emerge at the end of the sensorimotor period, however, signify an absent object and are internal representations of the absent object that is signified. Here the signifier and the signified are distinct unlike the sensorimotor example just given. Such symbolic representation is nonverbal, though speech is beginning to develop at the same time. In Piagetian terms symbolic representation is concerned to be idiosyncratic and private (Philips 1981). These symbols may be closely linked to the objects and events for which they stand. For example, Piaget (1951. Quotation from Bruner, Jolly and Sylva 1976 p. 573) describes his child's use of a toy donkey's tail as a pillow for pretend sleep:

> The object (the donkey's tail) chosen to represent the initial objective of the schema, and the make believe actions done to it, then constitute the 'signifier', while the 'signified' is both the schema as it would develop if completed seriously (really going to sleep) and the object to which it is usually applied (the pillow) . . . There is therefore representation, since the 'signifier' is dissociated from the signified . . .

Private symbols will give way to conventional 'signs' which are not directly linked to the object they signify, but are conventional ways of signifying aspects of the world again with signifier and signified dissociated. These conventional signs are taken in by the child and replace the private symbols. The child at this stage can distinguish what is being signified (an object, for example) from the symbol or sign itself (i.e. the signifier) and thus the way is opened to the child using language in its own right to think about and understand the world. We will have more to say about the link between cognitive development in the sensorimotor period and language and communication in the following section of this chapter. It should be clear, however, that if preoperational development is dependent upon Stages V and VI of sensorimotor development, as suggested in Piaget's account, then the practical implication for education of people who are profoundly retarded is very great.

Stages of Development

In the foregoing, we have described the main cognitive accomplishments of the sensorimotor and preoperational periods. Piaget has further divided these periods into more limited but distinctive stages, especially with respect to the former. Since much of the work with people who are profoundly retarded refers to sensorimotor stages, we need here to make some comment on such stages. Piaget's view that development occurs in distinct and identifiable stages reflects the fact that he regards development as occurring through structural alterations rather than through progressive increments of the sort we observe in straightforward learning. While, as Wohlwill (1973 pp. 190–204) points out, the concept of developmental stages is not unique to Piaget, it is his concept of stages that has occupied most attention in discussions among developmental psychologists. Certainly the concept is controversial as both Wohlwill and others (e.g. Brown and Desforges 1979) indicate. Since our purpose here is to provide a summary of Piagetian views as a background to their application in profound retardation, it is beyond our brief to enter into this controversy. It is also difficult to provide any simple definition of a developmental stage. Those wishing to pursue the issue in further detail are recommended to Wohlwill (1973), Chapter 9, from whom the following statement is taken:

> The underlying assumption is that in certain areas of development, particularly in the cognitive realm, but not necessarily confined to it, there exist regulating mechanisms that modulate the course of the individual's development so as to ensure a degree of harmony and integration in his functioning over a variety of related behavioural dimensions. The mechanism might be thought of in part as a

mediational generalisation process, permitting acquisition in one area, for example number conservation, to spread both to equivalent aspects of different concepts (e.g. conservation of length) and to different aspects of the same concept (e.g. cardinal-ordinal correspondence). The result is the formation of a broad structural network of inter-related concepts appearing, not all at once to be sure, but within a fairly narrowly delimited period, with further progress along any component concept or dimension being assumed to be deferred till the consolidation of this network — that is, the attainment of the 'stage'. (Wohlwill 1973 p. 192).

These consolidated networks, or stages, are associated with given age ranges in normal development, though the exact span should always be taken as very approximate. Indeed, different authors present different age ranges, and the following from Philips (1981, p. 45) differs from other tables you may encounter:

Sensorimotor Period — six stages		0–2 yrs.
1. Exercising the ready-made sensorimotor schemes	0–1	mo.
2. Primary circular reactions	1–4	mo.
3. Secondary circular reactions	4–8	mo.
4. Coordination of secondary schemes	8–12	mo.
5. Tertiary circular reactions	12–18	mo.
6. Invention of new means through mental combinations	18–24	mo.

Preoperational Period	2–7 yrs.

The Preoperational Period is sometimes further subdivided:

Preconceptual or Symbolic Substage	2–4 yrs.
Intuitive Substage	4–7 yrs.

There is some measure of agreement in studies of children that the actual achievements shown by them in these stages are observable and typically do not vary. This seems to be the case even where children are developing slowly and we shall consider this point later (Chapter 8) with respect to people who are multiply impaired and profoundly retarded.

Central to any account of changes between stages and the activity characteristic of them is the concept of the schemes to which we earlier referred. Such behaviours, repeatable and generalisable, take into account both the action and the object and are considered to be the *structure* of the *interaction* between action and object. It is schematic structures of this sort that develop and proliferate during the course of development and make possible an increasingly complex understanding of the world.

For Piaget, Stage I of the sensorimotor period involves the exercise of simple action schemes that bring the child into contact with the world. Though these actions are described as 'reflexive', they are reflexive in a wider sense than the neurological reflexes of the new-born that are of interest to the paediatrician. These early actions are truly schemes because they are repeated and generalised. The child, however, is dependent on making contact with the world in order to know it exists. In Stage II, Primary Circular Reactions, more clearly defined habits emerge which reflect the fact that the child is beginning to differentiate the nature of his or her world. In Stage III, Secondary Circular Reactions, these simple habits begin to give way to more clearly intelligent behaviour in which the same means of achieving a given end is applied to a variety of different ends and thus the child begins to differentiate the means by which an outcome is achieved from the outcome (end) itself. Uzgiris (1976), in a study of a small group of infants between 1 and 24 months, gives a fuller description of what is actually happening in Stages II and III. She points out that available schemes tend to be applied indiscriminately and that shifts between them tend to be rhythmic though the schemes themselves are not actually co-ordinated. For example, the child may mouth an object, then look at it, then shake it and so on. In applying several schemes to the same object the child comes to learn something of its properties. For example, banging a hard toy then squeezing it will result first in sound, and then resistance to squeezing. Exercising the same schemes with a soft toy will produce exactly the opposite outcomes. In addition, the child is also likely to apply the scheme of examining the object in the context of these activities. Thus, as Uzgiris puts it, it is at the intersection of these schemes that the child gradually comes to understand the properties of the objects. In addition, the child is beginning to develop procedures for recreating interesting spectacles resulting from the effect of his or her action on both objects and people. Through successive repetitions of different schemes, the basis for lengthier sequences of actions is laid down.

In Stage IV the secondary schemes begin to be co-ordinated into integrated patterns of action which are clearly directed to producing a particular outcome in the environment. Of this development Uzgiris (1976) comments that these patterns of behaviour are 'freely constructed in each situation, albeit from well practiced schemes, indicating the differentiation of means from goals' (Uzgiris 1976 p. 127). The range of schemes expands to include dropping objects, tearing material, etc. Uzgiris notes the importance of the child's caretaker at this stage in developing these sequences of component schemes. For example, the child drops an object, the caretaker picks it up, the child regrasps the object and then exercises the same scheme (dropping) or an alternative scheme. What, she notes, does *not* happen at this stage is the substitution or rearrangement of component schemes to effect an outcome when an earlier attempt has been unsuccessful. It is more likely that a complete new sequence of components will be constructed.

During Stage V, Tertiary Circular Reactions, existing schemes begin to undergo modifications as the child starts to deal with new aspects of reality. Trial and error learning is possible as the child modifies a scheme in the light of the outcome of an action. Again, Uzgiris's (1976) description of the development of the children she observed provides a fuller picture. She noted that at this level of sensorimotor development, behaviour is increasingly regulated by feedback on the outcome of the child's action. The child is, as it were, forced to deal with the real nature of objects and to become increasingly selective in his or her actions. Social interaction, too, facilitates this as children come to learn the socially defined function of objects. While behaviour is composed of schemes made up of several components, individual schemes become transferable from situation to situation. These complex schemes can be modified in a more selective fashion rather than restructuring the whole sequence as in Stage IV. Of these developments, Uzgiris comments that: 'The achievement of behavioral regulation by differentiated feedback would be expected to promote imitation of novel events and perfection of skilled actions' (Uzgiris 1976 p. 155).

With the coming of Stage VI, the child begins to work out new means of achieving a particular end, not through trial and error, but through combining mental representations of previous overt acts in order to arrive at a solution. Thus, we will observe quite direct solutions to problems posed by the environment. This stage has been described as the bridge to the preoperational period, the point at which the practical intelligence of infancy gives way to the representational intelligence of early childhood (Uzgiris 1976). It has also been taken up by students of child language as a critical phase in laying down the prerequisites of language acquisition, as we shall see.

It may be apparent that any full account of development in the sensorimotor period would relate change in specific domains, e.g. development of the object concept, to the characteristics of each stage and transitions between. Such an account is beyond the scope of this book and from a strictly practical point of view, the interested teacher will find the link expressed most clearly in Dunst's (1980) manual on the Uzgiris and Hunt Scales of Infant Psychological Development (Uzgiris and Hunt 1975) in which critical behaviours in the various domains are given stage placements. We will go into more detail on this type of assessment and its relation to development in subsequent chapters. It is now time, however, to describe the mechanisms of developmental change as proposed by Piaget.

Mechanisms of Developmental Change

Philips (1981) has given a clear account in Piagetian terms of the mechanisms underlying the various changes we have described. He points out that Piaget's account of development is not maturational, i.e. Piaget does not see development as the simple unfolding of a genetic plan or programme. Nor does he see development as simply the result of environmental influences. Philips describes Piaget's position as *constructivist*. The child '. . . *inherits* a genetic program that gradually (through a process called "maturation") provides the biological equipment necessary for *constructing* a stable internal structure — that "intelligence" then helps the organism adapt to *changes* in that environment' (Philips 1981 p. 9). The mechanisms with which we are concerned here are those that permit the construction of schemes as described above and in overall terms enable the child to construct reality.

There are two main functions involved in this process. These are adaptation and organisation. Through adaptation the child comes to relate to external events. We have described the kind of changes in schemes that come about as the child encounters the real world and these changes reflect this process of adaptation. Changes in the internal structure of the child's understanding of the world are the result of organisational change. Clearly such organisational change will in turn affect the child's adaptation to the world, and thus Philips (1981) points out that adaptation and organisation are '. . . aspects of a single mechanism . . .' (Philips 1981 p. 12).

These main functions underlie all developments, even beyond the periods with which we are mainly concerned here. Adaptation and generalisation are therefore constant, though the content with which they deal, i.e. the actual actions, does change as we have seen. What enables adaptation to take place? Anyone with even a passing knowledge of Piagetian theory will have encountered the terms 'assimilation' and 'accommodation'. It is these processes that underlie the child's adaptation to external reality. It is helpful to describe these terms in relation to simple schemes of the kind we might observe with a nursery toy. Let us imagine that a child has a well-established scheme of shaking an object he or she is holding. In the case of a rattle or a bell this may produce the appropriate sound and to an adult this constitutes 'appropriate use' of the object. This scheme can equally well be applied to other objects which from an adult standpoint are not really 'shakable', for example a fixed knob that will only produce sound if turned. When the child uses the shaking scheme he or she is *assimilating* the object into an existing scheme. In this case, the knob would be assimilated into an existing shaking scheme. The object would be changed by the action but the scheme could remain unaltered.

The child, however, finding that the knob does not rattle, might change the behaviour in the direction of a different action with the object. For example, a turning motion would be induced because only this movement *is* possible. Here the behaviour would have *accommodated* to the object and a new scheme (turning) would evolve. Subsequently other objects might be rotated and hence would be assimilated to the turning scheme. Thus, as with adaptation and generalisation, assimilation and accommodation are reciprocal — the occurrence of one process automatically has consequences for the other and they always vary together. Accommodation permits assimilation in future situations and this change reflects intellectual development. The balance between the processes is therefore critical to development. The child must have the opportunity of exercising existing schemes, i.e. to assimilate, but in the process must also have to accommodate to new demands if development is to take place. This balancing is referred to as *equilibration*. It has been suggested when a child *plays,* the activity is essentially assimilative, i.e. existing schemes are applied to objects and remain essentially unmodified. In contrast, when a child is requested to imitate then the resulting behaviour reflects accommodation. Whether this distinction is fully valid or as clear-cut as this has not been demonstrated. However, the distinction between the two activities clearly shows the essential contrast between the two processes. In the next section of this chapter, we will have more to say regarding the development of play.

During the preoperational period these mechanisms continue to provide the basis for cognitive development. While imitation in the sensorimotor period involves accommodation to an immediate event, deferred imitation requires accommodation to something happening in the present based on past accommodation. The move towards operational thinking is characterised by a growing balance between accommodation and assimilation towards a stable equilibrium that permits operations such as reversibility.

This highly abstract account describing mental operations can be reconsidered in a more obvious social-interactive way that we will argue later in the next chapter is of more immediate use in intervention work. In contrasting egocentrism with what she calls the norms of social exchange, Inhelder (1968) observes that the 'development of reasoning which takes place from the age of three or four to the age of eleven or twelve marks the gradual disappearance of one plane of thought (ego-centrism) in favour of the other (i.e. thought governed by the norms of social exchange)' (p. 62). It is co-operation with the environment that leads to these changes and the actual exchanges, informal and educational are observable social events.

The framework proposed by Piaget has led to the development of a variety of experimental studies on cognition, play, language and motor behaviour. It is beyond the scope of this chapter to review these, though some of their implications will be noted when we consider given curriculum areas. The framework we have provided, however, enables us to set about placing specific developments in other areas such as play, language and communication, and manipulative skill in Volume 2. Far from fully explaining developments in these areas we shall see that additional observations and concepts specific to these developments have to be brought into conjunction with Piaget's sometimes abstract and elusive ideas.

Play

It is only for convenience that we find ourselves giving some account of the development of play as an area in its own right. From Piaget's (1951) point of view and the many researchers he has influenced, play is an integral part of both the sensorimotor and preoperational periods. The changes during and between these periods reflect fundamental developments in cognition that are related to the development of symbolism and to language itself.

Piaget distinguishes between the two periods by contrasting the mastery play of the sensorimotor period with the symbolic play of the preoperational period. Leaving aside for the moment obvious behavioural differences between the play of, say, the 9 month old child and the 24 month child, it is possible to approach the distinction between the two types of play through a consideration of changes in the basic processes of assimilation and accommodation. While these complementary functions continue throughout childhood, the growth of intelligence reflects the increasing equilibration between these processes. From Piaget's point of view, Sensorimotor Stages I–V reflect a dissociation between assimilation and accommodation:

> After learning to grasp, swing, throw, etc., which involve both an effort of repetition, reproduction and generalisation, which are the elements of assimilation, the child sooner or later (often during the learning period) grasps for the pleasure of grasping, swings for the pleasure of swinging etc. In a word, he repeats his behaviour not in any further effort to learn or to investigate but for the mere joy of mastering it and showing off to himself his own power of subduing reality. Assimilation is dissociated from accommodation by subordinating it and tending to function by itself, and from then on practice play occurs. Since it requires neither thought nor social life, practice play can be explained as the direct result of the primacy of assimilation. (Piaget 1951. Quotation from Bruner, Jolly and Sylva 1976 p. 167).

The origins of play Piaget sees in the Primary Circular Reactions of Stage II are acts mainly of adaptive assimilation that can be continued as games for pleasure. In Stage III this state of affairs continues but the differentiation of adaptive or intellectual assimilation and play become more advanced. Critical to this advance is the fact that Secondary Circular Reactions are directed to objects rather than to the child's own body or to direct changes in sensorimotor experience. As soon as the child has accommodated to a new object and its properties the action '. . . will unfailingly become a game . . .' (p. 170). This has been referred to as the 'pleasure of being the cause'. It is related to a more obvious learning theory concept to be discussed in Chapter 9, i.e. contingency awareness, the educational implications of which are covered in Volume 2, Chapter 3. In Stage IV secondary schema are co-ordinated and applied to new situations and can be continued in a game-like way.

Fuller studies of Stage IV play have borne out Piaget's description and suggested that no qualitative changes take place in play. McCall (1974) studied infants at 1½, 10 and 11½ months. The child's play was closely linked to the sound produced by the toys presented and to their plasticity and complexity, but the children's activities did not differ over this period. Only small changes were seen in the creativity of their use of the toys. The move from this relatively long period of play of a specific form raises the next question posed by Piaget:

Why is it that play becomes symbolic, instead of continuing to be mere sensory-motor exercise or intellectual experiment, and why should the enjoyment of movement, or activity for the fun of activity, which constitute a kind of practical make-believe, be completed at a given moment by imaginative make-believe? The reason is that among the attributes of assimilation for assimilation's sake is that of distortion, and therefore to the extent to which it is dissociated from immediate accommodation it is a source of symbolic make-believe. This explains why there is symbolism as soon as we leave the sensori-motor level. (Piaget 1951. Quotation from Bruner, Jolly and Sylva 1976 p. 555).

Sensorimotor Stage V is regarded as transitional, with Tertiary Circular Reactions or 'experiments in order to see results' leading to chance combinations of actions that the child then repeats in a game-like fashion. These sequences of actions become rituals with an important consequence for symbolisation. Familiar, serious actions, e.g. wiping one's nose, are abstracted from their real functional context, and hence can evoke such actions symbolically. Of this development Piaget writes:

Of course, in such behaviours there is not necessarily as yet the con-sciousness of 'make believe' since the child confines himself to reproducing schemas as they stand, without applying them symbolically to new objects. But although what occurs may not be symbolic representation, it is already the symbol in action. (Piaget 1951. Quotation from Bruner, Jolly and Sylva 1976 p. 557).

In Stage VI, the game symbol as here described and as occurring in Stage V becomes dissociated from the game ritual and takes the form of a symbolic schema. At this point intelligence becomes mental as against being based on bodily action. At the same time, external imitation becomes internal or deferred. Piaget emphasises the pleasure shown by the child when symbolic play occurs as distinct from carrying out the action 'for real'. He gives the example of one of his own children using a cloth, a coat collar and a toy donkey's tail as symbols for a pillow when the child pretends to go to sleep with his head on one of these objects — smiling broadly to himself. Deferred imitation of a new model and symbolic play reproduce a situation in the presence of something other than that which gave rise to the original action. Thus in some sym-bolic play both deferred imitation and game symbolism may be seen. The relation between symbolic play involving assimilation and deferred imitation is illustrated further by Piaget when he describes how a donkey's tail is assimilated to a pillow, or a cardboard box to a plate, such symbolism involving both game-like symbolism which distorts objects and uses them at will, and a form of imitation since the child really does do the actions of going to sleep and eating meals. In fact this self-imitation is what makes the representation possible and permits pretence or make-believe. Thus, distorting assimilation and representational play go hand-in-hand.

While the critical period of transition from late sensorimotor to the preconceptual or symbolic sub-stage leads to the emergence of mental representation, further development and elaboration of play through the remainder of the sub-stage is to be expected.

Lowe's (1975) study of these developments leading to the development of her Symbolic Play Test (Lowe and Costello 1976), not only documents these changes in real play contexts, but points in a less abstract way to the kinds of play that can be observed and hence assessed and the psychological significance of changes in play. We shall describe this test in more detail in Chapter 7 and here we just note some changes that occur in the various play contexts employed by Lowe. These involve various combinations of dolls, household objects (cups, saucers, bed, etc.), as well as a lorry, trailers, etc. The children in Lowe's study ranged from 12 to 36 months, groups being assessed at each three-month interval. Even at 12 months these young nonhandicapped children were showing discriminating use of miniature objects such as the doll, spoon, cup or saucer and this extended to correct use of the toy brush and comb at 15 months. The most striking overall development was the shift from self-directed to doll-directed use of feeding and grooming utensils. Self-directed feeding and grooming peaked at 18 months. A similar pattern but at a much lower frequency occurred with behaviour directed to other people and dropped to its lowest level at 36 months. Concomitantly, play behaviour directed to the doll from 12 months onwards reaches a peak at 36 months. Doll-to-bed play developed later than play associated with feeding and grooming and it was not until 24 months of age that children showed a fully integrated sequence of putting the doll to bed. Still later was the full placing-doll-at-table-for-meal sequence. Lowe suggests that her study shows not only the rapid development of underlying concepts of use of objects, but that it also illustrates the way in which such play depends on the development of underlying concepts of use of objects and possible appropriate relations between them. This observation is important, because Piaget's account as we have illustrated tends to emphasise abstract underlying mechanisms. Though familiar events are used to illustrate the development of representation, he does not place the emphasis on the specific experiences and concepts that develop in a young child in a given environment as is the case with Lowe. In a sense, then, her account complements Piaget's by providing content for the form he suggests underlies the development of representational play. Certainly her cross-sectional summary over the three-month periods of the kind of play typically to be observed is valuable in giving pointers as to what to expect and in which direction to intervene.

Communication and Language

The Function of Communication

Studies of child language during the past ten years have increasingly emphasised the *use* to which young children put their communicative skills in order to control and cope with the world around them. These theoretical developments, which we shall describe more fully later, represent a reaction against what is now widely felt to be an overemphasis on language as a closed system of words and grammar, often in the past analysed independently from children's actual use of language. From the point of view of work with people who are profoundly retarded, this new emphasis is particularly welcome, since our aim is to increase their capacity to indicate their needs and experiences and to enable others to respond to them.

The function of *language*, therefore, is seen as being essentially one of *communication* and Lloyd and Beveridge (1981) indicate that to study communication, one has basically to take into account the situational and contextual factors in which both the expression and comprehension of language takes place between interacting speakers. Halliday (1973) has referred to such a view as the *functional* approach to language. By this he means that we must try '. . . to find out what are the purposes that language serves for us, and how we are able to achieve these purposes through speaking and listening, reading and writing. But it also means more than this. It means seeking to explain the nature of language in functional terms: seeing whether language itself has been shaped by use, and if so, in what ways — how the form of language has been determined by the functions it has evolved to serve' (p. 7). Halliday goes on to suggest that children know what language *is* because they know what languages *does*. There are many ways in which language is used by children,

. . . for the satisfaction of material and intellectual needs, for the mediation of personal relationships, the expression of feelings and so on. Language in all these uses has come within the child's own distinct experience, and because of this he is subconsciously aware that language has many functions that affect him personally. Language is, for the child, a rich and adaptable instrument for the realization of his intentions . . . (Halliday 1973 p. 10)

In this clear and nontechnical description, Halliday raises a number of central issues that have concerned students of early child language. First, he draws attention to the children's use of language to express 'experience' and 'intentions', i.e. to convey their evolving understanding of the world and the meaning it has for them. Second, he places this quite clearly in the child's social world and the communicative function emphasised by Lloyd and Beveridge is clearly spelled out.

Thus, language is a system of words and rules (i.e. syntax), the function of which is essentially social, i.e. to communicate with others. The growth of communication and the development of language as the result of social experience is described in the next section which is concerned with the social basis of language. The content of language is concerned with the meanings that an individual is attempting to convey, usually referred to as *semantic relations*. This content reflects the understanding an individual has about the world and hence is based on the development of cognition following on consideration of social aspects of communication. There are two aspects to this question: (i) the general cognitive developments and mechanisms underlying the ability to express certain semantic relations or meanings; and (ii) the specific meanings to be conveyed.

The Social Basis of Communication

Let us first, however, consider the social system that provides the framework for later (spoken) language acquisition. It is now abundantly clear that from the earliest weeks of life the infant develops an increasingly complex pattern of social interaction with his or her care-giver. In a host of studies, usually of mother-infant interactions, the baby emerges not as the passive recipient of maternal stimulation but as an equal and influential partner in the relationship. Both the timing and turn-taking in these interactions are sensitively phased from early in the infant's life. Such timing and phasing can be seriously disrupted in children at risk for moderate or severe intellectual delay. Studies by Jones (1977) and Berger and Cunningham (1981) (of infants with Down's Syndrome) have shown how even this earliest form of communication is already aberrant in such children. Though parallel studies have not to our knowledge been undertaken with children at obvious risk for profound retardation, it is evident that this disruption will be even more marked for such children, and in some instances observable interactions may appear nonexistent.

That these interactions persist and increase in complexity for nonhand-icapped children through the first year of life will be apparent to anyone observing young children with their parents. It is in this context that Bruner (1975a; 1975b) detects the origins of language, for, he suggests, the imputation of communicative intent to their babies and young children by mothers leads to maintenance and elaboration of such communicative exchanges. In these exchanges mother and child attend to common aspects of the situation, or, in Bruner's term, there is 'joint reference' to the situation as they attend to its common features. In such situations the child begins to 'traffic' with the adult in certain objects and relations between objects. While the adult is obviously already a member of the linguistic community, the child brings a more limited repertoire of com-municative skills to the situation. Bruner draws attention particularly to *indicating* and *naming*, for indicating is seen in joint visual regard of objects. Infants follow their mother's gaze as early as 4 months of age. Mothers, in turn, have their own implicit approach to teaching in this situation. They 'mark' objects by shaking or banging them, and place them to tempt the child to retrieve them. Reaching for the object along the line of regard is eventually replaced by a more peremptory reach: 'The extended hand becomes an external pointer for noting the line of regard rather than direction of activity' (Bruner 1975a p. 271). Such gestures become, by 8 months, conventional and correct signals between mother and child.

Various studies of individual children have described different aspects of this process. Carter (1975) documents the gradual evolution of the words 'more' and 'mine' from a single sensorimotor communication schema into adult phonetic forms, adult semantics, and the use of these words in more complex syntactic structures. Initially, gesture was seen as fundamental in requests of the 'more'/'mine' kind even when paired with vocalisations of 'm'. However, the need for gesture decreased from 12 to 14 months as specific words emerged for 'more' and 'mine' and the associated object. Throughout, the boy's mother modelled these words until by the end of the period they were clearly differentiated phonetically and at the pragmatic, semantic and syntactic levels. Similarly, Ninio and Bruner (1978) documented the achievements and antecedents of naming through the analysis of joint picture book reading. From 8 months of age the child participated in a dialogue with his/her mother and his/her eventual labels for pictures when they did emerge could be seen to be adult-like versions of earlier communicative forms such as smiling, reaching, pointing and babbling vocalisations. All these were consistently interpreted by the mother as intended labelling. These and other detailed observational studies of language development in context provide potentially valuable insights into the process by which the child's ability to refer to objects is socially created through the achievement of dialogue and point towards critical elements to which those intervening with language-delayed children might direct their attention.

Though gesture and other forms of signalling give way to verbal 'labelling', naming is initially not as specific as later object naming. Initially it is 'holophrastic', i.e. a single name can actually refer to a wide variety of situations highlighting some aspect of who is doing what with what object towards whom in whose possession and in what location and often by what instrumentality (Bruner 1975a). Thus, agent, object, recipient of action, location, possession and instrument are all involved. Bruner suggests that the differentiation of these elements into a system referring to specific aspects and relations in reality begins as early as 6 months through what he calls 'phonological marking'. Even then different sounds are used to differentiate different contexts, e.g. pitch variation in vocalisations may change according to whether an object is in the hand as against those involved in an interaction with the mother.

From the start, the child is well equipped with behaviours that have communicative value for the adult. For example, Bruner refers to the 'demand mode' which expresses discomfort, or vocalisation of pleasure. These early vocalisations evolve into the 'request mode' and by 8–10 months into the 'exchange mode' in which the child calls for an object, receives it, hands it back. From this emerges the reciprocal mode in which non-identical actions can be co-operatively combined in a given task. Here the mother's support assists the child to realise the task by providing a 'scaffolding'. The progress from demand to request to exchange to reciprocity during the first year is, Bruner believes, '. . . of central importance to the development of speech acts (or more properly), communicative acts, and as well to the later grasping of case-grammar in language' (pp. 277–8).

Bruner's view of the acquisition of case-grammar has been elaborated in a second paper (Bruner 1975b). Here he suggests that in *all* languages there are categories of agent, action, object of action, recipient of action, location, possession, etc. These categories reflect the structure of action and this the child learns independently of, and prior to, learning language. Thus, when the child first says, 'Mummy drink tea', he or she already has the concepts of an agent carrying out an action directed to a particular object. In terms of the parent-child interaction that we have discussed above, Bruner sees the mother interpreting the child's intentions and supplying the grammar. Bruner emphasises the role of attention in this process. The child must be able to attend to different parts and wholes within the total context in which the interaction takes place in order to be able to determine the possible topics of 'conversation' with his or her mother.

In reality, the mother-child 'situation' we have described is one familiar to us as *play* and many of the activities described are the traditional games and routes of infancy. Of this Bruner comments: 'It is that play has the effect of drawing the child's attention to communication itself, and to the strucutre of acts in which communication is taking place' (Bruner 1975b p. 10). In summary he concludes:

> The claim is that the child is grasping initially the requirements of joint action at a prelinguistic level, learning to differentiate these into components, learning to recognise the function of utterances placed into these serially ordered structures, until finally he comes to substitute elements of a standard lexicon in place of non-standard ones. (p. 17).

The process by which this substitution of standard elements occurs is in the second year of childhood and subsequently is obviously critically dependent upon the child being exposed in a suitable way to his or her native language as Macnamara (1972) implies. Chapman (1981), in a consideration of intervention with language-delayed children to which we shall return (Volume 2, Chapter 3), has reviewed the way in which linguistic input to the child occurs during the second year of life with respect to phonology, syntax and semantics.

In talking with their children, mothers tend to simplify phonology, substitute sounds and to reduplicate sounds. They are likely to exaggerate pitch, intensity, duration and stress, and talk at a slower rate, pausing at syntactically significant points (i.e. variations in the prosodic characteristics of language). Chapman suggests that these variations are not intended to enhance communication, though from the point of view of therapeutic intervention this is the role they may serve, but to convey *affect* to the infant.

The complexity of syntax is also varied by mothers. Utterances will be shorter, simpler and better formed than to older children and other adults. These changes reflect the mother's intention in the specific situation, for example to engage children in conversation or to get them to perform some task. Chapman notes that: 'Many students of child language believe that the simple well formed structure of the mother's input plays a critical role on the child's ability to learn language rapidly' (p. 210). From Macnamara's point of view it is critical to language acquisition that the child matches regularities between adult models and his or her own nonlinguistic models. Chapman herself emphasises the lexical aspect of this situation suggesting that if the mother's utterances contain fewer words there is a higher probability of the child associating the right words with the right aspect of the situation. To effect this association the mother must be aware of what the child is attending to in order appropriately to simplify her utterance.

Semantically, Chapman identifies differences in mother's speech to young children in word diversity, frequency, concreteness and a variety of other facets of word categories. Again, she suggests that these differences reflect the nature of the communicative situation, particularly the restricted topics of mother-child conversation. Restriction provides simplified input to ensure a match between the child's understanding of, and attention to, the situation, and the meaning of the mother's conversation.

These various phonological, syntactic and semantic events described by Chapman are related by her to Bruner's concept of 'scaffolding' and to the functional nature of language in this situation.

With respect to our opening observations on the relative contributions of cognitive, social and linguistic processes to the evolution of language, Bruner's position is: 'What may be innate about language acquisition is not linguistic innateness, but some special features of human attention that permit language to be decoded by the use to which it is put' (Bruner 1975b p. 2). He views the Piagetian account of the development of language from early sensorimotor schemes as inadequate because it fails to emphasise the function, or *pragmatic* nature, of language. This account, Bruner is suggesting, is too formal and insufficiently based in the real social and physical world of the child. It might be added, however, that though this criticism might reject Piaget's actual account of the emergence of language, it does not necessarily dispense with the need for the child to have acquired certain forms of sensorimotor functioning to be able to benefit from the more concrete experiences that Bruner describes. In other words, certain aspects of sensorimotor development may lead to *necessary*, though not sufficient, systems, for spoken language to emerge. It is essentially this position that Bates and her colleagues have considered and to which we now turn.

The Cognitive Basis of Communication

Underlying Mechanisms. Perhaps the most controversial issue in studies of early language development is the relation between cognitive development and the emergence of language and communication. Discussions of this question have typically concerned themselves with the question of cognitive prerequisites for language development. What *does* a child need to know about the world in order to acquire the various linguistic structures that constitute language?

The view that is most likely to be familiar to teachers working with people who are severely and profoundly retarded can be illustrated by Sinclair (1971), from a paper entitled 'Sensorimotor Action Patterns as a Condition for the Acquisition of Syntax'; Sinclair argues that the universality of language derives from universal structures of thought not linguistic universals. The latter exists because of the former. At the stage at which communicating through spoken language begins (15–18 months), '. . . the child possesses a set of co-ordinations of action schemes which can be shown to have certain structural properties which will make it possible for him to start comprehending and producing language' (p. 127).

Such a view has been called the *strong* version of the cognition hypothesis for language acquisition. Cromer (1979), who proposed this term, has suggested that it is an overstatement. It is also necessary to take into account, he argues, purely linguistic processes that are independent of cognition and make their own specific contribution to the development of language. He argues for a position '. . . incorporating both cognitive and more purely linguistic processes . . .' (p. 107) and refers to this as the *weak* form of the cognition hypothesis.

One of the fullest discussions of this question is that by Bates, Benigni, Bretherton, Camaioni and Volterra (1977). They caution, first, against any attempt to suggest that either cognition or social experience 'causes' language in any simple one-to-one fashion and indeed, against suggesting language 'causes' some aspect of cognition. They suggest instead that we view the linguistic, cognitive and social aspects of the situation in which children acquire language as systems which are dependent upon each other. Each system requires an input from another in order to build up its own structure. Bates *et al.*'s actual account of these dependencies will be summarised later.

Bate's own studies focus on what in pragmatics are known as

'performatives'. These refer to the act that a speaker intends to carry out with a sentence, for example declaring, asking a question, promising and so on. In her studies of child language, Bates has focused particularly on two types of performative, declaring and commanding, which are readily distinguishable in the young child's utterances. She also emphasises that when a performative or speech-act is uttered, the speaker is making the utterance in a context in which both speaker and listener have knowledge of the relation between utterance and context, i.e. the speaker 'presupposes' that he or she shares with a common listener a certain view of the relation between what is said and the situation. The familiar example to illustrate the idea of presupposition is the interchange: 'Have you got the time?' The questioner does not expect the answer 'Yes' because the presupposition is that listener will take this as a request for the time.

With regard to performatives such as a declaration in which the child comments on an object, e.g. 'Dog!' or commands 'Drink!' (as a request for drink), Bates *et al.* (1977) ask three questions: First, are there gestural forerunners or precursors to verbal comments and requests of the kind just noted? Second, are there cognitive prerequisites to such preverbal communications, and indeed social prerequisites? Third, what kind of performatives evolve from the above development, e.g. declaring, ordering, asking, etc.?

To answer these questions Bates and her colleagues undertook an intensive longitudinal study of a small number of infant girls. The expected continuity from gestural to linguistic performatives was indeed observed, and specific links between these developments and cognitive development found. The primary cognitive prerequisite for gestural performatives was acquisition of Piaget's Sensorimotor Stage V (see p. 43) — invention of new means to familiar ends, particularly developments in causality and means-end relations known as tool-use. Bates *et al.* (1977) illustrate this relation: 'In the 40 days in which the 10 to 11 month old subject used supports to pull objects, and tools or sticks to push other objects, she also began (i) to use objects as "tools" to obtain adult attention (showing, giving, communicative pointing) and (ii) to invoke adult help in obtaining objects' (p. 250). These authors refer to the child's use of objects to get adult attention as 'protodeclaratives', and it was in such situations that the first one-word labelling occurred. Similarly, 'protoimperatives' involved the child in getting the adult to obtain objects and again such situations were closely bound with the use of first words.

Nevertheless, words did not appear in these communicative schemes until Piaget's Sensorimotor Stage VI (see p. 43) when the capacity for mental representation and use of symbols had evolved. The first referential use of words was also noted at this stage co-occurring with non-verbal Stage VI behaviours including the beginning of pretend or symbolic play, deferred imitation and memory for absent objects and people, and the ability to follow invisible displacements. The authors concluded that:

> . . . the cognitive prerequisites for preverbal, intentional communication is in sensorimotor Stage V, the invention of new means to familiar ends. In particular, causal developments involved in tool use seems to be related to the ability to use objects to obtain adult attention and adult help to obtain objects. Because these intentional communications did not necessarily involve speech, this stage was termed the illocutionary phase in communicative development . . . the locutionary phase, involving the use of words in the same performative sequences, seemed to require further cognitive development characterised by Piaget Stage VI symbolic capacity. (p. 251)

These observations were confirmed in a follow-up study using the Uzgiris-Hunt Scale in which a respectable match was found between developments in cognition in Sensorimotor Stages V and VI and development in communication. Subsequent studies with language impaired and retarded children have confirmed Bates's observations. Snyder (1978) compared children (with language disability) with respect to declarative and imperative performatives in relation to the development of sensori-motor behaviour. Children who were language disabled had little difficulty in generating non-linguistic performatives but were unable to employ linguistic performatives. The best single predictor of the latter was Stage VI, means-end behaviour, in line with Bates's observations. None of the children who were language disabled had acquired Stage VI symbolic activities. Greenwald and Leonard (1979) studied children with Down's Syndrome from the same standpoint again comparing them with nonhandicapped children. Both those with Down's Syndrome and the nonhandicapped children scored at a higher level with respect to both imperatives and declaratives at Sensorimotor Level V of means-end behaviour, operational causality and object schemes in contrast to Level IV performance. Nevertheless, differences between children with Down's Syndrome and nonhandicapped children were noted that were not directly attributable to cognitive factors, and it is suggested that experiential factors may also play their part.

Before returning to Bates's general argument, some comment needs to be made on the place of object permanence in the acquisition of early language. Brown (1973) contended that object permanence predicts language acquisition because it bears on mental representation. This observation has had some influence in the field of severe and profound retardation as educators have become increasingly concerned with cognitive prerequisites of language. However, Bates's own data did not bear this out, and in Snyder's study, while none of the language impaired children had reached Stage VI in means-end behaviour, all had done so with respect to object permanence. While from the psychologist's point of view this provides supportive evidence for the critical role of means-end behaviour in early language development, it should not be taken as a relegation of the development of object permanence in the child's psychological growth. Clearly a full understanding of the nature of objects must have its place not only in the child's manipulation of the physical world but also in the understanding of the world that is expressed through language.

We have already commented on Bates's view of the way in which social and cognitive systems relate to the developing linguistic system. This is more a view of interdependent systems evolving in a mutually supportive way than of simple prerequisites being added successively in a linear fashion as in a developmental checklist. Bates goes on to suggest that both cognitive and linguistic development are dependent upon the development of *operative schemes* (see pp. 33–4). From this position it is predicted that developments in language, cognition and indeed social behaviour will occur at roughly the same time across children, though specific gains in each area might differ across children operating generally at Stage V. In a comparable way, referential speech and nonlinguistic aspects of Stage VI will also occur over the same period, underpinned by developments in operative schemes.

What, then, are the prerequisite cognitive skills that will permit the development of utterances of more than a single word? De Villiers and de Villiers (in press) suggest that the Stage VI behaviours that we have already noted as prerequisites for the emergence of language must also be seen as prerequisites for multi-unit utterances. They include the development of the object concept with an understanding that whole categories of objects can perform the same action while many actions can be performed by a single object. An understanding that objects can initiate change in other objects must be a further cognitive achievement required. Thus such prerequisites make possible the expression of relations between agents, actions and objects, as we shall discuss further in the next section.

Though there is less direct evidence from observation of children, Bates (1976) extends her account into the pragmatics of the preoperational period: 'In the preoperational period (from 1½ to 4 years) the child elaborates his capacity for internal representation (figurative knowledge) and operations on that representation (operative knowledge). The whole process of assimilation and accommodation that characterised sensori-motor adaptation to an object world is now repeated on a new and more flexible world of symbols' (p. 329). With regard to performatives, the child around 24 months can refer explicitly to the speech act itself, i.e. 'I said . . .'. Other overall changes in the structure of discourse also occur: (i) a dimensional concept of time emerges — 'tomorrow', 'Tuesday' and past and future tenses; (ii) the use of conjunctions to link utterances (e.g. 'but', 'or', 'else'); (iii) personal pronouns are mastered; (iv) sentences become embedded. Of these developments Bates comments: 'We have attributed these diverse developments not to a formal, specifically linguistic acquisition, but to a broad improvement in the child's cognitive system, an ability to control several procedures as objects subordinated to a higher organising procedure' (p. 330).

The Development of Specific Meanings. Both the account of social influences on the development of language and the contribution of cognitive development give some indication of the way understanding of the world evolves and the kind of meanings it has for the child. It is such meanings that become the subject of attempts at communication. The child experiences both events in the world and language related to those events. As Miller and Yoder (1974) point out: 'Through experience with objects and events around him, the child begins to perceive particular objects and relationships conceptually. At the same time experiencing the linguistic code of his community spoken around him' (p. 513). Thus, particular events are marked linguistically when they are understood. MacNamara (1972) describes this process more fully:

> . . . infants learn their language by first determining, independent of language, the meaning which a speaker intends to convey to them, and by then working at the relationship between the meaning and the language. To put it another way, the infant uses the meaning as a clue to language, rather than language as clue to meaning. (p. 1)

He thus assumes, in line with Piagetian theories such as Sinclair's (1971), that thought is in advance of, and independent of, language. By one year of age, MacNamara argues, when infants begin to understand language, they already have some understanding of the world and their place in it. Thus, as the mother supplies words and sentences for objects and relations already understood by children, they use the situation to relate linguistic regularities they hear to their existing knowledge.

Gregory and Mogford (1981) describe six categories of words in the vocabulary of young children (these categories were derived from Thatcher (1976) from work by Nelson (1973)):

General nominals — words naming a particular class of objects or events, e.g. 'chair'

Specific nominals — words naming a specific object or event, e.g. 'Daddy'

Action words — words describing or demanding action, e.g. 'Down'

Modifiers — words describing attributes or qualities, e.g. 'Hot'

Personal-social words — used in social contexts to describe relationships or feelings, e.g. 'Thanks' or 'Ouch'

Function words — with a purely grammatical function, e.g. 'For'.

Any given *word* can have different functions and the classification is based on function. For example, 'Down' could be an action word if the child was being held and wanted to be put down or a specific nominal if it referred to a given place, e.g. the house cellar.

A more elaborate classification of functions is given by Miller and Yoder (1974) which illustrates further how semantic functions are mapped onto language and used expressively by the younger child. Their table, based on several studies which show the development of single word utterances for a variety of functions, for functional two-word relations and for three- and four-term relations, is reproduced in Table 3.1. Thus, the child's understanding of an agent (e.g. Daddy or Mummy) carrying out an action (e.g. reading) appears as Noun-Verb semantic relation that can be expressed as 'Daddy read'. What is important here is that such semantic relations are not restricted to any single agent or action but to any agent and action for which a suitable noun and verb have been learnt. We will see in Volume 2, Chapter 4 how the development of such structures can be taught through appropriate intervention techniques. Similarly, Miller and Yoder's (1974) description points towards the content and sequence of language intervention targets that will be discussed further in that chapter.

Table 3.1. Functions Expressed in Early Production Stage 1

Relational Functions Single Word Utterance Level

Recurrence	Request	More
	Comment	
Nonexistence	Existence expected	No
Disappearance	Existence in immediately preceding context	Away A gone
Rejection		No
Cessation	Ongoing event ceased	Stop
Existence	Objects or people pointed out, noticed, or found	There
	Events that were sudden or startling	Uh Oh

Substantive Functions

Comments	Attaching a linguistic sign or label to the perceived event of:	Mama
Greetings		Dada
		Mimi
		Baby
Vocatives	To call for someone (less frequent than comments or greetings)	Mama Dada Mimi
Agent	Agent of an intended or immediate action	Mama Dada Mimi Baby
Object	(Infrequent occurrence) object of an action	Mama Dada Mimi Baby
Action	Marking of action or event states	Tumble Back Catch Turn Tire
Possession	Objects associated with:	Daddy
	Objects belonging to:	Mommy

Functional Relations, Two-word utterances

Existence	This (a, the, that, it, there) + substantive word
Recurrence	More (another) + substantive word; used as request or comment
Nonexistence	No (away, all gone) + substantive word; used also to express disappearance
Rejection	No + substantive word
Denial	No + substantive word (late)

Semantic Relations

Agent-action	N + V	Daddy hit, Adam put, Eve read
Action-object	V + N	Hit ball, put book, read book
Agent-object	N + N	Mommy sock, Mommy pigtail, Mommy milk

Table 3.1. continued

Possessive	N + N	Daddy chair, Mommy lunch, Adam checker
Locative (two forms)	N + N	Sweater chair, book table, bear raisin
	V + N	Walk street, go store
Attributive	Adj + N	Big train, Red book
Experiencer-state	I (me) +	hear, want, love, need
Datives of indirect objects	Give Mommy	
Commitatives	Walk Mommy	
Instrumentals	Sweep broom	

Three-term Relations

Type I	
Agent-action-object	Appear to be combinations of semantic relations expressed earlier in
Agent-action-locative	Stage 1 with repeating term omitted; i.e., agent-action, (Adam hit) +
Action-object-locative	action-object (hit ball)→agent-action-object (Adam hit ball) with redundant action (hit) deleted
Type II	
Non phrase expansion within two-term relation	Two-term relations expanded from within always express one of the following: attribution, possession or recurrence; example: action-locative (sit chair)→(sit Daddy chair) locative expanded as possessive

Four-Term Relations

At the end of Stage 1, four-term relations are of the same two types as described for three-term relations.

Source: Miller and Yoder (1974).

Fine Motor and Manipulative Development

The hand has been described as the instrument through which human intelligence is expressed, and Piaget (1953) has observed: 'With the mouth, the eye, and the ear, the hand is one of the most essential instruments of which the intelligence, once it has been established, makes use' (p. 88). Everyday observations tell us that it is through use of their hands that children show increased control of their world, through which they express a developing competence in understanding the world. Use of the hands to express understanding and the creation of understanding through use of the hands, is a two-way activity of great importance to early development. In this section we will describe the development of certain aspects of hand use in their own right, and in the following the part played by manipulation in cognitive development. We can then point out some further links in this two-way influence and in the following chapters note how different kinds of impairment influence the link.

Newly born babies at the outset are already active in the use of their hands. Indeed they are active in this respect long before they are born, quite independent of direct stimulation. The hand, too, will respond to stimulation at birth. An adult finger or appropriate object moved across the baby's palm from the ulnar (non-thumb) side to the radial side (thumb side) will produce sustained flexion of the fingers which close around the object. Touwen (1976) has described in detail the assessment of this palmar grasp reflex and its dissolution. In neurologically intact infants it occurs in all assessments during the first two months and is present in the majority until 5 to 6 months. From the third month, however, it begins to give way to weak often brief grasping of the object. By 8 months this weak reflexive grasp has virtually disappeared and cannot be elicited. From this stage only voluntary grasping is observed and Touwen noted that it becomes increasingly difficult to distinguish the reflex from voluntary grasping and that the amount of the latter may itself affect the developmental course of the reflex.

It is important to emphasise that voluntary grasping does not emerge from the palmar reflex, or put another way, the reflex is not a prerequisite for voluntary grasping. Touwen considers that while the palmar reflex may be partly responsible for the success of the first attempt at grasping, this grasping cannot solely depend on reflex mechanisms. Voluntary grasping emerges as an adaptive behaviour in its own right and both types of grasp co-exist for several months, the reflex weakening as we have indicated. In children who are retarded this weakening can be protracted, as Cowie (1970) has shown with Down's Syndrome infants. Melyn and Grossman (1976) note that persistence of the palmar grasp reflex can impair the development of voluntary grasping, a particular concern for those working with children who are retarded and motor-damaged.

Before moving on to consider voluntary grasp it is of interest to ask why a palmar reflex is found at all in human infants, given that it is not a developmental precursor to voluntary grasping. Prechtl (1981) has pointed out that there is comparability between infants of related species, and that evolution does not necessarily select out a given characteristic when it becomes irrelevant to development. Prechtl suggests that the palmar reflex is highly adaptive in young apes and monkeys because it enables them automatically to cling to their mothers. Indeed, during feeding the grasp will increase in strength. Thus, the palmar reflex has persisted from an earlier evolutionary stage, and it is to other mechanisms that we must look for the development and utilisation of voluntary grasp.

We will first briefly sumarise some of the main developments noted during the first two years of life. These have been carefully described with respect to neurological development by Touwen (1976), and in what follows we draw directly on his behavioural observations. It is important to note that though we are here emphasising *manipulative* development, this is clearly related to arm use and indeed to posture and we will have occasion to comment on these grosser aspects of motor development.

Touwen (1976 pp. 38–41) describes the main phases of goal-directed motility of arms and hands and illustrates the ages at which children typically display these patterns. The basic observations made are:

0. No goal-directed motility of arms and hands.
1. Looking at and playing with the hands. The infant moved one or both hands in front of his eyes and watched them intently. Mutual touching and/or grasping of the hands also scored 1.
2. Grasping objects. The infant approached the object with one or both hands and touched it, with or without actually getting hold of it. Although both assymmetrical and symmetrical arm/hand mobility could result in a score of 1 or 2 (depending on the final result of the movement), it was found that playing with the hands and this type of grasping objects mainly involved symmetrical arm/hand activity.
3. Playing with the feet. The infant touched or grasped one or both feet, with one or both hands. This behaviour was scored separately because of being so spectacular, even though this score was obtained by only a minority of the infants and usually occurred in conjunction with score 2 or with one of the following scores.
4. Holding one object. The infant was able to grasp and hold one object with one hand.
5. Holding an object in each hand. After grasping the first object the infant was presented with a second one: he managed to grasp and hold this second object without dropping the first one.
6. Holding two objects in one hand. While holding an object in each hand, the infant was able to grasp a third object presented to him without dropping one of the others. In the majority of cases the infant shifted one of the objects from one hand to the other and grasped the third one with the free hand. Some of the infants shifted the object to the ulnar side of the palm, held it with palm

and fingers and grasped the third object with the thumb and index
finger of this hand. (pp. 38–9)

While during the first month all children received a '0' score, from
about the third month a significant majority, i.e. 80 per cent of children,
were looking at and playing with their hands ('1'). Grasping objects was
observed during the fourth and fifth months with a majority going beyond
this phase by the sixth month. Touwen considers '4' (holding an object)
to be indicative of well-developed voluntary motor behaviour, while '5'
and '6' reflect the differentiation of manual manipulative capacities
(p. 39). From 10 months onwards a majority of children have reached
this phase. By around 16 months phase '6' behaviour is almost exclusively
observed in all children. Touwen notes that this final change in which
children hold two objects in one hand was closely related to the development of steady sitting.

This general description of arm and hand motility can be com-
plemented by assessment of voluntary grasping. Again, Touwen provides
a series of descriptions that cover the child from birth to around 18
months:

0. No grasping of the object.
1. Palmar grasp: when grasping the infant used the whole palmar
    surface of hands and fingers.
2. Radial palmar grasp: the infant mainly used the radial half of his
    palm, including thumb and index finger.
3. Scissor grasp: the infant grasped the object between the volar
    surfaces of his extended thumb and index finger.
4. Inferior pincer grasp: the infant grasped the object between the
    tip of his index finger and the volar side of his thumb.
5. Pointing: the infant appeared unable to grasp, but he pointed and
    eventually touched the object with an extended index finger ('tip-
    ping'). Sometimes this pointing was followed by an inferior or
    good pincer grasp.
6. Pincer grasp: the infant grasped the object neatly between the
    tips of index and thumb. (p. 41)

The increasing ability to employ fine prehension reflects a well-
documented developmental trend dependent upon maturation of the motor
cortex. It must be emphasised that palmar grip necessarily persists in
order for the child to hold large or heavy objects. Indeed, in part, competent prehension is dependent upon an optimal combination of grips

and their anatomical basis has been described by Napier (1980). We will return to the organisation of skilled sequences of grips and hand actions later in this section. Here we will consider the cognitive basis for and significance of manipulative activities as described by Piaget and experimentalists who have explored issues raised by him.

Piaget also begins his own account (Piaget 1953 pp. 88–121) with reference to 'impulsive movements' and 'pure reflex'. As noted earlier, however, Piaget is not referring specifically to reflexes in the neurological sense just described, but to the repertoire of movements with which the infant is born. These movements are observable while the child is still in the womb (Nijhuis, Prechtl, Martin and Bots 1982). Such impulsive movement becomes prolonged in Piaget's second stage of prehension and he refers to this stage as '. . . *the first circular reactions related to hand movements, prior to any actual coordination between prehension and sucking or vision'* (p. 90). Note that here Piaget is referring to the stages described here. The prehensile stages described occur, of course, during the sensorimotor period and can be mapped onto it, and serve as useful illustrations of the nature of infant development during this period. Here actions are carried out for their own sake, i.e. an object will be grasped and held without any attempt being made to bring it to the child's mouth or to look at it. Around the third month, finger-thumb opposition develops through the complementary processes of assimilation of objects to existing palmar grips and gradual accommodation of the grip to objects demanding finger prehension, or as Piaget puts it: 'The hand takes the form of the thing . . .' (p. 98).

In the third prehensile stage, the co-ordination between prehension and sucking occurs. For Piaget, sucking and prehension represent schemes that are exactly analogous with respect to enabling the child to develop through interaction with the world. Having grasped objects for the sake of grasping, the child moves towards combining the grasping scheme with the sucking scheme. Initially this is only partial in that: 'The hand takes hold of the objects and the mouth attracts the hand' (pp. 101–2). However, these schemes become assimilated to each other (i.e. reciprocal assimilation): 'The mouth seeks to suck what the hand grasps just as the hand seeks to grasp what the mouth sucks' (p. 102). At the same time, co-ordination between hand and vision begins to evolve, with the child observing its hand and even initiating movements of the hand while looking at it. However, true co-ordination does not yet occur, as the child does not know how to grasp what it sees, or hold what it grasps in front of the eyes.

It is in the fourth stage that prehension occurs simultaneously with the child's perception of the hand, the child grasping a *seen* object, not only those grasped or sucked. However, the child will only grasp an object which is seen in the same visual field as the hand. It is in the fifth stage that the child grasps what it sees without the limitation that hand and object must both be in the visual field. Here, according to Piaget, reciprocal assimilation is complete. He describes this achievement as 'the definitive triumph of prehension' (p. 119). It is of interest here to consider this achievement more broadly with respect to the development of the object concept. With the co-ordination of grasp, sucking and vision, progress towards a full object concept has been made during the first 4 to 5 months of life. Piaget writes: 'When an object can be simultaneously grasped and sucked or grasped, looked at and sucked, it becomes externalised in relation to the subject quite differently than when it could be only grasped' (p. 121).

Piaget's observations were made on his own children and experimental confirmation awaited an important study by White (1971). White's account is of the development of nonhandicapped infants raised in an institution. It begins with the assumption that at the outset the infant has reflexive grasps in response to touch (White 1971 p. 63) and some innate visual attentional behaviour (p. 63), the two being initially independent. Attentional behaviour improves through the first 3½ months, partly as a result of improved visual accommodation (pp. 56–9).

Reaching develops through the child regarding his or her own hands, thus generating eye-hand co-ordination. At this stage rapid swiping at objects occurs though the hand is closed prior to contact (pp. 58, 62, 64). Next, the child catches sight of its own hand and begins to look from it to the object, developing an integration of eye-hand and eye-object behaviour (pp. 60, 63, 64). Mutual hand grasping then 'spontaneously' occurs and the child discovers that the seen hand is the grasping hand. Further co-ordination between eye-hand, eye-object, and tactual-motor behaviours lead to visually controlled reaching (p. 64). This involves the hand opening prior to grasping, and the behaviour starting from outside the visual field.

White's account of visually directed reaching (and hence Piaget's conception of development) has been criticised in detail by Bower (1974). Bower (1979) has argued that reaching and grasping are basically genetically determined, though susceptible to environmental influences. White's infants were studied while lying on their backs, but Bower points out the importance of posture in the hand use displayed by the young baby. Where hands and head have to be used to maintain posture, the baby does show evidence of reaching and grasping during the first four weeks of life. If given the opportunity to practise these prehensile skills, they will persist, but more typically the child abandons the attempt to grasp objects until around 16 weeks, when reach and grasp again comes into evidence. These attempts during the fourth month, like those during the first, tend to be relatively unsuccessful, especially with respect to grasping. Reaching at this stage has been referred to as 'Phase 1' reach and grasp. The actual reach action tends to be ballistic, i.e. the child does not observe visually the course of the movement and adjust it, but rather moves the arm directly without such monitoring. The actual grasp is visually controlled, the hand closing on the object when it is seen to be within grasp. The action from about 20 weeks on, however, tends to take on different forms. In this 'Phase 2' reaching, the movement of the hand comes under visual control, that is, the child monitors where the hand is getting to by watching it. When the hand reaches the object there is a pause of less than half a second before the grasp is made. This grasp only tightens when the object is felt. Thus the movement of reaching shifts from being felt proprioceptively, i.e. through receptor cells in muscles and joints, to being under visual control, while the grasp alters from having been determined by the child seeing the object to feeling contact with it.

Two aspects of the maturational influences on reaching and grasping suggested by Bower are of special interest with respect to visually handicapped children. Bower notes that in the absence of objects to look at and reach for, for example, in a deprived institutional setting, babies will often look at their hand held in front of their face and reach for it with their free hand. Blind babies have also been observed to 'look at' and 'track' their hand, though obviously unable to see it. Similarly, both sighted and blind children will reach for an object they can only hear, but not see, in the early months. At about 20 weeks this co-ordination between sound and reach disappears in both groups. Bower (1979) reports work by Urwin (1973) in which blind children were given special training in reaching to sound to establish whether this channel of interaction with the outside world could be kept open beyond 20 weeks. Despite this, the ability to reach to a sound-producing object still disappeared.

Rather than reflecting the gradual construction of development described by Piaget, Bower emphasises its differentiation and maintenance through experience, and claims that White's observations are not valid. (For a full discussion of this argument see Hogg 1975 pp. 14–16.) while it is not possible to reconcile these contrasting views, detailed analyses of the sort provided by White and by Bower have the important function of alerting teachers to critical components of developmental achievements such as visually directed reaching. They also lay emphasis on certain general prerequisites for acquisition of developmental skills.

With the co-ordination of separate motor and visual schemes we move into the third stage of sensorimotor development of Secondary Circular Reactions described earlier. This in turn is followed by the fourth stage in which secondary schema are co-ordinated and applied to new situations (see pp. 42–3):

> Now, in order that two schemata, until then detached, may be co-ordinated with one another in a single act, the subject must aim to attain an end which is not directly within reach and to put to work, with this intention, the schemata thereto related to other situations. Here there exists simultaneously the distinction between the end and the means, and the intentional coordination of the schemata. The intelligent act is thus constituted, which does not limit itself merely to reproducing the interesting results, but to arrive at them due to new combinations. (Piaget 1951 p. 211)

With the fifth sensorimotor stage, Tertiary Circular Reactions occur in which new means are discovered through active implementation. As we have also seen, Stage VI will exhibit the invention of new means through mental combinations.

During the preoperational period cognitive development will permit increasingly complex and organised forms of manipulation which reflect growing problem solving abilities. Woodward (1972) considered such development in both children who were retarded (some with multiple impairments) and various groups of nonhandicapped children. She focused on the preconceptual or symbolic sub-stage with children of 18 months to 4½ years or 5 years of age. All had at least attained Sensorimotor Stage VI object concept and some had reached the intuitive preoperational stage, though none showed concrete operational thinking. Her study concentrated on a familiar preschool task-nesting beakers and she describes the various strategies from simple placement of one beaker in another and its removal through to selection of beakers successively and their successful nesting. This progress is dependent on two developmental changes. The first to a goal-directed outcome involving all beakers and the second to a series of paired checks in which the child evaluates the next placement either by picking up the next beaker and trying it or by a visual check. Before this stage is reached the child will make incorrect placements and have to remove beakers to realise the goal. Success around 5 years does not indicate operational thinking but does show an elaboration of means-ends behaviour indicative of sustained planning and use of feedback. A higher order plan would reflect realisation of the goal without successive checking (whether visual or otherwise). Other changes in manipulation in the service of construction are described by Goodson and Greenfield (1975) where it is shown how increasing complexity in the hierarchical organisation of material can be observed.

While a full programme anticipating a particular outcome does not appear to emerge in complex sequences of behaviour until later in the preoperational stage, anticipation of actions certainly does. A further study by Woodward and Hunt (1972) shows how anticipation continues to develop before that time in nonhandicapped and handicapped children with severe retardation. (It does not appear that any of these children were profoundly retarded, though full details are not given.) All children were presented with arrays of material, sometimes with instructions as to what to do, and sometimes not. The material will be familiar to many teachers: fitting tasks (pegboard, rings and stick, formboard); material for spontaneous handling (four sets, two colour variable with shape and size varying, one colour with shape and size variable, 100 identical counters); spatial order task (matching colour sequence on a rod); positioning tasks (fitting cubes into a tray). Anticipation was shown, for example, in the way in which children orientated blocks to be placed, a behaviour that increased from under 3 to over 3 years of age.

As in the nesting task described above, correction of errors was also noted. Here Woodward and Hunt make an important point with respect to error correction with different types of material. In a nesting task, for example, or a formboard, an error is immediately indicated to the child by the physical properties of the object — a square peg will not fit in a round hole. However, in the absence of such feedback, error correction was not seen in children in this preconceptual phase of the preoperational stage. In colour matching or spatial order tasks (sequences of different items that have to be matched to a standard), no self-correction was seen in either the children who are nonhandicapped or those who are handicapped. This indicates that the overall planning of the sequence is absent at this stage, matches being made piecemeal and without spontaneous use of information from the outcome.

Other important insights emerge from this study with respect to the way in which the child selects and arranges material. Over the period studied selectivity increases. With the exception of children who are characterised by the 'in-out' pattern with the pegboard, all showed spantaneous selectivity for at least one set of material. Arrangements were achieved mainly by placement of an object next to another, edge to edge or on top of each other. Regular arrangements were typically made on the basis of such spatial juxtapositions rather than through matching common attributes. The arrangements were classified as vertical structures (towers), horizontal lines and edge-matched groups of contrasted elements, the last varying in complexity. Typically there was a relation between the number of sets of material the child used, how many elements of a set, and the variety and complexity of structures. Thus breadth and complexity of selective behaviour is increasing during the preoperational stage.

However, while these cognitive developments will be reflected in increasingly competent and complex fine motor behaviour, they say little about the organisation of that behaviour from a motor skill standpoint. This issue has been approached by others than Piaget who have drawn on a wider literature of skill development. Here we must back-track again to the point at which the child is successfully reaching for and grasping objects. Embedded in the changes that occur in Phase II, reaching is a significant change that may relate to the way in which skilled action becomes more complex and effective. The 'break' of half a second between reaching and grasping shows the whole action has been differentiated into distinct components. Bower suggests that this distinction opens the way to grasping and releasing, and assumedly to adjustments of the hand on the object. Elliott and Connolly (1974) have proposed that skilled action, e.g. a child picking up a toy, placing it in a given place, holding it while a moveable part is adjusted, and so on, reflects the development of a variety of separate components that can be related in such a way that the child achieves a particular end. One important set of such components are the various grips the child uses. As we have seen earlier, these become increasingly 'fine' as they move from palmar grips, in which the object is in contact with the palm, to digital grips that employ finger-thumb opposition. The appropriate use and sequencing of the different types of grips to achieve different outcomes underlies skilled performance.

Connolly's description of the development of fine motor skill may be likened to the working of a computer program. The overall program is brought into play to achieve a particular outcome. To do this, it calls up a variety of smaller sub-programs, assembles them, and then the program is run. The sub-programs are the various component behaviours (grips, movements) that the child has developed. As the child becomes more skilled, so more and more components and ways of combining them are evolved.

In fact, it is more likely that the development of the child's skilled activity is much more flexible than this. While a motor program or scheme may direct the general course of the activity, it is possible that the program only specifies a general way of solving the problem and is not as rigid as the computer example would suggest. While we can to some extent identify component actions needed in a skill, these are likely to be much more variable in their form and execution than we would expect of simple, rigid sub-programs. This was found to be the case with relatively young nonhandicapped infants by Moss and Hogg (1983). Far from 12–18 month old children becoming more rigid in their pattern of action as they become more skilled, as the computer analogy would suggest, they became more variable and more creative in their use of their hands even when achieving the same result. This observation, taken with recent developments in the theory of skill learning, has important implications for how we teach skilled actions and we will return to this in our discussion of programme development in Volume 2, Chapter 5.

In using terms such as motor 'plans', 'schemes' and 'programs', we are emphasising the child putting together an organised sequence of actions that will bring about a particular outcome. Success and failure or changing circumstances will lead to changes in the motor plan. In addition, the action will be modified or revised on the basis of information received as the child carries out the action. Such modification is dependent upon 'feedback', i.e. visual or bodily information which is matched to the intended action. We have already seen how such information is used in the development of reaching and grasping and in nesting beakers. Connolly (1970) has described how, as the child develops, the ability to process such feedback increases, i.e. the child's span of attention is broadened. He has also noted that as the child becomes more skilled in action, so attention to the task decreases. At some stage in many skills we all find that we do not need to attend to what we are doing. The action can be 'run off' without conscious control. Skilled action of the kind we have described will always be limited in its expression by the child's understanding of the world. However, the very exercise of such skill will itself enhance and develop this understanding. As the child develops cognitively, so the ends he or she sets out to achieve become more complex. The role of skilled action of this sort in enabling a person to deal with the world continues throughout the whole of our lives.

In what we have written so far, we have tended, with a few exceptions, to emphasise manipulative activity in its own right. We have pointed out in passing, however, that a variety of other processes have to be sustained for the hands to realise an intended action. Prechtl (1981) has placed the action of voluntary grasping of a small object within what he calls the 'complex neural mechanisms which evolve as an assemblage of independently developed modules' (p. 207). He indicates that such an action is:

> . . . dependent on a whole series of independent mechanisms such as visual depth-perception with binocular vision and eye-movements, a finely graded control of body posture, the ability to execute an antici-patory shift of the centre of gravity before the arm reaches out, and servo-loops for smoothly directed arm movements and fine finger movements, for all of which the function of the neuronal connections from the motor cortex to the cervical motor neurones are essential. A failure in the development of one single component impairs the total final complex mechanism. (p. 207)

Prechtl goes on to invoke additional experiential factors of the sort we have described above in our Piagetian account. Prechtl's description of the general basis of manipulative action draws attention to the place of gross motor control in adaptive behaviour and it is to select aspects of such development that we now turn.

Gross Motor Development

The ability to maintain one's posture and the capacity to alter and reorient-ate one's position in space are in a very real sense the foundations on which so many of the other developmental adaptations we have described rest. Situations where communicative, cognitive or manipulative demands are being made on us demand stability of head, trunk and arms. Move-ment in the environment leads to changes in our relation to objects and people and enables us not only to realise out specific objectives but also results in changing experiences which have important cognitive and perceptual consequences.

In the preceding sections we have concentrated in the main on psychological events that are thought to underlie development, touching on neurological aspects only briefly in relation to prehensile develop-ment. While experience and psychological processes are undoubtedly involved in the development of posture and mobility, study of these developments has focused more explicitly on the development of the child's nervous system and musculature. These changes, on which the gross motor abilities noted above depend, involve not only qualitative changes in specific parts of the nervous system (e.g. myelination of nerves, growth of the brain), but the development of critical connections between various parts of the brain on which behaviour is dependent.

In people who are profoundly retarded with obvious physical impairments such as cerebral palsy or spina bifida, damage to these systems will exist and motor behaviour will consequently be impaired. Despite, however, the relevance of an understanding of developmental neurophysiology to the development of such people, a detailed account of this is beyond the scope of this chapter. We assume that teachers and parents working with such children will have access to physiotherapists and paediatricians who will have illuminated the specific physical difficulties that the child has and how best therapy can improve functioning (see Volume 2, Chapter 5). The teacher, while being concerned with and perhaps involved in improving basic motor ability, will also be looking to encourage use of available gross motor abilities through appropriate programmes (see Volume 2, Chapter 5). A detailed knowledge of neurophysiology will not, however, be required, and comment on this basis for motor behaviour will be limited in what follows. Here we shall summarise the main course of development of several aspects of posture and mobility based on a detailed study of infants by Touwen (1976): *Neurological Development in Infancy* (Spastics Medical Publications with Heinemann). In this book Touwen follows the course of a variety of aspects of motor development and comments on the processes underlying them. Here we shall note the main steps in acquiring stable sitting and standing posture and mobility.

Posture

Posture of Head, Trunk and Arms in Prone Position. Touwen describes seven developments through which children are likely to pass in reaching the stage at which they can support themselves on their hands with their arms extended. These are:

1. The infant lifted his head and kept it lifted for some seconds without using elbows or hands. The upper part of the thorax was either slightly lifted or not lifted at all. Absence of head-lift in the prone position did not occur among infants of this study due to the selection criteria for neurological optimality.
2. The infant lifted the head and the upper part of the thorax, apparently supporting himself on his elbows, but he did not topple over

when this elbow support was pulled away.

3. The infant lifted his head and upper part of the thorax, part of the time supporting himself on his elbows, part of the time without supporting himself. In the latter case he extended and spread his arms in a 'plane-like fashion' — a position described by Illingworth (1966) as 'swimming'.

4. The infant lifted his head and upper part of the thorax without supporting himself on elbows or hands ('plane' or 'swimming' position).

5. The infant lifted head and thorax, part of the time without any support, part of the time supporting himself on his (opened) hands and extended arms. Intermittently he supported himself on his elbows, which seemed to be a transition to support on extended arms. He toppled over if this support was pulled away.

6. The infant supported himself on his hands and extended arms almost exclusively. During this phase he might begin to draw his knees under his abdomen.

7. The infant supported himself on extended arms and flexed knees.

Scores 2 and 7 were considered as first and final changes respectively (pp. 41–2)

Part of Touwen's analysis of this and other scales relates the achievement of a particular ability in one area to achievements in others. In this instance, achievement of '7' above was related to important developments in sitting, walking and standing. He comments that:

One may contend that the development of the balance required for the all-fours position is a prerequisite for the development of adequate sitting. The ability to achieve an all-fours position also reflects an adequate sense of motor control needed for an efficient development of vertical posture. (p. 46)

This observation draws attention to the fact that, although we can usefully distinguish behavioural milestones in a number of areas of motor development, a smaller number of common motor processes will underlie these diverse developments and deficits in such processes will make themselves felt across a wide range of behaviours.

In the carefully selected children studied by Touwen (all screened so as not to be at risk for subsequent handicap), most infants had acquired this ability by 16 months. He points out that some authors have used delay in development in maintaining this posture in the prone position as a key indicator of abnormal retardation. He cautions, however, that a single indicator of this sort should only be taken in combination with other indices.

Sitting Up. This assessment began with the examiner holding the child's wrists and Touwen lists four categories:

   0. No active flexion of the elbows and/or retraction of the shoulders during pulling into sitting position. The head remained in one line with the trunk.
   1. Slight active flexion of the elbows and/or retraction of the shoulders, with evident flexion of the head. The infant was not able to reach a sitting position without the examiner's help.
   2. Evident active flexion of the elbows and retraction of the shoulders. The infant still needed the examiner's help during the last part of the movement. Evident head and trunk flexion.
   3. The infant was able to sit up without any active help of the examiner.

Scores 1 and 3 were regarded as indicators of the first and final changes respectively. (p. 55)

Touwen found marked variation in the age at which children were able to sit independently with a small minority achieving this by 32 weeks, but half not doing so until the end of the first year of life. Some only achieved independent sitting at about 65 weeks. A close reflection was found between the final change of sitting and the onset of standing up and of walking.

Duration of Sitting. Children's ability to sit independently increases with age, and Touwen followed the progress of infants in his sample from an inability to sit without support to full independent sitting:

   0. The infant was unable to sit without support.
   1. The infant was able to sit free for some seconds.
   2. The infant was able to sit free for about 30 seconds.
   3. The infant was able to sit free for about one minute.
   4. The infant was able to sit free for longer than at least one minute.

Scores 1 and 4 were considered as the first stages and the final changes respectively. (p. 57)

In reality, Touwen considers the ability to sit for 30 seconds independently as fully developed sitting. Shortly after this achievement infants will very soon be able to actually sit up themselves. A small minority of infants were able to achieve '1' around 5 to 6 months with improvements towards '4' occurring from 7 to 9 months. All children passed '3' or '4' in the twelfth month and all had passed '4' by the fourteenth month.

Posture of the Trunk During Sitting. Development of upright posture during sitting has a similar time course to the achievement of independent sitting itself. Touwen suggests that improving posture itself reflects the development of balance which in turn increases the duration of sitting. He distinguishes five steps in postural improvement in sitting:

0.   The infant was unable to sit without support.
1.   The infant sat with rounded back and supported himself on his arms.
2.   The infant sat with rounded back without supporting himself on his arms.
3.   The infant sat with straight back with no evident lumbar kyphosis or lordosis.
4.   The infant sat upright with evident lumbar lordosis.

Scores 1 and 4 were considered to reflect the moments of the first and final changes respectively. (p. 60)

We have already noted the importance of posture not only in its own right but in relation to other acts the child may engage in such as manipulation. Touwen noted that during the period when the infant can sit independently with a straight back, voluntary use of one or two hands begins to develop. Similarly, these developments in posture were also related to the infant's ability visually to follow a moving object by turning the head and trunk.

Standing Up. It is evident that the development of balance is critical to independent standing and that relations with other aspects of motor development demanding balance will be found. We will return to this point below. It is also of interest that the child can achieve the standing position through independent movement and Touwen's scale reflects this:

0. The infant was unable to stand up.
1. The infant was able to get into a kneeling position while support-
    ing himself with one or both hands.
2. The infant was able to get into a standing position while support-
    ing himself during standing. He was not able to sit down without
    help.
3. The infant was able to get into a standing position while support-
    ing himself during standing. He was able to sit down without help.
4. The infant was able to stand free.

Scores 1 and 4 were considered to reflect the first and final changes
respectively (p. 61)

Great variation was found in the achievement of the various phases
in this study. Standing with support varied from 36 to 72 weeks and while
one infant could stand at 44 weeks, about 80 per cent had not reached
this step until 18 months.

Mobility

Movement in the Prone Position. By movement in prone we are referring to the gradual progression the infant makes to crawling or creeping
on all fours. Touwen describes this progression in the following way:

0. No unequivocal change of spatial position.
1. Wriggling or pivoting movements, without specific use of arms
    and/or legs, resulting in spatial displacement. Moving backwards
    also scored 1.
2. Abdominal progression using the arms only.
3. Abdominal progression using the arms and legs.
4. Progression by way of abdominal creeping and creeping on all
    fours.
5. Creeping on all fours exclusively.

Scores 1 and 5 were regarded as first and final changes respectively.
(p. 47)

Relations exist between the mature phase of locomotion in prone and
walking unsupported, the development of steady sitting and the onset
of standing, developments that Touwen suggests reflect the development

of voluntary motor behaviour based on the maturation of specific brain mechanisms, and brain-spinal cord connections, while certain critical aspects of movement co-ordination are present at birth. Again, we will have more to say about the underpinnings and prerequisites of movement development below.

Rolling from Prone to Supine. Mobility of a different kind is involved here and as the following descriptions of Touwen's categories indicate, is related to the ability to sit up independently:

0.   The infant was not able to return into supine position.
1.   The infant rolled back into supine axially.
2.   The infant could turn from prone into supine position, sometimes by rotation of the trunk on the pelvis.
3.   The infant returned into supine position exclusively by means of trunk rotation. If the infant did not return into supine, but instead got into sitting posture (which usually happened as soon as the infant was able to sit up independently), this was also scored 3, as trunk rotation is evidently involved in this process.

Scores 1 and 3 were considered as first and final changes respectively. (pp. 52–3)

According to Touwen it appeared easier for an infant to push up on extended arms and then rotate the top half of the body on the pelvis so as to turn on the back, than in supine position to lift the head and shoulders and rotate them on the pelvis to turn to prone. By 13 months over 80 per cent of infants sat up from prone rather than returning to supine.

Rolling from Supine to Prone. The course of rolling from supine to prone is described by Touwen as follows:

0.   No rolling behaviour. The infant remained in supine position.
1.   The infant turned from supine into prone position by way of axial rolling, initiated by head rotation, but without evident hip rotation.
2.   The infant used rotation of the body on the pelvis during rolling behaviour.

Scores 1 and 2 were considered as first and final changes respectively. (pp. 50–1)

For most healthy children the developmental course of this ability is fairly brief, occurring between 4 and 7 months, though '2' can entail a more protracted period with 80 per cent passing at 7 months and 100 per cent of children only passing at 14 months.

Walking. Walking independently is one of the most significant of early gross motor skills for parents and educators. It is also an ability in which there can be marked variation as to the age at which the child achieves the later stages of the development course described by Touwen:

0. The infant was unable to walk.
1. The infant could walk if his mother held him by both hands.
2. The infant could walk if his mother held him by one hand.
3. The infant walked free for a few paces.
4. The infant walked free for at least seven paces consecutively.

Scores 1 and 4 were regarded as first and final changes respectively. (p. 63)

Within this course, Touwen found that the median for walking with both hands held was 12 months while for free walking it was 16 months.

The Basis for Posture and Mobility

We have already indicated that we do not intend going into the neurophysiological basis of the behavioural developments described above. However, much of what Touwen and others have written regarding these developments is relevant to our understanding of impairments of function and their remediation.

First, Touwen (1976), Prechtl (1981) and others are insistent that it is not appropriate to regard the infant's nervous system as simply an inadequate or even defective adult nervous system. It has, they argued, its own special properties which are well adapted to the environment. It is certainly not a bundle of reflexes:

From birth onwards the infant is very well able to cope with his infantile needs, in a far more differentiated way than would ever be consistent with the notion of a 'reflex-being'. Instead of being considered as a bundle of reflexes, the infantile nervous system must be seen as a complex information processing apparatus. (Touwen 1976 p. 52)

This is not to say that reflexes do not play their part in early development or that inadequacies in reflex functioning do not impair development. One important example of reflex activity which is involved in well co-ordinated motor organisation and is established in the spinal cord, are the leg movements present at birth. These involve crawling and stepping movements, i.e. basic patterns of gross motor behaviour closely akin to the late 'milestone' behaviours we have described.

This brings us to our second point, namely that such activities in themselves are not adequate to achieve these milestones. As Touwen points out: '. . . the mechanisms for maintaining balance during crawling or standing cannot express themselves because appropriate instrumentation (e.g. muscle power) is lacking' (p. 49). He goes on: 'Increasing muscle power and differentiation and organisation of the co-operating vestibular and cerebellar mechanisms which result in the improvement of maintenance of trunk and limb position are needed for the brain to generate efficient movement patterns' (Touwen 1976 p. 49). In terms of the organisation of a curriculum, this fact parallels the setting of educational aims in which a child must be able to organise the posture of trunk and limbs before the ability to crawl is taught and must be able to stand before walking.

What emerges from this view is that the unfolding of gross motor behaviour is dependent upon closely related developments in different areas. Touwen suggests a schematic developmental course '. . . in which standing and walking are preceded by steady sitting, while the development of balance (reflected by sitting behaviour) should at least have started before the all-fours position and creeping on all fours can be achieved' (p. 61).

In complementary fashion, deficits or delays in specific components will disrupt the achievement of a whole pattern of behaviour. Though dealing with children who are severely rather than profoundly retarded, Molnar (1978) has clearly demonstrated the way in which acquisition of specific postural mechanisms leads to the acquisition of major gross motor milestones as they complete the jig-saw of necessary components. A fuller account of this study appears in Chapter 8 while its remedial implications are covered in Volume 2, Chapter 5.

A further illustration comes from studies of 'teaching' walking. Cunningham (1979) observed that with instruction children with Down's Syndrome in his sample could walk with support at 17.4 months in contrast to those observed by Share and Veal (1974) who walked with support at 19 months. Nevertheless, independent walking was only achieved in both Down's Syndrome groups at 24 months, perhaps when the relevant automatic postural control mechanism had matured.

Movement and Perception

Earlier we commented on the adaptive value of movement and postural control, an obvious point and one of which we are all aware. Less obviously, however, movement has consequences that reach beyond those that are immediately apparent. It is also clear that voluntary, active movement is important for the development of sensory perception and beyond that for cognition. In a series of studies with both animals and humans, Held (1965) showed how important active movement was for the development of perception. This work began with two questions that have clear implications for those working with individuals who are multiply impaired. First, is visual stimulation enough in itself to lead to the development of normal perceptual processes? Or, second, is it necessary for the varied sensory experience to come about through active, voluntary movement?

Though the experiments described involved human subjects, it is a study with kittens that most clearly demonstrates that the latter suggestion is the correct one. Pairs of kittens from the same litter were placed in an apparatus surrounded by a circular wall on which clear, black vertical stripes were painted. The kittens were yoked together in such a way that one was free to walk round the apparatus voluntarily. This kitten's movements were transferred to the other who was passively rotated in a box, but who was able to see the stripes moving round just as for the active kitten. Thus their visual experience was almost identical, though in one it resulted from active movement, while for the other movement was passive. The kittens were subsequently tested on a number of simple sensorimotor tasks including such things as visually directed paw placement, visual tracking and so on. It was quite clear that, despite their comparable visual experience, the active kitten was far superior on these tasks. Held and Hein (1968) in reporting the original study comment that '. . . the variation in visual stimulation accompanying movement is essential for the development of certain coordinations . . . but this variation can be effective only when it is concurrent with and systematically dependent upon self-produced movements' (pp. 872–3). Other more complex studies with humans involving both vision and hearing amply bear this conclusion out.

Parallels with Piaget's account of sensorimotor development clearly exist. Piaget emphasises the active exercise of schemes as an essential condition for cognitive development, though he, of course, goes beyond the importance of physical movement to mental activity as well. For the child with little, or restricted, movement, then, there will be important sensory consequences that will influence a wide range of other activities. It should also be clear that whatever other value the passive visual stimulation of such children may have, this should not be expected to lead to development in anywhere near as effective a way as would occur for visual stimulation resulting from active movement.

Conclusion

We have in effect come full circle. We have moved from cognition to gross motor behaviour, only to find as we suggested earlier, that apparently distinct areas of development are inextricably related, influencing each other.

In the following chapters we set various kinds of impairment against this account of development. Inevitably many gaps exist in that developmental studies of impairment such as these are far more limited in number than are the studies that go to make up the full scope of developmental psychology.

References

Bates, E. (1976) *Language and Context: The Acquisition of Pragmatics*, Academic Press, London

Bates, E., Benigni, L., Bretherton, I., Camaioni, L. and Volterra, V. (1977) 'From Gestures to the First Words: On Cognitive and Social Prerequisites' in M. Lewis and L.A. Rosenblum (eds.), *Interaction, Conversation and the Development of Language*, Wiley, New York

Berger, J. and Cunningham, C.C. (1981) 'The Development of Eye Contact between Mothers and Normal Versus Down's Syndrome Infants', *Developmental Psychology, 17,* 678–89

Bower, T.G.R. (1974) *Development in Infancy*, W.H. Freeman, San Francisco

Bower, T.G.R. (1979) *Human Development*, W.H. Freeman, San Francisco

Bronfenbrenner, U. (1979) *The Ecology of Human Development: Experiments by Nature and Design*, Harvard University Press, Mass.

Brown, R. (1973) *A First Language*, Harvard University Press, Mass.

Brown, G. and Desforges, C. (1979) *Piaget's Theory: A Psychological Critique*, Routledge and Kegan Paul, London

Bruner, J.S. (1975a) 'From Communication to Language: A Psychological Perspective', *Cognition, 3,* 255–87

Bruner, J.S. (1975b) 'The Ontogenesis of Speech Acts', *Journal of Child*

Language, 2, 1–19

Bruner, J.S., Jolly, A. and Sylva, K. (1976) *Play: Its Role in Development and Evolution,* Penguin Books, Harmondsworth

Butterworth, G., Jarrett, N. and Hicks, L. (1982) 'Spatiotemporal Identity in Infancy: Perceptual Competence or Conceptual Deficit', *Developmental Psychology, 18,* 435–49

Carter, A. (1975) 'The Transformation of Sensorimotor Morphemes into Words: A Case Study of the Development of 'More' and 'Mine' ', *Journal of Child Language, 2,* 223–50

Chapman, R.S. (1981) 'Mother-child Interaction in the Second Year of Life' in R.L. Schiefelbusch and D.D. Bricker (eds), *Early Language: Acquisition and Intervention,* University Park Press, Baltimore

Connolly, K. (1970) 'Response Speed, Temporal Sequencing and Information Processing in Children' in K. Connolly (ed.), *Mechanisms of Motor Skill Development,* Academic Press, London

Cowie, V.A. (1970) *A Study of the Early Development of Mongols: Institute for Research into Mental Retardation, Monograph 1,* Pergamon Press, Oxford

Cromer, R. (1979) 'The Strengths of the Weak Form of the Cognition Hypothesis for Language Acquisition' in V. Lee (ed.), *Language Development,* Croom Helm, London

Cunningham, C.C. (1979) 'Aspects of Early Development in Down's Syndrome Infants', unpublished Ph.D. thesis, University of Manchester, Manchester

deVilliers, J.G. and deVilliers, P.A. (in press) 'The Acquisition of Language' in D.I. Slobin (ed.), *The Cross-linguistic Study of Language Acquisition,* Lawrence Erlbaum, Hillsdale, N.J.

Dunst, C.J. (1980) *A Clinical and Educational Manual for Use with the Uzgiris and Hunt Scales of Infant Psychological Development,* Pro-Ed, Inc. Austin, Tex.

Elliott, J.M. and Connolly, K.J. (1974) 'Hierarchical Structure in Skill Development' in K. Connolly and J. Bruner (eds.), *The Growth of Competence,* Academic Press, London

Goodson, D.B. and Greenfield, P.M. (1975) 'The Search for Structural Principles in Children's Manipulative Play: A Parallel with Linguistic Development', *Child Development, 46,* 734–46

Gregory, S. and Mogford, K. (1981) 'Early Language Development in Deaf Children' in B. Woll, J.G. Kyle and M. Deucher (eds.), *Perspectives on British Sign Language and Deafness,* Croom Helm, London

Greenwald, C.A. and Leonard, L.B. (1979) 'Communicative and Sensorimotor Development of Down's Syndrome Children', *American Journal of Mental Deficiency, 84,* 296–303

Halliday, M.A.K. (1973) *Explorations in the Function of Language,* Arnold, London

Held, R. (1965) 'Plasticity in Sensory-motor Systems', *Scientific American, 213,* 84–94

Held, R. and Hein, A. (1963) 'Movement-produced Stimulation in the Development of Visually Guided Behavior', *Journal of Comparative Physiology and Psychology, 56,* 872–6

Hogg, J. (1975) 'Normative Development and Educational Programme Planning for Severely Subnormal Children' in C.C. Kiernan and F.P. Woodford (eds.),

Behaviour Modification with the Severely Retarded, Associated Scientific Publishers, Amsterdam

Hogg, J. (1986) 'Assessing Early Cognitive Development' in J. Hogg and N.V. Raynes (eds.), *Assessment in Mental Handicap: A Guide to Tests, Batteries and Checklists,* Croom Helm, London

Illingworth, R.S. (1966) *The Development of the Infant and Young Child, 3rd edn,* Churchill Livingstone, Edinburgh

Inhelder, B. (1968) *The Diagnosis of Reasoning in the Mentally Retarded,* John Day, New York

Jones, O. (1979) 'Mother-child Communication with Prelinguistic Down's Syndrome and Normal Infants' in H. Schaffer (ed.), *Studies in Mother-child Interaction,* Academic Press, London

Lloyd, P. and Beveridge, M. (1981) *Information and Meaning in Child Communication,* Academic Press, London

Lowe, M. (1975) 'Trends in the Development of Representational Play', *Journal of Child Psychology and Psychiatry, 16,* 33–47

Lowe, M. and Costello, A.J. (1976) *Manual for the Symbolic Play Test: Experimental Edition,* NFER, Windsor

McCall, R.B. (1974) 'Exploratory Manipulation and Play in the Human Infant', *Monograph of the Society for Research in Child Development, 39,* Serial No. 155, 1–88

Maçnamara, J. (1972) 'Cognitive Basis of Language Learning in Infants', *Psychological Review, 79,* 1–13

Melyn, M.A. and Grossman, H. J. (1976) 'Neurophysiological Correlates' in W.M. Cruickshank (ed.), *Cerebral Palsy: A Developmental Disability,* Syracuse Press, New York

Miller, J.F. and Yoder, D. (1974) 'An Ontogenetic Language Teaching Strategy for Retarded Children' in R.L. Schiefelbusch and L.L. Lloyd (eds.) *Language Perspectives: Acquisition, Retardation and Intervention,* PRO-ED, Inc. Austin, Tex.

Molnar, G.E. (1978) 'Analysis of Motor Disorder in Retarded Infants and Young Children', *American Journal of Mental Deficiency, 83,* 213–22

Moss, S.C. and Hogg, J. (1983) 'The Development and Integration of Fine Motor Sequences in 12- to 18-month Old Children: A Test of the Modular Theory of Motor Skill Acquisition, *Genetic Psychology Monographs, 107,* 145–87

Napier, J. (1980) *Hands,* George Allen and Unwin, London

Nelson, K. (1973) 'Structure and Strategy in Learning to Talk', *Monograph of the Society for Research in Child Development, 38,* Serial No. 149, 1–135

Nijhuis, J.G., Prechtl, H.F.R., Martin, C.B. and Bots, R.S.G.M. (1982) 'Are there Behavioural States in the Human Fetus?', *Early Human Development, 6,* 177–98

Ninio, A. and Bruner, J. (1978) 'The Achievements and Antecedents of Labelling', *Journal of Child Language, 5,* 1–16

Philips, J.L. (1981) *Piaget's Theory: A Primer,* W.H. Freeman, San Francisco

Piaget, J. (1951) *Play, Dreams and Imitation in Childhood,* Routledge and Kegan Paul, London

Piaget, J. (1953) *The Origin of Intelligence in the Child,* Routledge and Kegan Paul, London

Piaget, J. (1955) *The Child's Construction of Reality,* Routledge and Kegan Paul,

London

Piaget, J. and Inhelder, B. (1956) *The Child's Perception of Space*, Routledge and Kegan Paul, London

Prechtl, H.F.R. (1981) 'The Study of Neural Development as a Perspective of Clinical Problems' in K.J. Connolly and H.F.R. Prechtl (eds.), *Maturation and Development: Biological and Psychological Perspectives*, Heinemann, London

Share, J.B. and Veale, A.M.O. (1974) *Developmental Landmarks for Children with Down's Syndrome (Mongolism)*, University of Otago Press, Dunedin

Sinclair, H. (1971) 'Sensorimotor Action Patterns as a Condition for the Acquisition of Syntax' in R. Huxley and E. Ingram (eds.), *Language Acquisition: Models and Methods*, Academic Press, London

Snyder, L. (1978) 'Communicative and Cognitive Abilities and Disabilities in the Sensorimotor Period', *Merrill-Palmer Quarterly, 24*, 161–80

Thatcher, J. (1976) 'An Analysis of the Structure, Function and Content of the Vocabularies of Babies: The First Hundred Words', M.A. dissertation, University of Nottingham, Nottingham

Touwen, B.C.L. (1976) *Neurological Development in Infancy*, Clinics in Medicine, No. 58, Spastics International Medical Publications with Heinemann, London

Urwin, C. (1973) 'The Development of a Blind Baby', unpublished manuscript, University of Edinburgh, Edinburgh

Uzgiris, I.C. (1976) 'Organization of Sensorimotor Intelligence' in M. Lewis (ed.), *Origins of Intelligence: Infancy and Early Childhood*, Plenum Press, London

Uzgiris, I.C. and Hunt, J.McV. (1975) *Assessment in Infancy: Ordinal Scales of Psychological Development*, University of Illinois Press, Chicago

White, B.L. (1971) *Human Infants: Experience and Psychological Development*, Prentice-Hall, Englewood Cliffs, N.J.

Wohlwill, J.J. (1973) *The Study of Behavioral Development*, Academic Press, London

Woodward, W.M. (1972) 'Problem Solving Strategies of Young Children', *Journal of Child Psychology and Psychiatry, 13*, 11–24

Woodward, W.M. and Hunt, M.R. (1972) 'Exploratory Studies of Early Cognitive Development', *British Journal of Educational Psychology, 42*, 248–59

4 THE DEVELOPMENTAL CONSEQUENCES OF VISUAL IMPAIRMENT

General Development

The impact of visual handicap on the development of a child obviously increases with the severity of the impairment. Much of the evidence we consider here comes from studies of totally blind children or those with only light perception, though parallel findings with partially sighted children sometimes exist. Reynell (1978) has described patterns of development in both blind and partially sighted children using the Reynell-Zinkin Mental-Development Scale devised specifically for use with such children (Reynell and Zinkin 1975).

Delays were noted relative to sighted children for both these groups, with the more severe delay emerging for the blind child in most (though not all) areas of development:

(i) Social adaptation was assessed by a scale concerned with response to people, self-help, etc., and was found to be equally delayed for blind and partially sighted children, relative to their sighted peers. The level of social adaptation achieved by the sighted children at 3 years was reached by the visually impaired groups at 4–5 years.

(ii) Sensorimotor understanding, involving performance that indicates that the child understands the properties of objects and relations between them, followed a similar pattern, though here blind children achieved the level of sighted children somewhat later than did partially sighted children. It was not until around 5 years old that the visually handicapped groups began to achieve the level reached by their nonhandicapped peers at around 3 years.

(iii) Exploration of the environment by visually impaired children followed a pattern similar to sensorimotor development.

(iv) Verbal comprehension was assessed through a consideration of both early responses to sound, recognition of phrases and understanding of words as object labels, as well as understanding of complex directions. The divergence between the sighted children and their visually impaired peers began to emerge at the stage of understanding object labels, and it was not until around

5 years of age that the latter had reached the level achieved just after 3 years by the former. Though the partially sighted children remained consistently in advance of the blind children in their comprehension, this effect was very slight compared to the marked delay shown by both visually impaired groups.

(v) The structure of expressive language was explored through assessment of early sound-making, through one word utterances and word combinations. Towards the end of the first year of life the sighted children begin to get ahead of their visually impaired peers. After this they remain six to eight months ahead. Differences between the impaired groups are very slight, with the blind children actually leading the partially sighted group during the second year at the stage of jargon and 'situation' words.

(vi) The expression of language content is again delayed in the visually impaired children with only the most marginal advantage to the partially sighted children. Nevertheless, visually impaired children reach the level acquired by sighted children at 4 years of age by their fifth year.

We may see, then, that the apparently highly specific handicap of visual impairment has a marked effect on a variety of different aspects of development. We can also see that this effect may truly be referred to as a 'delay' since the impaired children generally do achieve the ability of their sighted peers at a later age. This normative information, however, tells us little about the processes involved that lead to delay. Nor does it illuminate the way in which development in one area can affect development in another. To gain some understanding of these processes it is helpful to start with an area of development that clearly begins to follow the normal course but then goes radically awry in blind children, i.e. gross motor development.

Gross Motor Development

Adelson and Fraiberg (1974 and 1976) have shown that many aspects of gross motor development in blind children fall within the normal range. This applies particularly to postural development involving head and trunk control, and reflects the essentially normal neuromuscular development of these children. Thus the child sits alone momentarily, takes stepping movements when the hands are held, and stands alone, at ages within the normal range. Despite this, the developments in mobility that might follow these milestones are markedly delayed. The blind child does not elevate his/her body when laid prone, pull to standing, or walk alone at the stage when postural control and neuromuscular development would permit these activities. The consequence is, then, that, without early intervention, the child is immobile and in remaining immobile is denied a whole range of crucial experiences critical to the developing child's attempt to construct a 'picture' of the world.

And yet most blind children do become mobile and learn that objects beyond their immediate reach can be attained through bodily movement in space. While the sighted child achieves this through co-ordination of movement in visual space, the blind child has to use sound as a substitute. For the former, creeping, crawling or hitching to get a seen object will occur around 7 months. For the latter, only when he or she learns to localise an object in space on the basis of sound will the blind child move off to obtain the 'heard' object. Though there is no such thing as 'auditory space', the blind child has had to create a framework comparable to the visual space in which the sighted child develops. Of this development Adelson and Fraiberg (1976) noted: 'Once reach on sound has been achieved [the blind child] can be lured into motion and can begin to cope with the relatively less difficult problems of balance, co-ordination, speed and safety' (p. 14).

Fine Motor Development

In the same way that delay in the acquisition of gross motor skills inhibits the visually impaired child's opportunity to explore the world, so do similar delays in fine motor development. Directed reaching for objects can be delayed for several months as can persistent reaching for objects that are difficult to obtain (Norris, Spaulding and Brodie 1957). Fraiberg (1968) draws attention to the fact that blind children do not bring their hands together in the midline and finger them as occurs with sighted children. This suggests, she noted, that this behaviour is under the control of vision and may be a direct precursor of visually directed reaching: 'Sustained hand regard and an alternation of hand regard and visual fixation of an object facilitate the co-ordination of vision and prehension and prepare for intentional reaching in the subsequent stage' (p. 281). This subsequent stage occurs around 5 months in sighted children but much later in blind children. 'There is no adaptive substitution of sound for vision at this stage', writes Fraiberg (p. 281).

Fraiberg goes on to document the course by which the blind child learns to reach for objects with which he or she has had contact. If such an object is taken from the child and put on a table top with which the child is in contact, then he/she will explore the surface to try to retrieve the object. At this stage, from 6 to 8 months, however, the child will not reach on the basis of sound alone for an object with which recent contact has not been maintained. The actual range during which reaching on the basis of sound was noted was wide among Fraiberg's children — from just under 7 months to almost 12 months. Such reaching, as we have seen, is inherently bound up with the development of mobility. Fraiberg writes that: *'We have no baby in our series who learned to creep before he gave us a demonstration of reaching on sound cue alone'* (p. 285). Again, we see how important it is to consider the interdependence of different areas of development that traditionally we discuss and teach as if they were isolated from each other.

In certain respects, blind children do not differ markedly in other aspects of fine motor development. Fraiberg (1968) reports that pincer grip (finger thumb opposition or adult digital grip) is as developed by 10 months in blind children as for sighted children by 10 months, though it is somewhat awkward and uncertain. We might speculate that it is the deprivation of visual feedback that leads to such awkwardness, the consolidation of the motor program or schema depending mainly on proprioceptive and tactile feedback. Similarly the child will finger holes in a pegboard in order to explore them tactually at 10 months. Gottesman (1971) has studied the further development of the hands as a source of tactile and haptic information, and found that such development is essential as for sighted children. He explored with blind children (having light perception only, or less), the three stages of haptic perception described by Piaget and Inhelder (1948). In Stage I, sighted children are able to recognise familiar objects by touch alone (2–4 years) while at 4–6 years rectilinear and curvilinear shapes can be crudely differentiated (Stage II). In Stage III (6–8 years) sighted children can distinguish between complex forms through precise detailed exploration. Gottesman found that blind children were essentially similar to sighted children with respect to these stages and the age at which they were attained. Reviewing a variety of other studies on the theme of tactile discrimination, Warren (1977 p. 16) confirms this finding noting that there are no striking differences between the sighted child and his or her blind peer.

Cognitive Development

Developmental psychologists have emphasised the extent to which the child's construction of reality is dependent upon active manipulation of, and movement in, the world about him or her. In considering both gross and fine motor development in blind children we have seen how this interaction is impaired and how such children, in addition to having to come to an understanding of the world on the basis of restricted sensory information, are additionally disadvantaged by delay in motor development. We have also seen from Reynell's (1978) study that early cognitive development is indeed impaired, but it is to the nature of this impairment that we now turn.

Several authors (e.g. Gottesman 1976; Stephens 1972) have emphasised the potential impairment of cognitive development through this restricted movement as a consequence of, and in addition to, the reduced experience occasioned directly by visual deprivation. In terms of sensorimotor development as described earlier, Gottesman (1976 p. 94) quotes from an unpublished lecture by Piaget who comments:

> Blind infants have the great disadvantage of not being able to make the same co-ordinations in space that normal children are capable of during the first year or two, so that the development of sensory-motor intelligence and the co-ordination of actions at this level are seriously impeded in blind children. For this reason, we find that there are even greater delays in their development at the level of representational thinking and that language is not sufficient to compensate for the deficiency in the co-ordination of actions. The delay is made up ultimately, of course, but it is significant and much more considerable than the delay in the development of logic in deaf and dumb children.

Warren (1977) has summarised the development of blind children through the sensorimotor period (see Chapter 3, pp. 40–4). During Stages I and II, Reflexive Responding and Primary Circular Reactions respectively (0–4 months), no differences are expected or observed because actions are essentially directed to the self rather than the outside world. The next Stages III, Secondary Circular Reactions (4–8 months), and IV, Co-ordination of Secondary Circular Reactions (8–12 months), will be delayed because these entail the child interacting with the outside world and are heavily dependent on vision. This failure to interact in an outer directed way is clearly exemplified in the delay in directed reaching we have already described. Despite the lack of vision, however, the organisation of co-ordinated secondary circular reactions do begin to emerge towards the end of the first year as auditory-tactile connections are established. Again, we have seen the nature of these connections in our earlier discussion of reaching for an object on the basis of sound. Warren notes that there is little information from research on Stage V, Tertiary Circular Reactions (12–18 months), though he suggests that restricted mobility may lead to less opportunity to apply active trial and error to objects and situations in the environment.

With respect to Stage VI involving the internalisation of thought, Fraiberg (1968) has considered the full achievement of the object concept by blind children. She suggests that this is delayed in such children until 3 to 5 years of age in contrast to 2 years of age in sighted children, and that this delay results from the compounding effect of two mutually reinforcing retarding influences, i.e. the blind child fails to engage in sustained search behaviour which in turn leads to failure to develop the mature object concept which in turn leads to absence of search. 'The failure of search', writes Fraiberg (1968), 'leaves the blind child with a temporary handicap in cognitive development; he cannot believe that an object exists when it does not manifest itself to him, and this conceptual problem becomes a temporary barrier to the development of spatial concepts and the notion of causality' (p. 287). Similarly, Rowland (1983) reports on marked delays in three blind children she studied. Nevertheless, under conditions where development is being enhanced optimally through appropriate parent-child interactions, Urwin (1983) observed at around 18 months of age '. . . play and changes in search behaviour which indicated that the children knew of the continued existence of objects apart from their own actions and independent of specific locations' (p. 150).

Of Period II, the preconceptual sub-stage of the preoperational period, Stephens (1972) in a discussion of the development of blind children emphasises the development of language: 'Preconcepts are defined as the notions the child attaches to the first verbal signs he learns to see' (p. 110). Clearly delays in the sensorimotor period will lead to delays in this preconceptual stage. In addition, suggests Stephens, there will be further disruption of language development because of the differential experience of blind and sighted people of the objects to be named. As we saw earlier, links between sensorimotor development and language development are part of the Piagetian account of early development, and at this stage, i.e. preconceptual, we find ourselves moving into an account of language development in blind children. Before considering this further, however, we will note Stephens's comments on the way in which the mechanisms underlying development proposed by Piaget are impaired and how cognitive delay is caused.

Stephens suggests that, in line with Piaget's earlier comment, visually impaired children do not fully experience the relation of objects to themselves. As a result of this, rupture is experienced in the equilibration between the two processes, assimilation and accommodation: 'Although the blind child has at his disposal the intellectual instruments necessary for the integration of external facts, he is deprived, in the main, of the means which the sighted have to aid in the adjustment to reality' (pp. 109–10). Disequilibrium therefore exists between the available potential for assimilation and the profoundly deficient control of the accommodation system.

Language Development

Urwin (1983) points out that whether we emphasise the cognitive or the communicative aspect of early language development, we would expect blindness to pose considerable problems for infant development. She notes the important role of vision in Piaget's theory and the implication that cognitive development will be slowed down by visual impairment. The role of vision in early communication may be seen from the accounts given in Chapter 3 of Bruner's description of exchanges between mother and child and the importance of gesture as a precursor to spoken words in the work of Bates and her colleagues.

We have already seen from Reynell's (1978) assessment that both comprehensive and expressive language is delayed in blind and partially sighted children. The impact of the handicap appears to be greater for comprehension than for expression. Indeed, in the early expressive phase when children babble, Warren's (1977) review suggests that blind and sighted children do not differ, an observation also confirmed by Reynell's assessment (Reynell 1978 p. 300 Figure 5). Nevertheless, acquisition of first words is certainly slower in blind than in sighted children (Warren 1977). Burlingham (1961) has reported that mothers of congenitally blind children comment how slowly their children add to their vocabulary during the 16 to 18 month period when sighted children typically show a marked spurt. Indeed, the mothers also reported that even where words had occurred, there could be some slipping back. Reynell's work also indicated that during the first five years, blind and partially sighted children fall behind their sighted peers in naming familiar objects, describing the use and position of objects and in their ability to describe on-going events. Mills (1983) shows that blind children are also disadvantaged with respect to learning phonemes the articulation of which cannot be seen because they are unable to use such visual information.

The passage from early delays to essentially normal functioning is in reality more complex than these studies would suggest. First, in line with the ecological approach to development described in Chapter 3, the course of language development in blind and partially sighted children can be influenced significantly by environmental factors, most noticeably the form of interaction with parents. Urwin (1978a) describes the impact of parental strategies on the development of language of two blind and two partially sighted children that modifies the picture we have presented above. We describe this aspect of her work in the following section. Here we will note her findings on the strengths and weaknesses of the children's communicative and linguistic development.

The three children in Urwin's study (1978a; 1983) were followed until approximately 20–22 months with follow-ups at 2 years and 2 years 3 months. Despite lack of vision, these children learnt turn taking and use of gesture to gain adult attention. As with children who are not impaired, gesture or early vocalisation with a communicative function led into and occurred with the children's early words. Such communications successfully maintained interactions with others and facilitiated maintenance of conversation. The first words used emerged in affective or routine activities over which the child had some measure of control — as often occurs with children who are not impaired.

Urwin (1983) suggests the importance of object permanence in language development when she notes that developments in pretend play and search for objects at 18 months coincided with a rapid expansion in vocabulary and the first word combinations. While this finding suggests that representation need not necessarily be delayed in blind children, some restrictions in language development were found. Ability to initiate interactions was somewhat restricted, being dependent on physical imitation up to the end of the first year. Similarly, joint attention with the mother to far-off objects presented problems since joint visual looking or pointing were not possible. These two difficulties did at first restrict the children's use of language in initiating play until well into the second year. With the emergence of language, however, ways of initiating interactions do emerge — particularly the frequent use of people's names.

Naming of objects, however, presented further difficulties. While these could be named when the child was in physical contact with an object (or in the case of the partially sighted child when it was held close to the eyes), the children did not name or request objects until after 18 months. Urwin (1983) points out, however, that this should not necessarily be taken to indicate some kind of cognitive deficit but notes that:

> For them to name and request objects is perhaps more akin to sighted children's referring to things which are absent or concealed, with the minimum support from the immediate context. This use of language is not observable with any degree of frequency in the early stages, suggesting that apparently similar phenomena may represent more complex developmental achievements on the part of blind children. (p. 152)

Overall, Urwin (1983) argues that the status of the children's language is, after the first two years, 'relatively satisfactory', and despite the lack of vision; alternative routes to language are found. Similarly, Warren's (1977) review of the limited information available suggests that there is no consistent developmental lag with respect to use of sentences and syntax in blind children. It appears, then, that we can truly refer to 'language *delay*' with respect to visual impairment. Andersen, Dunlea and Kekelis (1984), however, suggest that whether or not we regard the devlopment of language in visually impaired children as just slow or as deviant depends upon the level of linguistic analysis employed. They studied six children among whom vision extended from congenital blindness to normal vision. They show that at one level of linguistic analysis their findings are similar to those of others, including Urwin's. However, they indicate several differences between the visually impaired children and those with normal vision, first with regard to the body of words learnt (the child's lexicon), and second with regard to the role adapted by the child in exchanges with others.

With respect to the lexicon, Andersen *et al.* reported that for the visually impaired children in their study, this was broadly comparable to that of the non-impaired children. However, a number of differences were noted. In the lexicon of the visually impaired child: (i) there were no idiosyncratic forms of words and no drop outs as in the case of the non-impaired children; (ii) '. . . words for actions were restricted to self actions among the blind children, while sighted children use their terms to refer to a variety of activities involving other people and objects, as well as their own activities' (p. 654); (iii) blind children's use of functional relational words related to their own needs, e.g. 'more' for a biscuit for themselves, but not to changes in the world about them, e.g. 'more' when the number of objects has increased. The authors conclude that the categories represented in the early vocabulary of blind and sighted children may be similar. However, behavioural and linguistic evidence both suggest that the process that enables young sighted children to understand what the features are of something to which a word refers and extend use of the word is different from their sighted peers. With respect to role reversal, i.e. the ability to use 'I' and 'you' interchangeably in a conversation ('I' from my own point of view becomes 'you' in another person's conversation), the authors suggest that this ability is also impaired through lack of vision.

From the perspective of this chapter, it is the causes of these delays and possible differences that is of critical significance for working with the child who is mentally handicapped and blind, and it is an understanding of these that will enable us to avoid the compounding influence of visual impairment. Some understanding of how visually impaired children, who are not retarded do achieve relatively satisfactory language development emerges from a consideration of their patterns of interactions with their parents.

Mother-Child Interactions

As we have seen in Chapter 3, it is now widely accepted by developmental psychologists and linguists that the basis of spoken language is created during the prelinguistic period, and that this basis is being laid down from the earliest days in the infant's life. From then on a pattern of interaction and communication begins to develop between parent and child. This is characterised by sustained eye contact between parent and child, turn taking in responding to, and eliciting reactions from, each other, and growing sensitivity to what facial expressions and sound communicate. The role of vision in this sensitive and developing pattern of prelinguistic communication is central, and Fraiberg (1979) has considered the process by which blind infants and their mothers develop their own communication system in the absence of the infant's vision. 'What we miss in the blind baby, apart from the eyes that do not see,' she writes, 'is the vocabulary of signs and signals that provides the most elementary and vital sense of discourse long before words have meaning' (p. 152). There are many aspects of this prelinguistic communication that are impaired in this situation. Fraiberg notes the importance of 'eye language' in initiating social exchanges. The absence of this in blind children places the onus of starting an interaction on the parent, and in addition can convey a general lack of interest to the parent.

Similarly, the infant will not respond simply to the presence of the parent's face. A smile from the parent will have no effect, while the blind child's smiling is typically less frequent, and more muted, than for a sighted child. In addition, the richness of facial expression in sighted children is lacking in the blind child compared to a sighted 6–12 month old.

Given the importance of vision in eliciting a variety of reactions from the infant, it may well be that the sparseness of vocalisation in blind infants noted by Fraiberg results from the child's inability to see what would, in the sighted child, trigger vocalisation. This sparseness means that the child fails to communicate its feelings through vocalisations, and such communication is also reduced with respect to facial expressions. Yet we cannot assume that the child is not experiencing the full range of emotions felt by the sighted child. Fraiberg notes that careful attention to the hands indicated that the child was expressing feeling through gesture: 'It was — and still is — a bizarre experience for us to read hands instead of faces in order to read meaning into emotional experience' (Fraiberg 1979 p. 161). It is when the child begins to orientate towards objects and people in the world that it becomes possible to interpret these manual expressions of feeling.

It may be that the function of hand movements during speech continue to be of special significance in blind people. In a study with young congenitally blind adults Blass, Freedman and Steingart (1974) found a relation between finger-to-hand movements, e.g. stroking the finger-tips, and language production. They suggest that such activity can facilitate the encoding of thoughts into language, and reflects the significance of touch as an important part of the blind person's sensory experience. They also suggest that such hand movements may be an outgrowth of sensorimotor schema. Manual activity, once a primary means of exercising schema, far from being replaced by the development of symbolic activities, continues in parallel as a facilitator of thought. An important aspect of this interpretation is that such activity is therefore adaptive and should be distinguished from disruptive stereotyped behaviour of the sort discussed later in this chapter and in Chapter 8 and in relation to people with profound retardation and multiple impairments in Chapter 7, Volume 2. With respect to individuals with profound retardation it also raises the question of the changing developmental status of manual activity. What might be regarded as disruptive and maladaptive at one developmental stage in a child's life, may at another have functional significance and be a prerequisite for further development.

It is at this point that the ecological perspective on language development comes even more into focus. Fraiberg (1979) asks whether the child's lack of vocalisation leads in turn to the parent saying less to the child. Certainly a number of writers have suggested that the problems created in language development by the absence of vision can be accentuated by the parent's overall response. Burlingham (1965) suggests that the parent's perception of the child as helpless may lead to anticipation of the child's requirements, thus reducing the child's need to use language to get what it wants. This sort of behaviour may be seen as what Rapin (1979) regards as overprotectiveness, but withdrawal by the parent would also lead to reduced language experience (Burlingham 1961).

The way in which the pattern of interaction between mother and blind infant can be distorted has been shown in a careful observational study by Rowland (1983). Here three girls, 11, 15 and 16 months at the start of the study, were observed interacting with their mothers. The probability of infant and mother reacting to the other's behaviour in a specific way was determined. There was a striking lack of responsive behaviour by the infant to specific maternal behaviours while the mothers themselves responded rapidly and frequently to infant behaviours, particularly the infant's smile. To this infant behaviour there was a high probability that the mother would vocalise to, or touch, her child. For two of the children maternal response to infant vocalisation was very low, though for the most able infant, who was using actual words, her mother's response to her vocalisation was high. For the first two mothers who were low in their response to vocalisation, their response to their infants' gestures was high. Where infants did respond to their mothers the match response was smiling at her vocalising rather than vocalising or gesturing in response.

These distortions in social relations can be avoided, despite absence of vision. The role of parents and educators in enabling the child to acquire language becomes a critical objective. That this can be achieved in an effective way is suggested by Fraiberg's (1979) account of how the communication system between parent and blind child does evolve. We have already noted how such children may communicate through gesture, and Fraiberg points out how parents can be taught to understand this 'language'. She also notes how lack of smiling to visual stimuli such as the parent's face can be overcome through other means such as intense tactile and physical stimulation to elicit smiling. In more general terms, Wills (1956) writes about the help needed by the child to build up a working knowledge of the world:

. . . the mother of the blind child might have to perform two distinct roles: she has on the one hand to establish a good bodily relationship with her blind child through her handling and care, but she also has to provide the right kind of auxiliary ego for him, not in the usual sense of supplying control, but in the sense of giving him meaningful experiences of the world, something that the mother of a sighted child can do automatically on the basis of her own experience. (pp. 360–1).

Wills's latter point draws attention to the important fact that the experience of the world of the sighted and the nonsighted person differs in several critical respects and we have already seen Stephens's (1972) observation of this influence on preconceptual development (p. 93).

Burlingham (1965) makes the important point that the language offered by a parent to the blind child may fail to provide an appropriate label for the child's *own* experience, i.e. the label offered is appropriate to visual experience. It is likely, as Burlingham (1961) suggests, that such inappropriate words might well be learnt by the child on the basis of intensive reinforcement of imitations. It is this, she suggests, that probably leads to what has been referred to a 'parroting' or 'blindisms', i.e. the use of words by the blind child to refer to aspects of the world outside his/her actual sensory experience. In the field of blind education, this issue has generated much controversy. Do blindisms distort the blind person's understanding of the world? Should the language offered to the blind person uniquely reflect his or her own direct experience? These issues are beyond the scope of this book, but the response of educators of the blind in recent years to them is relevant to working with people with mental handicap with visual impairment. Reviews by both Dokecki (1966) and Warren (1977) advocate that visual terms and concepts should not be excluded from the language experience of blind children. A language that truly reflects the surrounding world should be taught, but that this should be firmly rooted at some point in the child's actual experience of the world. Landau (1983) in a detailed case study comments on one child that '. . . free use of visual terms has allowed [the child] both to make crucial linguistic distinctions for her own means of perceiving, and to understanding what is meant by the other, visual means of perceiving' (p. 75).

The preceding discussion conveys both the somewhat negative view of language development and social interaction in visually impaired children that prevailed in the literature for many years, as well as the conviction that early intervention is both desirable and effective. That such interaction is best realised through parent-child interaction is illustrated in Urwin's (1978b) studies which we have already seen point towards relatively satisfactory language development in the children she observed. The crucial factor in the parent-child interactions, according to Urwin, 'concerned the extent to which all the parents made use of non-visual communicative systems themselves, and discovered alternative cues to the infant's attention, involvement and intention' (p. 148). Among these strategies Urwin notes: (i) mothers would watch their babies' faces closely 'mirroring' changes in facial expression and bodily movement; (ii) touching, stroking, tickling and gross body play were used, sometimes in the context of familiar games such as 'pat-a-cake' and 'ride-a-cock horse'; (iii) through such games anticipation and expectancy could be built up, leading to shaping the child into developing an active role; (iv) vocalisation, too, was encouraged through talking to their child and by marking, questioning and imitating the child's preverbal vocalisations. Towards the end of the first year, all those children in Urwin's study were imitating vocally and engaging in dialogue-like exchanges. Urwin comments that some of the communicative shortcomings observed in Rowland's (1983) study did not occur with these parents and infants.

Rowgow (1980) has also emphasised the need for adults to adopt an active role in enabling the child who is blind and multiply handicapped to develop language, through developing a system of consistent and clearly defined responses to the child's behaviour, and establishing a system of signals based on the child's own interests. The lack of natural interchanges between parent and child, she argues, must be compensated for by a stress on mutual actions and reciprocal interchanges. We will return to models of co-active intervention as they are applied to visually and multiply impaired individuals in Volume 2, Chapter 5 where approaches to language are considered.

Self-reference and Identity

We mentioned earlier that in one particular respect, self-reference, blind children do confront a special problem in language development. Fraiberg and Adelson (1976) discuss this problem in detail and describe the nature of these special difficulties. Thus, the use of the personal pronoun which is used consistently by sighted children by 2–3 years will emerge much later in blind children, and is never acquired by some of them. The extent of this problem is shown in McGuire and Meyers' (1971) survey where a substantial proportion of totally blind children (46 per cent) referred to themselves in the third person.

This specific language difficulty reflects an important impediment to the child constructing reality. This differentiation of the child's self from the rest of the physical world is presented to the sighted child in an immediate and readily apprehended way. For the visually impaired child, awareness of self as distinct from the rest of the world, including other people is, therefore, not so readily attained. Fraiberg and Adelson (1976) have commented that to achieve this distinction is a prodigious feat '. . . without the one sensory mode that would describe, through the picture, the commonalities and the generalizations that lead to the concept "I" ' (p. 146). Fraiberg and Adelson see this as a special problem for blind children, in contrast to the deaf and thalidomide children who we consider in Chapters 5 and 6. This difficulty, reflected in language and with consequences for the development of the child's personality, will in turn also compound the child's problems of understanding the physical world. Fraiberg (1976) notes succinctly that: 'Our views are that since 'I' represents the child's capacity to see himself as an object, the visual impediment presents a problem in conceptualization of self in relation to objects' (p. 150).

Behaviour Disorders

In summarising studies of behaviour disorders in blind and partially sighted children, Jan, Freeman and Scott (1977) conclude that by whatever method of assessment, most studies agree that behavioural and developmental problems are much commoner among blind and visually impaired children, more so in the former. In addition, psychiatric disorder is significantly more common in children with multiple handicap and in children in whose central nervous system damage exists. They emphasise, however, that these behaviour problems arise as a result of interaction involving psychological, developmental, attitudinal and social factors which place the visually impaired child's functioning in jeopardy. Consequently, such problems are not inevitable and through suitable teaching and organisation of their environment *can* be avoided.

One major developmental disadvantage, lack of mobility, is clearly restricting as it limits access to the outside world, and reduces the amount of information the child acquires about the world. But it is not for this reason alone that Adelson and Fraiberg (1976) comment that: 'The blind child's special pattern of gross motor development claims our attention because the periods of development that are normal for the blind child probably represent periods of serious developmental hazard.' (p. 10).

It is also clear that it is during these periods of immobility, though with the capacity for movement, that passivity can lead to disorders in personality development. In the period before the blind child has constructed a spatial map of the world on the basis of near-to objects that can be experienced through touch, and far-off events experienced through hearing, it is self-stimulation that often fills the void. Burlingham (1965) suggests that '. . . it appears that this void is filled in part by the child's attentiveness to the sensations arising from his own body' (pp. 203–4).

If we observe the actual behaviours that visually impaired children use to create these bodily sensations, then we are immediately struck by strong similarities with many of the self-stimulatory activities engaged in by children who are profoundly retarded. Among these is body rocking. Adelson and Fraiberg (1976) note that in both sighted and visually impaired children the period between neuromuscular readiness to become mobile and actually moving off is occupied by a marked increase in motor activity. Often this activity takes the form of body rocking. This reduces when the child attains mobility, and is therefore obviously protracted in the visually impaired child for whom mobility is delayed.

If rocking as a result of immobility declines with the onset of movement, other forms of self-stimulation by blind chldren do not necessarily disappear spontaneously. This self-stimulatory activity takes many forms: hand waving in front of the face, eye rubbing and poking, body rocking, head turning and rolling. These actions, all carried out repetitiously and at high frequency, have been referred to as 'blindisms', a quite inappropriate term as they are observed in a variety of sighted groups including children who are autistic and also those who are retarded. Indeed, as children exhibit increasing degrees of developmental delay, so the extent of stereotyped behaviour and self-stimulatory activity increases (Berkson and Davenport 1962). Given the prevalence of such behaviour by children who are profoundly retarded with and without visual impairment, it is particularly relevant to ask what has been learnt about the development of such behaviour from studies of blind and visually impaired children. We can approach this topic from two related standpoints. The first is concerned with the function of stereotypic and self-stimulatory behaviour: Under what conditions do blind children exhibit the behaviour? The second is to do with the particular sensory experiences that lead to the behaviour: Do the behaviours result directly from visual deprivation, or are other aspects of sensory experience, such as touch, involved too?

Warren (1977) reviews some of the hypotheses that have been put forward to account for stereotypic behaviour and self-stimulation in visually impaired children. It should be said at the outset, these explanations are not necessarily alternatives, and in various circumstances may all have some truth. As Baumeister and Forehand (1973) suggest: 'At one level or another, they all make some sense' (p. 57). To Warren the most compelling hypothesis is that these behaviours serve to increase the general level of sensory stimulation. Where the child is in an environment in which there is little external stimulation, then he or she will increase it for him/herself. As Baumeister and Forehand (1973) conclude, several studies have supported such a view, and in Volume 2, Chapter 7, where reduction of these behaviours is considered, we will look at some of these reports.

In contrast, it has been suggested by Knight (1972) that stereotypies will be increased or induced if a child is put under stress by the environment. This view is related to the proposal that anything that increases the child's arousal level will also enduce stereotyped behaviour which will have the effect of reducing stress or arousal by filtering out some of the excessive stimulation. It is, of course, possible that stereotyped behaviour and self-stimulation do indeed reflect both an arousing function and a decrease in arousal. Stone (1974) proposes that there are indeed two types of stereotypies, one which alerts the child and one which permits withdrawal. In a study of three blind retarded children he suggests that the former behaviour is more complex and ritualistic but less rhythmical than the latter, and that different patterns of EEG are associated with the two types of stereotypies. Warren (1977) comments that these suggestions may '. . . be interpreted as attributing to the blind retarded child a fairly active role in the manipulation of his level of consciousness in order to regulate the extent of his contact with reality' (p. 77).

All the above hypotheses hinge on the notion that the behaviours are in some way regulating the internal state of the child by controlling environmental input. There is also a body of literature, however, that indicates that such behaviours are subject to learning and change in the same way as other aspects of behaviour. Baumeister and Forehand (1973) review these studies and point out that while it is undoubtedly possible to show that stereotyped behaviours are subject to the principles of learning, this does not necessarily mean that this was how they were developed in the first place. Their overall conclusion, however, is sympathetic to the view that the behaviours are essentially normal but have been conditioned to such a high level of activity that they have ceased to be adaptive to the child. Such a view obviously is of great importance for intervention and we shall consider these findings in Volume 2, Chapter 7.

If we return to the question of the nature of the stimulation experienced by the stereotyping or self-stimulating blind child, we must ask the question: What kind of sensory stimulation? It is clear that among the repetitive activities we listed above several sensory modalities are involved. Provided some vision remains, certain activities, e.g. waving the fingers before the face, may stimulate rudimentary visual experiences. Others, such as body rocking, will alter the experience of balance, i.e. they are essentially vestibular, while others again, e.g. rubbing the hands together, may be tactile or cutaneous (stimulating through the skin). Again the conclusion must be that the nature of the sensory stimulation may vary for different children and for the same child from time to time.

Thurrell and Rice (1970) studied eye rubbing in three groups of blind and visually impaired children. One was totally blind, one had some residual light vision, while the third, though also impaired, had some usable vision. They hypothesised that where children had some residual capacity for receiving stimulation via the optic apparatus, they would be more likely to eye-rub to gain some visual experience than those without such residual function or those for whom vision still served some use. As rated by judges, this hypothesis was born out. The blind and functional-vision groups both showed less eye rubbing than the group with some residual capacity to receive ocular stimulation but no functional vision.

It seems, then, that visual deficits can be related to self-stimulatory behaviour. However, Prescott (1976) has argued persuasively that much stereotyped and self-stimulatory behaviour reflects not visual deprivation, but what he calls somatosensory stimulation. This term embraces all bodily sensation from the feeling of movement and balance (kinesthetic-vestibular stimulation) to sensations received through the skin (cutaneous stimulation) and touch (tactile stimulation). His argument is, in fact, that a visual defect can result in the child being deprived of somatosensory experience, and problems in development that we might assume are the direct result of visual deprivation are in reality the result of this handicap leading to reduced physical experience. We have already seen how this might come about. The prolonged immobility of the blind child, the initial lack of head turning and so on, all reduce vestibular experience. Problems in communication in early childhood resulting from the child's failure to respond may lead to the blind child getting less handling than his or her sighted counterpart.

Prescott goes on to argue that such deprivation will have direct influence on the cells of the brain and will later have behavioural consequences: 'Sensory stimulation is like a nutrient and just as malnutrition adversely affects the developing brain so does sensory deprivation (p. 68). One consequence of this deprivation, he suggests, is that cerebral and cerebellar cortexes may become 'supersensitive' or 'hyperactive' and interact in an abnormal way with other brain structures leading to body rocking and other abnormal motor patterns. Prescott draws on many sources of information to support his position. He notes Berkson's studies showing that visual deprivation itself does not lead to body rocking and that somatosensory deprivation does contribute. Berkson (1976) provides one piece of information that contributes to this conclusion. When monkeys are raised in isolation with a dummy mother (i.e. effectively a static doll), body rocking, a sign of emotional disturbance, is found However, if the dummy actually moves, then this consequence is avoided Berkson (1976) claims that:

> This suggests that the manifestation of body rocking in most normal infants in our society might reflect the fact that they are not regularly carried around on their mother's hip. It also suggests that body rocking of populations who are at risk for stereotyped movement (such as individuals who are blind and retarded) might benefit from carefully programmed rearing with movement stimulation, at low levels of arousal with opportunities to interact with the environment maximised. (p. 131)

But this is beginning to take us into the whole issue of intervention. All that we will add here is that Prescott's position is also supported by studies such as those of Adelson and Fraiberg (1976) in which stereotypes in blind children *were* reduced through sufficient somato-sensory stimulation. The implications of both Prescott and Berkson's position, as well as intervention studies that draw on them, will be considered further when we consider physical impairment in Chapter 6 and intervention strategies to deal with self-injurious behaviour and stereo-typing and self-stimulation in Chapter 7 of Volume 2.

We would emphasise that it would not be appropriate to try to lay the whole weight of an account of stereotyped behaviour at the door of deprivation in any one modality. Berkson (1976) himself concludes that: '. . . blindness does not appear to be a sufficient condition for the development of stereotyped movement' (p. 132), thus not precluding vision entirely from his account. Effects may well add together to increase the degree of stereotyped behaviour. Guess (1966), for example, certainly showed greater stereotypy in blind retarded than sighted retarded children, but also found that when stereotypies and self-stimulation were taken together, nonambulant children showed more such behaviour than those who could walk.

It would appear then, that the development of stereotyped and self-stimulating behaviour in blind children serves a number of functions and involves several modalities. It is not appropriate to try to intervene with an individual child in order to reduce behaviours on the basis of theory alone. In Volume 2, Chapter 7 we will discuss how we can analyse what it is that maintains these and other behaviours in individual children, and we will see that the value of such theories is in directing our attention to the particular aspects of the situation that we must observe and manipulate.

Concluding Comment on Blindness

In our pursuit of an understanding of the impact of blindness on development we have found that we have progressively moved to the implications of the information for intervention with children, whatever their overall degree of intellectual impairment. We have also seen the interdependency of various distinguishable aspects of development among themselves and in relation to the child's social and physical environment. It will have become apparent in the concluding discussion of self-directed behaviours that such behaviour is not inherently undesirable in its own right, but presents a major problem when it prevents the child interacting with his or her environment. Warren (1977) comments on the extent to which such behaviour prevents the shift from self-directed to outer-directed behaviour which is critical, in Piagetian terms, to the child's sensorimotor development and in turn, to language and preconceptual development. Adaptive and non-adaptive behaviour are not, therefore, distinct areas requiring independent programming, but as we shall see, interacting aspects of development, or its failure, to be treated within the same framework.

References

Adelson, E. and Fraiberg, S. (1974) 'Gross Motor Development in Infants Blind from Birth', *Child Development, 45,* 114–26

Adelson, E. and Fraiberg, S. (1976) 'Sensory Deficit and Motor Development in Infants Blind from Birth' in Z.S. Jastrzembska (ed.), *The Effects of Blindness and Other Impairment on Early Development,* American Foundation for the Blind, New York

Andersen, E.S., Dunlea, A. and Kekelis, L.S. (1984) 'Blind Children's Language: Resolving some Differences', *Journal of Child Language, 11,* 645–64

Baumeister, A.A. and Forehand, R. (1973) 'Stereotyped Acts' in N.R. Ellis (ed.), *International Review of Research in Mental Retardation: Vol. 6,* Academic Press, London

Berkson, G. (1976) 'Stereotyped Behaviors in Humans' in Z.S. Jastrzembska (ed.), *The Effects of Blindness and Other Impairments on Early Development,* American Foundation for the Blind, New York

Berkson, G. and Davenport, R.K. (1962) 'Stereotyped Movement of Mental Defectives: 1. Initial Survey', *American Journal of Mental Deficiency, 66,* 849–52

Blass, T., Freedman, N. and Steingart, I. (1974) 'Body Movement and Verbal Encoding in the Congenitally Blind', *Perceptual and Motor Skills, 39,* 279–93

Burlingham, D. (1961) 'Some Notes on the Development of the Blind', *Psychoanalytic Study of the Child,* 16, 121–45

Burlingham D. (1965) 'Some Problems of Ego Development in Blind Children', *Psychoanalytic Study of the Child, 20,* 194–208

Dokecki, P.C. (1966) 'Verbalism and The Blind: A Critical Review of the Concept and the Literature', *Exceptional Children, 32,* 525–30

Fraiberg, S. (1968) 'Parallel and Divergent Patterns in Blind and Sighted Infants', *Psychoanalytic Study of the Child, 23,* 264–300

Fraiberg, S. (1976) 'Language and Self-Representation in the Blind Child' in Z.S. Jastrzembska (ed.), *The Effects of Blindness and Other Impairments on Early Development,* American Foundation for the Blind, New York

Fraiberg, S. (1979) 'Blind Infants and Their Mothers: An Examination of the Sign System' in M. Bullova (ed.), *Before Speech: The Beginning of Interpersonal Communication,* Cambridge University Press, Cambridge

Fraiberg, S. and Adelson, E. (1976) 'Self-Representation in Young Blind Children' in Z.S. Jastrzembska (ed.), *The Effects of Blindness and Other Impairments on Early Development,* American Foundation for the Blind, New York

Gottesman, M. (1971) 'A Comparative Study of Piaget's Developmental Schema of Sighted Children with that of a Group of Blind Children', *Child Development, 42,* 573–80

Gottesman, M. (1976) 'Stage Development of Blind Children: A Piagetian View', *New Outlook for the Blind, 70,* 94–100

Guess, D. (1966) 'The Influence of Visual and Ambulation Restrictions on Stereotyped Behavior', *American Journal of Mental Deficiency, 70,* 542–7

Jan, J.E., Freeman, R.D. and Scott, E.P. (1977) *'Visual Impairment in Children and Adolescents',* Grune and Stratton, New York

Jastrembska, Z.S. (ed.) (1976) *The Effects of Blindness and Other Impairments on Early Development,* American Foundation for the Blind, New York

Knight, J.J. (1972) 'Mannerisms in the Congenitally Blind Child', *New Outlook for the Blind, 66,* 297–302

Landau, B. (1983) 'Blind Children's Language is Not "Meaningless" ' in A.E. Mills (ed.), *Language Acquisition in the Blind Child: Normal and Deficient,* Croom Helm, London/College-Hill Press, San Diego

McGuire, L.L. and Meyers, C.E. (1971) 'Early Personality in the Congenitally Blind Child', *New Outlook for the Blind*, 65, 137–43

Mills, A.E. (1983) 'Acquisition of Speech Sounds in the Visually-handicapped Child' in A.E. Mills (ed.), *Language Acquisition in the Blind Child: Normal and Deficient*, Croom Helm, London/College-Hill Press, San Diego

Norris, M., Spaulding, P. and Brodie F. (1957) *Blindness in Children*, University of Chicago Press, Chicago

Piaget, J. and Inhelder, B. (1948) *The Psychology of the Child*, Basic Books, New York

Prescott, J.W. (1976) 'Somatosensory Deprivation and its Relationship to the Blind' in Z.S. Jastrzembska (ed.), *The Effects of Blindness and Other Impairments on Early Development*, American Foundation for the Blind, New York

Rapin, I. (1979) 'Effects of Early Blindness and Deafness on Cognition' in R. Katzman (ed.), *Congenital and Acquired Cognitive Disorders*, Raven Press, New York

Reynell, J. (1978) 'Developmental Patterns of Visually Handicapped Children', *Child: Care, Health and Development*, 4, 291–303

Reynell, J. and Zinkin, P. (1975) 'New Procedures for the Developmental Assessment of Young Children with Severe Visual Handicaps', *Child: Care, Health and Development*, 1, 61–9

Rowgow, S.M. (1978) 'Considerations in the Assessment of Blind Children who Function as Severely or Profoundly Retarded', *Child: Care, Health and Development*, 4, 327–35

Rowgow, S.M. (1980) 'Language Development in Blind Multi-handicapped Children: A Model of Co-active Intervention', *Child: Care, Health and Development*, 6, 306–8

Rowland, C. (1983) 'Patterns of Interaction Between Three Blind Infants and Their Mothers' in A.E. Mills (ed.), *Language Acquisition in the Blind Child: Normal and Deficient*, Croom Helm, London/College-Hill Press, San Diego

Stephens, B. (1972) 'Cognitive Processes in the Visually Impaired', *Education of the Visually Handicapped*, 4, 106–11

Stone, A. (1974) 'Consciousness: Altered Levels in Blind Retarded Children', *Psychosomatic Medicine*, 26, 14–19

Thurrell, R.J. and Rice, D.G. (1970) 'Eye Rubbing in Blind Children: Application of a Sensory Deprivation Model', *Exceptional Children*, 36, 325–30

Urwin, C. (1978a) 'The Development of Communication Between Blind Infants and Their Parents: Some Ways into Language', unpublished doctorial dissertation, University of Cambridge, Cambridge

Urwin, C. (1978b) 'The Development of Communication Between Blind Infants and Their Parents' in A. Lock (ed.), *Action, Gesture, Symbol: The Emergence of Language*, Academic Press, London

Urwin, C. (1983) 'Dialogue and Cognitive Functioning in the Early Language Development of Three Blind Children' in A.E. Mills (ed.), *Language Acquisition in the Blind Child: Normal and Deficient*, Croom Helm, London/College-Hill Press, San Diego

Warren, D.H. (1977) *Blindness and Early Childhood Development*, American Foundation for the Blind, New York

Wills, D.M. (1965) 'Some Observations on Blind Nursery School Children'
Understanding of Their World', *Psychoanalytic Study of the Child, 20,* 344–6

5 THE DEVELOPMENTAL CONSEQUENCES OF AUDITORY IMPAIRMENT

Much of what we have noted concerning the consequences of visual impairment has been concerned with its impact on the development of communication. It will come as no surprise that in studies of hearing impaired children this issue assumes an even more explicitly central role. Though we have seen that the development of communication is not exclusively dependent upon hearing spoken language, visual and motor influences are also important, the deprivation resulting from *not* hearing language spoken has devastating consequences for many hearing impaired children. As reflected in educational attainment, particularly with reference to spoken and written language, many deaf individuals fall far short of their hearing peers even after years of specialised education. The conditions under which these consequences may be mitigated will constitute an important element in this review as they have obvious implications for intervention with people who are both hearing impaired and profoundly retarded. Before addressing these implications, however, it is worthwhile considering briefly two issues that recur in studies of deaf children which have significance for working with people with profound retardation.

A central preoccupation in discussion of the educational consequences of hearing impairment is the issue of whether such children should be exposed exclusively to spoken language or whether the teaching of manual communication (signing) is acceptable. This debate, sometimes referred to as 'the hundred years war' (or even 'the two hundred years war'), has, at least to the outsider, generated extraordinarily intense passions and vitriolic argument. Even the apparent rapprochement offered by 'total communication' approaches involving learning of both spoken and signed languages has not escaped assaults from both sides. In Volume 2, Chapter 4 we address this issue with respect to non-oral communication approaches.

Related to the question of the mode of communication is a more fundamental psychological issue, namely the relation between language and thought. The question posed is, whether thought processes are so inherently dependent upon language that the language-deficient child will inevitably be cognitively impaired, or whether adequate cognitive functioning can develop in the absence of spoken language. This is obviously a complex question and one on which research will continue for a long time to come. In a major review of work on deaf children on linguistic deficiency and thinking Furth (1971) points towards considerable independence between the development of thought and language. We will comment further on this below when we consider the early development of deaf children. Again, for our present purpose, his conclusion is important as it suggests that whatever communicative deficiencies a person who is retarded may exhibit, movement through the sensorimotor period and early preoperational period can be enhanced in its own right, however far behind such development communicative skills may lag.

Cognitive Development

While the consequences of serious brain damage or a known history of family deafness might lead to early detection of hearing impairment, typically several months can go by before the hearing impaired child is diagnosed. Rapin (1979) observes that '. . . the deaf child usually sails through infancy much as his hearing peer' (p. 205). The studies reviewed by Furth (1971) only begin with children of 3 years 6 months but by implication suggest that sensorimotor and preconceptual development does not diverge significantly from that of nonhandicapped children. Similarly, Meadow (1980) writes that conceptual development (with special reference to concept attainment) is comparable to hearing children during early development and probably beyond the end of the preoperational stage.

Liben (1978) also points to the relatively late identification of deafness as a major cause of the lack of research on the effect of hearing impairment on sensorimotor development. In particular she notes the effect of hearing impairment on exploratory behaviour:

> . . . it is clear that sound also has important implications for the quantity, quality and effectiveness of the child's experience with objects. With the absence of severe attenuation of sound, the deaf child is deprived of knowledge about the sound-making qualities of objects and actions. Furthermore, in so far as noises made by objects and by actions upon objects excite the child towards exploration, the absence of an auditory channel might be expected to limit the motivation for exploration and, hence, retard cognitive growth. (p. 22)

Thus, the development and combination of schemes dependent upon auditory consequences would be precluded. Furthermore, insofar as auditory experience enables the child to develop spatial sense, development in this domain may also be impaired by lack of hearing.

When assessed on standard tests of children's cognitive development the impact of hearing loss does not seem great, despite Liben's (1978) conclusion that auditory feedback provides important information about objects. Gregory and Mogford's (1983) use of Lowe and Costello's Symbolic Play Test (see Chapters 3 and 7) with young deaf children suggests that in terms of overall scores little difference is observable from the play of hearing children. However, a more detailed analysis did point to some qualitative contrasts in the play of hearing and nonhearing children.

Motor Development

Studies of motor development in deaf children do indicate that common aetiological factors may well underlie a variety of disturbances in their motor development. Boyd (1967) used the Osteretsky Scale to explore gross motor development and found poorer equilibrium, co-ordination and speed of movement in deaf children relative to their hearing peers. Direct tests of perceptual-motor functioning by Gilbert and Levee (1967) pointed to similar poorer performance in deaf children. It is important to note, however, that these correlations between hearing impairment and motor ability appear to reflect some common aetiological origin rather than a developmental effect on motor development of the hearing impairment itself. Where brain damage affecting motor performance exists, this will clearly affect the ease with which alternative modes of non-oral communication can be employed. Kimura (1981) reviews several cases of manual signing disorders in deaf people after central nervous system damage. Clearly the presence of such damage during learning of a sign language would be expected to have a detrimental influence.

Language and Communication

It is with this topic that we obviously come to the core of handicapping consequences for hearing impaired children. As in our consideration of visual impairment, we need to approach this issue from several different viewpoints, always bearing in mind their interdependency with respect to a full account of the development of communication.

Vocalisation in the early months, prior to the emergence of babbling, is observed in both hearing children of deaf parents and deaf children of deaf parents. In responding to vocalisation in their blind or nonhandi- capped children, parents will maintain this behaviour during the first half of the first year of life.

Menyuk (1977) reviews studies that indicate differences in vocalisa- tion in deaf children. From 3 to 7 months vocalisation (which cannot be considered babbling) in hearing impaired infants decreases, notably at around 5½ months. Periods of silence increase in contrast to their steady decrease in hearing children. Qualitative differences in the kinds of sounds made are also noted.

In Chapter 3, we commented on some of the functions of babbling and its significance with respect to both the comprehension and produc- tion of speech sounds. Of deaf children Menyuk (1977) writes: 'The babbling period which was previously labelled ''prelinguistic'' is a period during which the normally hearing infant makes both perceptual and productive categorizations of the speech signal, and these categorizations may be crucially important for later language development' (p. 625). However, she continues, we know little about how much auditory information is being lost by deaf children. Gilbert (1982) points out that at present there is no study showing whether the babbling that follows early vocalisation is similar to or different from that of hearing children. In the post-babbling stage, however, phonological divergencies will be noted in addition to syntactic and semantic problems (Nober and Nober 1977). Depending on the degree and nature of hearing impairment, it must be assumed that one aspect of spoken language is already deviant from the earliest months, and that this will have consequences for subsequent linguistic development.

This assumption has not been invariably accepted in the past. Tate (1979), for example, argues that despite reduced linguistic input, the language of the deaf child develops along the same lines as the hearing child, generating sentences and making errors in the process. Gregory and Mogford (1981) disagree strongly with this conclusion, arguing that it cannot simply be claimed that deaf and hearing children set out on the language acquisition path from the same place, and that it is only inadequate verbal input to the deaf child that leads to deviant development. They investigated the development of eight prelingually deaf children of hearing parents through observation of free play, interviews with their mothers and diary records. They produce evidence of deviant language development from two sources, the rate of acquisition and the content of early vocabulary.

Two profoundly deaf children by Gregory and Mogford's sample had not yet reached the 10-word milestone by the age of 4 years and were not included in their general analysis. Of those with mild to severe loss, the first word appeared at 16 months, five months after it had appeared in three hearing infants. The 100-word milestone was passed at 34 months instead of 20 months and a positive correlation between degree of hearing loss and time taken to reach all milestones (except the first word) found.

Apart from these differences in time taken to acquire milestone vocabularies, Gregory and Mogford suggest that the actual process of acquisition differs between hearing and nonhearing children. While the latter children learn in the context of interactions with their parents in the way described in Chapter 3, mothers of deaf children 'work' on the production of words as a performance. While from the 18 months/50 words level hearing children's vocabulary 'snowballs', the increase in deaf children is a steady 10 words per month.

Two-word utterances are produced by hearing children around 18 months of age, by deaf children, at 30 months. Again, the age at which two-word utterances begins correlates with extent of hearing loss. Nevertheless, both groups begin their two-word utterances at the same, i.e. at the 50-word, level. However, in the case of deaf children the onset of syntactic development is not associated with a dramatic increase in vocabulary size.

With respect to vocabulary content, Gregory and Mogford base their analysis on the six categories listed and defined in Chapter 3: general and specific nominals, action words, modifiers, personal-social words and function words. They determined the proportion of such words at 50-word and 100-word levels and compared deaf and hearing children. For both groups, general nominals constituted the largest group, function words the smallest. Deaf children had:

(i)   fewer nominals at 50- and 100-word stages;
(ii) a greater proportion of personal-social words at both levels;
(iii) a greater proportion of action words at the 50-word level;
(iv) a greater proportion of modifiers at the 100-word level.

Though differences in developmental level might partially account for these differences, the authors conclude: 'Deaf children do seem to use their language to talk about different things from hearing children. The language that arises through interaction for hearing children seems to be a language of predominantly joint reference to objects, the language that is elicited from deaf children seems to be one concerned with labelling features of social relationships and activity as much as labelling objects' (p. 230). On the basis of both the rate of acquisition of vocabulary and its content, the authors conclude that their results point towards fundamental differences in the language of deaf children, in a way that parallels findings on language acquisition in visually impaired children described in Chapter 4.

The origins of such differences might in part derive from the impact of lack of hearing in early social interactions. Gregory and Mogford note that turn taking is highly independent on sound and is therefore probably disrupted by lack of hearing. Similarly during joint reference activities between parent and child, sound both marks and directs joint attention. In anticipation games (such as 'Round-and-round-the-garden') vocalisations mark features of the game. Thus, the authors argue:

> . . . the preverbal period has elements, many of them relying on the articulatory/auditory channel, which are important in the later development of communication . . . The picture emerges of the preverbal child knowing about language before he comes to use it himself. This knowledge may well be missing in the deaf child. (p. 233)

Some support exists for this view. Charles (1978) and Gregory, Mogford and Bishop (1979) have shown that vocal clashes occur more frequently in deaf child-parent interactions than in interactions between hearing pairs. Similarly, these authors have described problems in anticipatory-play between parents and deaf infants.

Despite the disruptive effect of absence of sound in these interactions, we have seen that the origins of communication do not reside in vocalisation alone even in hearing children. Gestures also serve a communicative function, and we noted Fraiberg's (1979) eloquent description of understanding the blind child through observation of his or her hands. Gesture also develops naturally in deaf children. Schlesinger and Meadow (1972) speculate on the neurological basis for the association between manual activity and speech, pointing to the anatomical proximity of the speech and motor areas in the brain and their neuronal similarity. That such gestures persist and evolve in deaf children is noted by Hoemann (1972) who comments on the natural use of gestures by deaf preschool children.

What aspects then of communication are enhanced through parents' responsiveness to the child's early gestures? This question opens up two lines of consideration which in reality are inseparable. The first concerns the question of refining and enhancing manual communication itself, and the second the nature of the parent-child interaction.

To consider these questions we must briefly address an issue that has received increasing attention during the 1970s, i.e. the status of sign languages. We shall have more to say on sign languages in Volume 2, Chapter 4, when we discuss non-oral communication in people who are mentally retarded. Here it is only necessary to point out that some manual sign systems (not all) do in fact constitute true languages parallel in important respects to spoken language. The American Sign Language (AMESLAN) has received special attention in this respect. Meadow (1980) has reviewed linguistic studies of AMESLAN and concludes: '. . . that it does have all the characteristics of language, although there are some differences deriving from the crossing of modalities — that is, from sound and voice to sight and movement' (pp. 18–19). An important implication of this is that we can consider the development of deaf children's (manually signed) language in relation to the development of spoken language in hearing children.

The classic study that undertook this comparison was carried out by Schlesinger and Meadow (1972). They documented the acquisition of signing by two deaf children of *deaf* parents. Ann was followed from 8 to 22 months. The actual acquisition of signs (words) more than compared favourably with that of hearing children. By 18 months Ann had acquired 117 signs compared with 50 words for a hearing child. Of equal interest was the fact that the use of these signs reflects similar linguistic processes to those of the hearing child. Overgeneralisation of signs was noted, e.g. Ann signing 'dog' on seeing a lion. Holophrastic use of signs was also employed, with the sign for 'smell' meaning variously 'I want to go to the bathroom', 'I am soiled please change me' and 'I want the pretty smelling flower'. Immature variations in signing comparable to 'baby-talk' were also noted. Similarly, the acquisition of single 'words' was comparable to hearing children and growing maturity in signing (with respect to configuration, placement and movement) comparable to the production of speech sounds observed.

Karen, also the child of deaf parents, was studied at a later age in order to explore the birth of grammar. Two-sign utterances and pivot-open constructions of the kind observed with hearing children were found, though in line with other workers, Schlesinger and Meadow (1972) note that 'pivot' could not be strictly defined as such as it was often used alone or in conjunction with other pivots. Again, as with other studies of hearing children, the pivot grammar was used to convey a variety

118   *Auditory Impairment*

of meanings including locative, genetive, attributive and relations between agent and object.

Several other studies have confirmed that deaf children of deaf parents exposed to a conventional sign language progress through the stages of language acquisition as do hearing children (Newport and Ashbrook 1977; Hoffmeister and Wilbur 1980; Kantor 1982; Caselli 1983). Further studies of deaf children with hearing parents employing both signing and oral language are also reported by Schlesinger and Meadow (1972). Here we have in effect children being raised in a bilingual culture. Meadow (1980) reviewing this work concluded that children raised in this way followed the same order of grammatical emergence in signed and spoken English that hearing children exhibit. In addition Meadow (1980) notes that vocabulary growth, grammatical complexity and syntactic structure all progress in the same way as for the hearing children.

In answer to our earlier question, it is clear that the development of natural gesture into a formal language through the teaching of a sign language led to effectively normal linguistic development: '. . . in spite of the difference in modality, the milestones of language development may be the same in the deaf child as in the hearing child' (Meadow 1980 p. 22).

In contrast, exposure to oral-only language will enormously impoverish the deaf child. As Meadow (1980) notes, language acquisition will be painfully slow and linguistic retardation will continue through adolescence and present problems for most deaf adults.

Where a deaf child of hearing parents is not exposed to a formal gestural system, they will, however, spontaneously develop their own 'home sign' system (Tervoort 1961; Lenneberg 1964; Fant 1972; Moores 1974). Even where the absence of formal signing in part is compounded by lack of oral input through profound deafness, a gestural, communicative system similar to that of children raised in normal linguistic environments will evolve (Feldman, Goldin-Meadow and Gleitman 1978; Goldin-Meadow 1979). These studies and others undertaken by these authors (Goldin-Meadow and Feldman 1975, 1977; Goldin-Meadow 1982) found that in the six children they studied, lexical, syntactic and semantic properties developed comparable to those found in nonhearing impaired children, though the actual linguistic form that evolved did show clear differences from normal models. Sign sentences with some, though not all, the structural properties of early child vocal language were observed. These findings are in contrast to those of Gregory and Mogford (1981) noted above, in which apart from pointing, no evidence of gestures was observed.

In a fuller study of Goldin-Meadow and Mylander (1984) investigating the extent to which environmental factors, notably modelling and shaping (immediate and general imitation of models — differential reinforcement of gestures), led to the development of the linguistic aspects of these home sign systems. They first considered the role of imitation since it was thought possible that the children might be receiving gestural input and their own gestural output was simply mirroring that of their mother. Immediate imitation was scant, however (0–7 per cent), and Goldin-Meadow and Mylander discount this explanation. Like hearing children, they conclude that the production of sentences is not by and large dependent on imitation of a communication partner's sentences or their structure.

Alternatively, it is possible that imitation in a more general sense may have occurred, with the parents' gestures forming a system that served as a general model for the child. Goldin-Meadow and Mylander therefore analysed the gestural systems of the parents and compared these with those of the child. For example, the pattern of sign order can be compared. Little comparability of structure was found, however, though less structural aspects of the gesture systems (e.g. the content of communications) did bear some similarity. Typically the children in the study produced their own novel, structural sign sentences.

With respect to the possibility that the children's gestural system was shaped through differential responding to sign sentences, Goldin-Meadow and Mylander confirmed the picture found in studies of hearing children's language. Adult approval or disapproval related not to the correctness of the form of the gestures, but to how true the statement was. Parallel responses did not relate to the correctness or otherwise of the formal properties of the children's sentences.

Goldin-Meadow and Mylander concluded that even under conditions of massive linguistic deprivation a language system can evolve. Their findings confirm the picture that has evolved from studies of spoken child language, i.e. that there are properties of language systems that are highly resilient and which are actively generated by the child. Bates and Volterra (1984) have questioned some aspects of this study, suggesting that other forms of input (e.g. school teachers and peers) might have had an influence and that maternal input may have been more complex than assumed. This might have involved complex multi-modal messages dependent on combinations of vocalisation, gesture and context.

In the case of deaf parents of deaf children, the compatibility of their common communicative systems results in many academic and social advantages displayed by such children relative to their deaf peers with hearing parents. It is unlikely, however, that such benefits stem purely from linguistic compatibility. Blanton (1968) drew attention to the role of language in affective development and raised questions concerning the impact of early problems in deaf children's communication on social development. Conner (1976) comments that psychiatric studies of deviations in parent-child relationships probably begin as early as the first 3 or 4 months of life. Even at this stage of development, we have seen, the deaf child's vocalisation is deviating from normal, and we might assume that auditory stimuli that gain a hearing child's attention during parent-child interactions will also be effective.

Conner goes on to suggest that the enhanced development of deaf children of deaf parents might reflect not the compatibility of their communicative modes, but their greater warmth and acceptance of their child resulting from the fact that they are less traumatised by the occurrence of the handicap. This will permit from the outset a greater flow of communication with the vocal and auditory factors we have just noted playing an insignificant part. Similar acceptance would, of course, be reflected later in the first year of life as gestures take on a more formal communicative significance. In support of this view Conner cites a report by Greenstein (1975) on the development of deaf children from 10 to 40 months: 'The most important finding of this longitudinal study indicated that affective aspects of mother-infant interaction were more highly correlated with the child's language acquisition than were methods or types of the mother's presentation of language' (p. 10). Similar enhancement was also noted for warm *hearing* mothers of deaf children suggesting that it is the nature of the interaction rather than the parent's hearing status which is more crucial. Central to this interaction and language acquisition, Conner notes, is the amount of visual regard through eye contact, a source of communicative contact which as we have seen is devastatingly absent in blind infants and children.

One element of the early interaction liable to go awry when it is disturbed is the role-taking by parent and child that we noted in Chapter 3. This occurs in the case of hearing impaired infants and is to be seen too in their early social interchanges with their peers. Kitana, Stiehl and Cole (1978) report on such disruption and the way in which it can lead not only to communication difficulties, but also to inappropriate behaviour on the part of the deaf child.

At the preschool age, interactions between mother and child continue to differ. Schlesinger and Meadow (1972) compared such interactions in deaf and hearing preschool children. Mothers of the latter were significantly more permissive, nonintrusive, nondidactic, creative, flexible and approving of their child, though they did not enjoy their child significantly more, and mothers of deaf children were able to ensure co-operation in the video-studio as well as mothers of the hearing child. From the point of view of the child, the less their hearing impairment, the more akin their interactions were to those of the hearing children. However: 'Deaf children with fewer communicative skills appear to be less happy, to enjoy interaction with their mothers less, to be less compliant, less creative, and to show less pride in mastery than either their deaf peers with additional communicative skills or hearing children' (p. 104).

Other Aspects of Parent-Child Interaction

Given the disruption of the parent-child interaction and parental perceptions regarding the hearing impairment itself, it is to be expected that differences in the style of parenting will also be noted. In discussing the effect of blindness on parent-child relationships, the possibility of the parent becoming overprotective was mentioned. Meadow (1980) suggests that this is also the case with parents of deaf children, and that this contributes to the social immaturity noted in many deaf preschool children, an immaturity that is greater the poorer the communicative competence. Meadow draws on evidence from Chess, Korn and Fernandez' (1971) observations on children damaged as a result of maternal rubella. Here a striking percentage of children were not permitted to do for themselves a variety of self-help activities of which they were perfectly capable. In addition to overprotectiveness, Schlesinger and Meadow (1972) note greater repressiveness and willingness to use physical punishment than mothers of hearing children, though they emphasise that this does not indicate any less enjoyment of the children. Clearly all the above observations represent generalisations that will be modified by the degree of impairment, particularly with reference to parental attitudes to the impairment. There is also suggestive evidence that patterns of interaction are far more immutable and can be influenced by intervention (Ling and Ling 1976; Bycock and League 1971).

Behaviour Problems

Rutter, Tizard and Whitmore (1970) report that they found 15.4 per cent of hearing impaired children exhibited behaviour disorders in contrast to 6.6 per cent in the general (nonhandicapped) population. This falls close to the mean of a variety of other studies noted by Meadow (1980) who suggests a range of 8–22 per cent. Though in general terms we can agree with Schlesinger and Meadow's (1972) suggestion that '. . . absence of communication in the global sense leads to behaviour problems . . .' (p. 121), the actual genesis of behaviour problems in deaf children appears to have received little study. That the pattern is a complex one is suggested by Schlesinger and Meadow's observation that as a problem evolves it enhances communicative difficulties creating a mutually reinforcing spiral. The key role of communication is also suggested by the fact that behaviour problems are greater for deaf children of hearing parents than those of deaf parents (Stokoe and Battison 1975).

It is equally clear, however, that when deafness is found as part of a wider pattern of multiple handicap, the possibility of other determinants is raised, a major concern to us here given the population with which we are ultimately concerned. In their extensive study of emotional and behavioural problems in 43,946 hearing impaired children involved in special education programmes in the United States, Jensema and Trybus (1975) found links between such problems and other handicaps. Behaviour problems were highest among multiply handicapped children:

> Students with other reported handicaps in addition to their hearing impairment had higher percentages of emotional/behavioural problems. Students with three or more additional handicapping conditions had a lower percentage of emotional/behavioural problems than did students with two additional handicaps, a fact which may be related to the difficulty of differential diagnosis in students exhibiting such extensive impairment in other respects. (p. 9)

Vernon (1969) has explored this issue in some detail, approaching it from the standpoint of aetiology. His hypothesis was that hearing impairment resulting from hereditary causes would be less likely to lead to additional disabilities of the sort that accompany deafness resulting from causes leading to more extensive organic damage. Thus, in contrast to children deafened through maternal rubella, meningitis, prematurity or Rh Factor (erythroblastosis fetalis), children with hereditary deafness will show least behavioural evidence of brain damage. With respect to behaviour problems, Vernon's results suggest that these are dependent not only on the relative presence or absence of brain damage, but also on its nature. Thus, while his overall findings indicated brain damage in both rubella and Rh factor deafened children, teachers' ratings of emotional and behavioural difficulties were far greater for rubella children than for the Rh group. Vernon suggests that in the latter group damage has been done primarily to areas related to motor behaviour in contrast to damage in rubella that affects the regulation of behaviour. A more direct measure of behaviour problems relating to children being dropped from educational programmes because of behaviour problems broadly confirmed this finding. 17.9 per cent of rubella children were dropped in this way, though none were in the Rh group. Children in the hereditary group showed little evidence of brain damage and were rarely dropped (6.2 per cent). Children whose deafness resulted from, or was associated with, premature birth, also tended to exhibit behaviour problems, greater disturbance being associated with lower birthweight.

Concluding Comment

This last discussion has effectively carried us to the threshold of a consideration of the nature of multiple handicap and the problem of the relation between behaviour-environment interactions and organic damage.

We could, in the light of Vernon's study, have pursued this topic with respect to other areas of development, notably language. Suffice it to make the point here, that in considering the relation of specific handicaps to development, and in attempting to illuminate the problems of people who are profoundly retarded and multiply impaired with this information, the possibility of multiple causality must be borne in mind.

As with the handicapping consequences of visual impairment, we have seen in the case of deafness the interdependence of several aspects of development. For such children it is clear that the fundamental contribution to difficulties that may occur results from disruption of the communicative network in which the hearing child develops. From this can stem not only the obvious failures in language development, but affective problems in the mother-child interaction, and wider failures in socialisation. While cognitive development is not necessarily impaired, it is clear that where understanding of the world is made dependent on language, cognitive deficits will be observed.

From the point of view of intervention much that is encouraging comes from these studies. The communicative, academic and affective advantages shown by deaf children of deaf parents, and also those with hearing parents who encourage manual signing, indicate just how dependent development is on the child's place in his or her social ecology rather than the child being merely a passive victim of a handicapping condition.

124   *Auditory Impairment*

References

Bates, E. and Volterra, V. (1984) 'On the Invention of Language: An Alternative View', *Monograph of the Society of Research in Child Development, 49,* Serial No. 207, 130–42

Blanton, R.L. (1968) 'Language Learning and Performance in the Deaf' in S. Rosenberg and J.H. Koplin (eds.), *Development in Applied Psycholinguistics Research,* Collier-MacMillan, London

Boyd, J. (1967) 'Comparison of Motor Behavior in Deaf and Hearing Boys', *American Annals of the Deaf, 112,* 598–605

Bycock, J.R. and League, B. (1971) *Assessing Language Skills in Infancy,* Tree of Life Press, Gainesville, Florida

Caselli, C.C. (1983) 'Communication to Language: Deaf Children's and Hearing Children's Development Compared', *Sign Language Studies, 39,* 113–44

Charles, J. (1978) 'A Comparison of Mothers' Speech to Deaf and Hearing Children of Two Different Ages', unpublished dissertation, Department of Psychology, University of Nottingham, Nottingham

Chess, S., Korn, S.J. and Fernandez, P.B. (1971) *Psychiatric Disorders of Children with Congenital Rubella,* Brunner/Mazel York, New York

Conner, L.E. (1976) 'New Directions in Infant Programs for the Deaf', *The Volta Review, 78,* 8–15

Fant, L.J. (1972) *Ameslan: An Introduction to American Sign Language,* National Association for the Deaf, Silver Spring, Md.

Feldman, H., Goldin-Meadow, S. and Gleitman, L. (1978) Beyond the Herodotus: The Creation of Language by Linguistically Deprived Deaf Children' in A. Lock (ed.), *Action, Symbol and Gesture: The Emergence of Language,* Academic Press, London

Fraiberg, S. (1979) 'Blind Infants and Their Mothers: An Examination of the Sign System' in M. Bullova (ed.), *Before Speech: The Beginning of Interpersonal Communication,* Cambridge University Press, Cambridge

Furth, H.G. (1971) 'Linguistic Deficiency and Thinking: Research with Deaf Subjects', *Psychological Bulletin, 76,* 58–72

Gilbert, J.H.V. (1982) 'Babbling and the Deaf Child: A Commentary on Lenneberg *et al.* (1965) and Lenneberg (1975)', *Journal of Child Language, 9,* 511–15

Gilbert, J. and Levee, R.F. (1967) 'Performances of Deaf and Normally Hearing Children on the Bender-Gestalt and the Archimedes Spiral Tests', *Perceptual and Motor Skills, 24,* 1059–66

Goldin-Meadow, S. (1979) 'Structure in Manual Communication System Developed without a Conventional Language Model: Language Without a Helping Hand' in H. Whitaker and H.A. Whitaker (eds.), *Studies in Neurolinguistics: Vol. 4,* Academic Press, London

Goldin-Meadow, S. (1982) 'The Resilience of Recursion: A Study of a Communication System Developed without a Conventional Language Model' in L.R. Gleitman and E. Wanner (eds.), *Language Acquisition: The State of the Art,* Cambridge University Press, Cambridge

Goldin-Meadow, S. (1985) 'Language Development under Atypical Learning Condition: Replication and Implications of a Study of Deaf Children of Hearing Parents' in K.E. Nelson (ed.), *Children's Language: Vol. 5,* Erlbaum,

Hillsdale, N.J.

Goldin-Meadow, S. and Feldman, H. (1975) 'The Creation of a Communication System: A Study of Deaf Children of Hearing Parents', *Sign Language Studies*, 8, 255–34

Goldin-Meadow, S. and Feldman, H. (1977) 'The Development of Language-like Communication without a Language Model', *Science*, 197, 401–3

Goldin-Meadow, S. and Mylander, C. (1983) 'Gestural Communication in Deaf Children: The Non-effects of Parental Input on Language Development', *Science*, 221 (4608), 372–4

Goldin-Meadow, S. and Mylander, C. (1984) 'Gestural Communication in Deaf Children: The Non-effects of Parental Input on Early Language Development', *Monographs of the Society for Research in Child Development*, 49, Serial No. 207, 1–120

Greenstein, J.M. (1975) 'Methods of Fostering Language in Deaf Infants', Final report to HEW, Grant no. OEG-0-72-5339, June 1975

Gregory, S. and Mogford, K. (1981) 'Early Language Development in Deaf Children' in B. Woll, J.G. Kyle and M. Deucher (eds.), *Perspectives in British Sign Language and Deafness*, Croom Helm, London

Gregory, S. and Mogford, K. (1983) 'The Development of Symbolic Play in Young Deaf Children' in D. Rogers and J.A. Sloboda (eds.), *The Acquisition of Symbolic Skills*, Plenum Press, London

Gregory, S., Mogford, K. and Bishop, J. (1979) 'Mothers' Speech to Young Impaired Children', *The Teacher of the Deaf*, 3, 42–3

Hoemann, H.W. (1972) 'The Development of Communication Skills in Deaf and Hearing Children', *Child Development*, 43, 990–1003

Hoffmeister, R. (1978) 'The Development of Demonstrative Pronouns, Locatives and Personal Pronouns in the Acquisition of American Sign Language by Deaf Children of Deaf Parents', unpublished doctoral dissertation, University of Minnesota

Hoffmeister, R. and Wilbur, R. (1980) 'The Acquisition of Sign Language' in H. Lane and F. Grosjean (eds.), *Recent Perspectives on American Sign Language*, Erlbaum, Hillsdale, N.J.

Jensema, C. and Trybus, R. (1975) 'Reported Emotional/Behavioral Problems among Hearing Impaired Children in Special Educational Programs: United States, 1972–73', Gallaudet College Office of Demographic Studies, No. 1, Series R, Washington, D.C.

Kantor, R. (1982) 'Communicative Interaction: Mother Modification and Child Acquisition of American Sign Language', *Sign Language Studies*, 36, 233–82

Kimura, D. (1981) 'Neural Mechanisms in Manual Signing', *Sign Language Studies*, 33, 291–312

Kitana, M.K., Stiehl, J. and Cole, J.T. (1978) 'Role Taking: Implications for Special Education', *Journal of Special Education*, 12, 59–74

Lenneberg, E.H. (1964) 'Capacity for Language Acquisition' in J.A. Fodor and J.J. Katz (eds.), *The Structure of Language: Readings in the Philosophy of Language*, Prentice-Hall, Englewood Cliffs, N.J.

Liben, L.S. (1978) 'Developmental Perspectives on the Experiential Deficiencies of Deaf Children' in L.S. Liben (ed.), *Deaf Children: Developmental Perspectives*, Academic Press, London

Ling, A.H. and Ling, D. (1976) 'Communication Development of Normal and

Hearing Impaired Infants and their Mothers' in Z.S. Jastrzembska (ed.), *The Effects of Blindness and Other Impairments on Early Development*, American Foundation for the Blind, New York

Meadow, K.P. (1980) *Deafness and Child Development*, Edward Arnold, London

Menyuk, P. (1977) 'Effects of Hearing Loss on Language Acquisition in the Babbling Stage' in B.F. Jaffe (ed.), *Hearing Loss in Children*, University Park Press, Baltimore

Moores, D.F. (1974) 'Nonvocal Systems of Verbal Behavior' in R.L. Schiefelbusch and L.L. Lloyd (eds.), *Language Perspectives: Acquisition, Retardation and Intervention*, University Park Press, Baltimore

Newport, E.L. and Ashbrook, E.F. (1977) 'The Emergence of Semantic Relations in American Sign Language', *Papers and Reports on Child Language Development, 13*, 16–21

Nober, E.H. and Nober, L.W. (1977) 'Effects of Hearing, Loss on Speech and Language in the Post-babbling Stage' in B.F. Jaffe (ed.), *Hearing Loss in Children*, University Park Press, Baltimore

Rapin, I. (1979) 'Effects of Early Blindness and Deafness on Cognition' in R. Katzman (ed.), *Congenital and Acquired Cognitive Disorders*, Raven Press, New York

Rutter, M., Tizard, J. and Whitmore, K. (1970) *Education, Health and Behaviour: A Psychological and Medical Study of Childhood Development*, Wiley, London

Schlesinger, H.S. and Meadow, K.P. (1972) *Sound and Sign: Childhood Deafness and Mental Health*, University of California Press, Berkeley

Stokoe, W.C. and Battison, R. (1975) 'Sign Language, Mental Health and Satisfactory Interaction', unpublished paper, Linguistics Research Laboratory, Gallaudet College, Washington, D.C. Cited by Meadow (1980)

Tate, M. (1979) 'Comparative Study of Language Development in Hearing Impaired Children and Normally Hearing Infants', *The Teacher of the Deaf, 33*, 5

Tervoort, B.T. (1961) 'Esoteric Symbolism in the Communication Behavior of Young Deaf Children', *American Annals of the Deaf*, 436–80

Vernon, M. (1969) *Multiply Handicapped Deaf Children: Medical, Educational and Psychological Considerations*, Council for Exceptional Children Research Monograph, Washington, D.C.

6 THE DEVELOPMENTAL CONSEQUENCES OF PHYSICAL IMPAIRMENT

The aetiologies, patterns and degrees of severity of visual and auditory impairment are many and diverse. This multiplicity is even more apparent when we encounter physical impairment. The causes and manifestations of the two major categories of physical impairment, cerebral palsy and spina bifida, are sufficiently different that it is rare in the literature to find them even mentioned in the same breath. An equally distinct condition, impairment of a child as a result of the drug thalidomide being taken by the mother during pregnancy, is also usually considered in its own right. More generally, physical impairment can result not only from congenital influences, but also from temporary and imposed immobility as in the case of infants being immobilised through plaster casts, traction, splints and other restraint procedures. Less obviously, impairment can result from hospitalisation during infancy.

For our present purpose, this diversity is compounded by both the nature of the underlying causes of physical impairment on the one hand, and variations within conditions on the other. With respect to the former, damage to the brain and central nervous system may influence a variety of functions in addition to movement. Contrasted definitions of cerebral palsy reflect this distinction. On the one hand, Cruickshank quotes Perlstein (1949) as defining cerebral palsy as a 'condition, characterized by paralysis, weakness, inco-ordination, or any other abberation of motor function due to pathology of the motor control centers of the brain' (Cruickshank 1976 p. 1). On the other, Cruickshank himself suggests a wider practical definition:

> From such a view cerebral palsy is seen as one component of a broader brain damaged syndrome comprised of neuro-motor dysfunction, convulsions, or behaviour disorders of organic origin. In some cerebral palsied individuals only a single factor may appear; other individuals may be characterised by any combination of factors mentioned. (Cruickshank 1976 p. 2)

According to Cruickshank, the term 'mental retardation' would be embraced by 'psychological dysfunction'. It would be possible to parallel the contrasted definitions with respect to spina bifida.

Regarding different types of physical impairment within a general category, a variety of sub-categories may also be identified. Thus, Cruickshank (1976) presents information on vision, hearing and speech impairments in cerebral palsy with respect to spasticity, athetosis, rigidity and ataxia. Anderson and Spain (1977) related their findings with spina bifida children to presence and absence of a valve and the co-occurence of hydrocephalus. Lonton (1977) considers both intellectual and motoric functioning in relation to the location in the spinal cord of the myelomeningocele lesion and its extent. With respect to both these physically handicapping conditions, sub-classification and its relation to development and function are critical issues. In reality, however, to our knowledge, few studies exist that consider at an observational, or experimental, level the relation between such sub-categories and specific aspects of development of the sort with which we are concerned here. References to them in our subsequent account will therefore tend to be limited.

In this review, we have in fact taken the main categories noted above (i.e. cerebral palsy, spina bifida, thalidomide impairment and environmental restriction), in order to consider the effect of physical impairment on young children's development. Lagergren (1970) lists many other forms of physical impairing diseases and injury that might be relevant to such an account. However, with respect to early child development we have found few studies outside the categories noted that might be of help to us. Indeed, even from these categories remarkably little work on *early* development has been undertaken. What there is will be supplemented from time to time by a forward look at older children in these groups on the assumption that deficits in processes observed later in childhood will probably have played their part in impairing developmental processes in the young child and infant.

With respect to the person working with individuals who are profoundly retarded and multiply handicapped, it is important that he/she has an understanding of cerebral palsy and spina bifida in their own right though it is not our intention to provide this background here. In the following review we ensure that the particular condition with which we are concerned is distinguished. However, rather than review each category independently, we will focus on the *areas* of development in which we are interested with respect to all available information from the different groups. For example, we will consider studies of mother-child interaction undertaken with cerebral palsied, spina bifida and thalidomide children within a single developmental framework rather than review all aspects of development for a single condition. Indeed, this particular focus, i.e. mother-child interaction, provides a useful starting point. From it we can branch out into a consideration of sensorimotor development and language and communication. We can then move on to fine motor, perceptual and gross motor development and finally to behaviour disorders in physically impaired children, a topic which in effect brings us back again to early parenting.

Mother-Child Interaction

The presence of physical handicap in young infants and children can influence their relationships with the mother and other members of the family in a variety of ways. At the outset the unusual appearance of the child may play its part, in some cases leading to abbreviated, or distorted, contacts of the sort described by Roskies (1972) in the case of mothers of visibly deformed thalidomide-damaged babies. Cruickshank, Hallahan and Bice (1976) emphasise the importance of visible disability in impairing social relationships. With reference to cerebral palsied, spina bifida and thalidomide children they hypothesise that:

> . . . as the degree of severity of visible physical disability increases, the scope of personality characteristics and their degree of psychological severity increase. It is the nature of the visible physical disability to which society reacts and which tends to set the cerebral palsied child apart. Research is available to demonstrate that cardiac children with a non-visible physical disability, function as physically normal children do in several different types of personal-social situations . . . children with visible physical handicaps, including a group of cerebral palsied, were observed to be very different in personality characteristics to physically normal peers with whom the former had been matched by sex and chronological age. (p. 128)

Any physical distancing that might result from the child's appearance may be increased by periods of hospitalisation during the first year. Roskies (1972) comments on this situation with respect to thalidomide-damaged children and notes compounding factors such as the child's tendency to become more attached to other people than the mother. There are, too, longer-term consequences to such separations to which we will return at the end of this chapter.

Important, indeed crucial, though these broad setting conditions are for the development of the relationship between mother and physically impaired child, it is ultimately in the nature of their interaction that benefits and disadvantages may be seen. Despite the problems for the mothers described by Roskies (1972), she noted that there were surprisingly few repercussions on actual techniques of child rearing, and indeed as we shall see later, these mothers saw their children's development as being essentially normal in a variety of respects. However, distortion of the relationship as a result of the child's physical impairment can occur, and is documented in Shere and Kastenbaum's (1966) account of mothers' interactions with their cerebral palsied children. Like Roskies's study, this work merits considerable attention with respect to the entire field of mothers' relationships with their handicapped children and the role of the professional in that relationship. Between them they address a host of issues that professionals have failed to take into account in their enthusiasm for transferring their own professional skills to parents, issues which have only recently begun to receive attention in the literature on parental support.

Shere and Kastenbaum (1966) suggest that the development of the children in their study is in double-jeopardy from the consequences of the physical impairment itself, and from the potential emergence of an interactional pattern that might inhibit, rather than foster, psychological growth. Their concern was to investigate whether the interaction between the mother and her cerebral palsied child distorted the child's interaction with the world of objects and people in a way that inhibited cognitive growth. They took as their starting point the position we have described in Chapter 3 regarding the child learning through active co-ordination of movement and vision, though drawing on Dewey rather than Piaget. They note that this interaction will inevitably be impaired in cerebral palsied children:

> Although the infant may live in an environment that is stocked with a diversity of objects, these objects scarcely exist as 'real' entities permitting of interaction, pleasure and learning by doing. The objects provide visual stimulation of a relatively passive and unchanging character — and little more. (p. 259)

As with visually impaired children, this state of affairs can lead to a failure of self-differentiation by the child from both objects and other people. What, then, did they see as the implication of this state of affairs for the child's interaction with his or her mother? Shere and Kastenbaum presuppose that if a child is so impaired by cerebral palsy that he/she cannot move towards objects nor ask for them, then this impoverished environment can only be overcome if the mother adequately provides the child with objects. The key word here is 'adequately', and it is to evaluate such adequacy that their study is directed.

Through interviews, observations and evaluation of a parent guidance programme, Shere and Kastenbaum established the relation between the mother's concerns for her child and how she mediated between the child and the world of objects. The first and overwhelming concern of the mothers was for the physical well-being of their children. By the age of 3:0 years, they were noting (in the following order) insufficiencies with respect to the child's physical development and growth, the lack of responsivity to the mother's communicative attempts and the lack of reaching for objects. These concerns, advice given by professionals and the child's tendency to sickness all led to an emphasis on physical development as the major concern, with passivity being equated with the child's happiness. These views precluded any notion of play as valid and cognitively useful activity for the cerebral palsied child, and this was reflected in the way the child was dealt with. Thus, passive positioning predominated, e.g. in front of the television. When objects such as toys were introduced to the child they were to encourage movement and physical development in their own right rather than offering the possibility of learning and development through play. Overall, Shere and Kastenbaum comment that typically '. . . the child was kept in an almost barren environment which prevented him from gaining experience of the object world' (p. 285). Specific factors may curtail direct interaction between mother and child. Lencione (1976) comments on the fear expressed by mothers of putting their cerebral palsied child into extensor spasm through verbal stimulation.

We have dwelt on this study at some length not only because it is one of the few that has attempted to observe mother-child interactions where the child is seriously physically impaired, but because it again points to the unity of the infant's social relationships and developmentally critical experiences of the world of objects. Basically, the mother's view of the nature of the impairment conditioned the way she mediated the child's environment, in this instance in a way judged disadvantageous by Shere and Kastenbaum. Indeed, they note that most of the mothers did not perceive the child as being incapacitated with regard to coming into contact with the object-world around.

As with the mothers of the cerebral palsied children just described, those of the thalidomide-damaged children investigated by Roskies (1972) also saw the main area of abnormality affecting their children as motor behaviour, e.g. with respect to reaching, sitting, crawling and walking.

However, this state of affairs was seen essentially as arising from the child's phocomelia, i.e. the deformity in which the hands are attached to the shoulders and the feet are attached to the hips. With respect to intelligence, speech and emotional development, however, they saw their children as essentially normal. We will return to some aspects of these judgements when we consider specific areas of development later. With respect to the perceived motor abnormalities, some features of development in this area were particularly disturbing to the mother. Unusual sequences, e.g. walking before sitting independently, and unusual forms of prehension, e.g. picking up objects with toes, particularly aroused anxiety and confronted mothers with painful choices about how to deal with the behaviour. Nevertheless, Roskies notes that in general these differences did not lead to marked changes in the mother's habitual child-rearing techniques.

Later in this chapter we will discuss the influence on behavioural adjustment of the relation between the physical contact a child has with its mother and the bodily feelings that result, a topic introduced in connection with visual impairment in Chapter 4. It is obvious that where a child cannot move and grasp its mother, then again this experience will depend entirely on the mother's initiating contact. There is the suggestion in Shere and Kastenbaum's study that the passivity character-ising the cerebral palsied children might have led to reduced physical contact between mother and child. A similar state of affairs might also occur with children with upper limb dysfunctions of differing types. It is interesting to note that in Gouin Décarie's (1969) study of thalidomide-damaged children no relation did emerge between the types of malform-ation and emotional adjustment. A child suffering from severe malform-ations could show remarkable socialisation, while another less impaired child might reveal a lack of attachment to others. With the exception of one child, all children studied would cling to their mother even if in an unconventional fashion. Legs were mainly used, but digits would also be employed as might chin and shoulder.

This small, but important, group of studies amply illustrates the way in which the child's physical impairment, the mother's perception of it and the interaction between the two will condition the mother-child relationship and affect cognitive development. Such interactions, as Cruickshank *et al.* (1976) imply, will also occur in broader family and social contexts. The nature of these interactions will also be conditioned by social characteristics of the families as Lonton and Sklayne (1980) have shown with regard to the effect of social class on the intellectual skills of spina bifida children. Against this background, we may now consider some of the specific sensorimotor consequences of physical impairment.

Sensorimotor Development

Delay in both early and later cognitive development in many physically handicapped children is to be anticipated not only because of the reduced opportunity for interacting with the physical world, but also because of associated damage to brain and central nervous system. With respect to thalidomide-damaged children, it was the possibility of considering the developmental impact of physical impairment in its own right that led Gouin Décarie (1969) to study these children. All 22 in her study suffered from malformations involving either the upper extremities (hands and arms) or lower extremities (legs and feet) or both. The severity of their malformations varied. In particular she was concerned to establish what the effect of impaired prehension was on early sensorimotor development, given the importance of prehension in '. . . the elaboration of the fundamental categories of intelligence: object-concept, space, time and causality' (p. 171). Of special importance among these was the construction of the object concept and how this takes place, ' . . . in the case of individuals lacking even the possibility of co-ordination between essential schemes such as sucking and prehension' (p. 171).

For Gouin Décarie to answer the question of whether these physically impaired children do attain the object concept and when, she had to employ a variety of techniques of assessment that permit the child to demonstrate where in the six stages of sensorimotor development he or she was located. A variety of observational and psychometric techniques were employed including the use of her own object-concept scale and object relations scale (Gouin Décarie 1962). With respect to overall development, the children ranged from superior intelligence to developmentally retarded, 31 per cent having developmental quotients between 90 and 109. The overall distribution was skewed to a below average Developmental Quotient (DQ) of 90. There was no obvious correlation within this group of severity of impairment and DQ. A consideration of the component abilities making up the DQ produced what Gouin-Décarie calls '. . . a typical profile of the limb deficient infant and this profile is a rather unexpected one' (p. 177). With great consistency it was found that *language* was most affected, while *eye-hand* performance was highest. In accounting for this unanticipated observation, she returns to the social context of the mother and child and notes that it is the adult failure to compensate for the child's deficiencies which has led to increased manual activity. Reduced language input from adults, on the other hand, cannot be compensated for by the child in this way.

With respect to the development of the object concept, Gouin Décarie employed assessments of object permanence as the critical test. The children were allowed to use any means, e.g. use of mouth or toes, to remove a screen to reveal the object. In her group of 22 17 month to 3 years 8 months old children she found 19/21 had reached Stage VI. One had achieved Stage V and one, Stage IV. The last two were amongst the youngest, though this alone could not account for the delay. She concludes that thalidomide-damaged children do acquire the full object concept within the normal range. How, then, does this tie in with the fact of physical impairment?

Eleven of the children studied could actually bring their hands with ease to their midline, while this was also possible with difficulty for eight others. Three children had no hand-hand or hand-mouth contact, and among these were two of those who had failed to reach Stage VI. 'In other words', writes Gouin Décarie, 'most of the subjects did not, in fact, lack the fundamental schemes required for the construction of the object-concept . . . and secondly, all of them could use substitute channels that led to such co-ordination as "toes-mouth", "eyes-toes", "shoulder-chin-eyes", "digits-toes", "eyes-digits", etc.' (p. 181). Thus alternative schemes to those permitted by prehension can achieve the object concept by different routes from those conventionally followed. This finding also points to the influences underlying the high 'eye-hand' score on the developmental test.

From Gouin Décarie's study, then, we can see that in the absence of marked brain damage, children who are clearly physically *impaired* are not necessarily *disabled* with respect to the motor prerequisites of cognitive development, and are not, in a whole range of activities, subsequently handicapped. Will the cerebral palsied child with severe involvement of limbs be more adversely affected in interaction with objects during the sensorimotor stages?

Eagle (1985) argues that research on sensorimotor development and its dependence on movement would be more illuminating if this issue were explored with severely involved quadraplegic children. She employed measures of object permanence based on the Uzgiris-Hunt Ordinal Scales of Development (see Chapters 3 and 7) to investigate this in 34 children who nevertheless varied in their degree of physical impairment. Intellectually this group cannot be regarded as normative as 10 were profoundly retarded, 16, severely to moderately retarded, and only 8, mild to normal intelligence. She found that the best predictor of the achievement of object permanence was Mental Age (MA), severity of physical handicap only being related to the development of object permanence because less severity is associated with higher MA. Eagle concludes: '. . . that at least some of these severely involved quadraplegic children reached the highest level of object permanence does indicate that early levels of cognitive development *can* be reached even when sensorimotor experience has been *profoundly* reduced or *distorted*' (p. 280), though, of course rate of attainment may be much slower than is normative.

Whether the object concept can develop independently of any form of intentional movement, including early eye movements, must remain an open question. Eagles concludes, however, that cognition can develop in the context of profoundly disturbed intentional movement of the limbs, even when eye movement as well is seriously affected.

The possibility of cerebral palsied children utilising nonmotoric methods to cognitive ends has been studied by Melcer (1966) in the development of means-end behaviour (cited by Cruickshank *et al.* 1976 p. 173). That either alternatives to motor behaviour or optimal use of available motor ability are employed to carry the child through the sensorimotor and preoperational stages can be inferred from studies of older cerebral palsied children who do possess higher-order concepts of functional relations and class membership (Lencione 1976).

In considering the early development of spina bifida children we must follow a similar logic as we have traced no experimental or observational studies of the progress of such children through the sensorimotor and preconceptual stages. The medical and educational significance of spina bifida ranges from the negligible consequences of spina bifida occulta through to children with encephalocele and with myelomeningocele with hydrocephalus. Encephalocelic and myelomeningitic children account for around 90 per cent of spina bifida children (Tew 1973). Despite the motor and perceptual anomalies shown by myelomeningitic children, the average intelligence of these children falls not so far from the average IQ of 89 (Tew 1973). Typically, verbal IQ is advanced over performance IQ, 94 and 85 in Tew's study. He also reports a similar pattern of abilities for children with encephalocele though here full-scale IQ was only 52. Despite this general skew towards lower intelligence, it is also the case that some children with spina bifida perform on such tests at or beyond average ability. Concluding a full review on this topic, Anderson and Spain (1977 pp. 117–44) summarise five

points related to the intellectual development of spina bifida children:
(i) Intelligence tends to be below average. (ii) Variation is found with
occurrence/non-occurrence of hydrocephalus and the severity of this
condition. (iii) Intelligence does not vary with the severity of physical
handicap unless there is hydrocephalus. (iv) Differences in intelligence
are related to the nature of the central nervous system lesion. (v) Verbal
skills tend to be less affected than performance skills.

It is clear then that for the majority of spina bifida children progress
is made through the phases of early development in which we are
interested. For many, the development of language is not impaired to
the point at which they are linguistically handicapped, though their ability
to manipulate the world of objects lags behind. The immobility of many
of these children will clearly reduce the extent to which they can interact
with the world around them, though as with cerebral palsied and
thalidomide-damaged children, this will be alleviated by greater use of
their hands and arms. As we shall see, though upper-limb involvement
is not typically as apparent for the spina bifida child as it is for the
hemiplegic or quadraplegic cerebral palsied child, difficulties do exist
that might inhibit sensorimotor interactions, a state of affairs compounded
by perceptual problems to be described later.

Before moving to a more direct consideration of motor and perceptual
aspects of physical impairment and their consequences for development,
however, we will consider the immediate outgrowth of early social
interaction and sensorimotor development, namely language.

Language Development

From the model of development we have described, it is to be anticipated
that any consequences of physical impairment that lead to abbreviated
or abnormal interactions between child and mother, and reduce sensorimotor experiences, will in turn affect the emergence of language. At
the outset, then, it is interesting to comment on language development
in thalidomide-damaged children as we have seen the remarkable capacity
of most of these children to establish normal affective relations with their
mothers and to progress through the sensorimotor period to Stage VI.

The mothers studied by Roskies (1972) saw their children as being
essentially normal in the development of their communicative ability.
In 14 out of 18 instances they reported their children's first words between
6 and 12 months, the other four occurring at 18 to 24 months. Roskies

comments that what deficits did exist tended to be related by the mothers to periods of hospitalisation. As Gouin Décarie (1969) reported, however, language was unexpectedly delayed when formally assessed. Developmental testing yielded a developmental quotient of only 73 (compared to 95 on eye-hand use). We have already noted that Gouin Décarie attributes this to reduced language input by the parents.

In relation to cerebral palsy, delays in early language development are typically, though not inevitably, noted. Denhoff (1976) found 11 per cent of children in the sample produced single words by 9 months, 15 per cent, by 10 months, though 74 per cent were delayed beyond the expected 12-months norm. The average for production of single words was 27.1 months. With respect to two and three word utterances, 31 per cent had produced these by the expected 24 months, and a further 23 per cent, by 30 months. The remaining 46 per cent produced two and three word sentences after this age. The overall mean was 37.4 months.

Lencione (1976) in a review of retrospective studies in this area indicates that they demonstrate that while the degree of competence in producing speech sounds was usually delayed or distorted, the acquisition of the phonological system followed essentially the same course as for nonhandicapped children.

A more detailed study of language in cerebral palsied children was undertaken by Love (1964), though in citing this we again jump forward from early language development to that of 10–15 year old athetoid and spastic children. These were compared with other physically handicapped children exhibiting no obvious speech or hearing problems. The cerebral palsied and physically handicapped groups differed in expressive naming but not in receptive vocabulary, nor in their descriptive language. Love concluded that disorders of comprehension and the formulation of oral symbols often attributed to cerebral palsied children were not found here. Lencione (1976) states that Love's study gave '. . . strong indications that for those children who had acquired expressive language, syntactical and semantic behaviours were similar to those of normal speakers' (p. 183). As Lencione concludes, however: 'To date, there is very little scientific data concerning the development of linguistic processes in children with cerebral palsy' (p. 205), especially with reference to the 'manner' in which symbolic skills emerge.

This conclusion can be equally applied to language acquisition in spina bifida children. We have already indicated that for many such children verbal behaviour approaches that of their nonhandicapped peers, and is usually in advance of their performance abilities. Anderson and Spain

(1977) note that children without shunts have normal vocabulary at 3:0 years as assessed on the Reynell Developmental Language Scale (Reynell 1969). With shunts, only one third of the children fall within the normal range. With respect to syntax, all children in Spain's (1974) study of the three groups of children, i.e. encephoceles, spina bifida with shunt and spina bifida without shunt, had a grasp of syntax normal for their age. This applied even to those with poor performance ability with low overall verbal scores. With respect to comprehension, spina bifida children with performance developmental quotients of over 80, with or without a shunt, scored at or above average on the Reynell Comprehension Scale, though those below 80 and with a shunt were well below the norm.

These findings will lead the teacher of people with profound retardation and spina bifida to anticipate a variety of specific strengths and weaknesses in the development of their language. These teachers will also have encountered what Anderson and Spain (1977) call the 'hyperverbal' person with spina bifida. They define hyperverbal behaviour as fluent speech coupled with poor understanding, and note that it is found particularly in hydrocephalic children, such children tending to be more handicapped both neurologically and physically.

In addition to the impairing effects on language of the conditions described so far, there is also evidence to suggest that language can be affected through periods of immobilisation and sensory restriction. Sibinga, Friedman, Steisel and Sinnamon (1968) studied a group of children with phenylketonuria (PKU) who had undergone relatively brief periods of isolation, confinement and restrictions of stimulation (even in a single modality) before they were 3 years of age. In contrast to PKU children who had not experienced one of these conditions, such children were 20 points or more lower on both the full Wechsler Intelligence Scale for Children (WISC) (51.9 vs 71.9) and Peabody Picture Vocabulary Test (53.7 vs 78.9). Again, detailed explanation of this finding is lacking, though the authors satisfactorily rule out alternative explanations such as other intrinsic differences between the groups.

A further influence of restraint on speech has been reported by Sibinga and Friedman (1971). They studied language development in children with a history of immobilisation. They report an unexpectedly high incidence of articulation problems and language delays in children who had been immobilised for medical reasons during the first six months of their lives, e.g. in splints. It is suggested that such impairment reflects interference with the motor processes underlying speech production. It should be mentioned, too, that impairment of the motor basis of articulation will be more grossly apparent where direct neurological damage exists, particularly in the case of cerebral palsied individuals (Lencione 1976; Melyn and Grossman 1976). Wider specific consequences of impairment to movement will now be further considered.

Fine Motor Development

The works and creations of the human hands may never cease to be a source of wonder — but equally, the remarkable capacity of human beings to develop and evolve their intellect and their understanding of the world in the absence of normally functioning hands is equally as impressive. We have already seen the adaptive use to which thalidomide children put their vestigial upper limbs, and their remarkable eye-hand abilities. Where manipulative control is entirely lacking, as in some cases of cerebral palsy, we shall see (Volume 2, Chapter 3) that alternative modes of interaction with the environment can be established to substitute in a developmentally advantageous fashion.

Children with spina bifida appear to occupy an intermediate position with respect to normal competence in hand use and severe impairment of the kind found in some instances of cerebral palsy. For some time it was assumed that spina bifida children typically exhibited dysfunction of the lower limbs alone, and perhaps the severity of this impairment masked less dramatic dysfunction of the upper limbs. Anderson and Spain (1977) point out that at 1 year of age, however, apart from locomotor delay, it is in eye-hand co-ordination that these children most lag behind. This is even more marked at 3:0 years when children with shunts show poor manipulative ability — especially in a task such as bead threading. Overall, their results:

> . . . do indicate very strongly that visuo-motor co-ordination skills and the ability to organize motor actions in space are impaired and this may give rise to difficulties in carrying out many everyday actions such as getting a shirt on the right way round and doing up the buttons or catching a ball, and in school will certainly affect attainments, particularly number work and writing. (p. 136)

In reviewing manual skills in spina bifida children, Anderson and Spain (1977) comment on the abnormally low proportion of right-handers, while Lonton (1976) notes the abnormally high proportion of left- and mixed-handers. Possibly this reflects neurological abnormality accentuated by the child's need to use his or her hands for bodily support while sitting — thus reducing the opportunity to use them to play with objects. Again, the presence or absence of a shunt has important consequences for manual activity. Employing an adaptation of a standard test of hand function, Anderson and Spain report that children: (i) without shunts scored as well as controls in timed items; (ii) with shunts were slower regardless of overall ability; (iii) with shunts had difficulty in touching thumb to finger, in picking up small objects and in positioning pegs in a board — a difficulty even experienced by children with clear hand dominance. In an experimental task described in the next section, Anderson and Plewis (1977) comment on the awkwardness of prehension and the immaturity of the grip employed to hold a pencil. This grip was either too loose or too tight, and there were problems in controlling force and movement. Some explanation of this difficulty will be offered in the following section on perception and physical impairment.

With respect to these manual difficulties it is only possible to speculate on their specific impact on early sensorimotor development. We would hypothesise that they are insufficiently gross (in comparison, for example, with not being able to move about) to greatly delay the development and relating of action schemes. Their effects, it would seem, would be more likely to manifest themselves in tasks involving fine control and co-ordination of the sort valued later in childhood and noted by Anderson and Spain.

Perceptual Development

If it has proved difficult to discuss fine motor development without reference to perceptual aspects of manual activity, it is certainly not possible to consider perceptual aspects without in turn being drawn into accounts of hand use. At the basic perceptual level both cerebral palsied and spina bifida children have problems that affect their perception. With respect to sight, Cruickshank (1976) presents figures indicating that in a total population of cerebral palsied children 22–28 per cent had defective vision. In the population of particular concern in this book the figure will be dramatically higher. Even in the IQ range 30–50, Black (1980) found only 20.4 per cent of a group of 6–16 year old cerebral palsied children had normal eyes when ophthalmologically examined. Nearly 50 per cent of these had refractive errors and over 50 per cent had squints. Similarly, with respect to spina bifida, Tew (1973) draws attention to the high incidence of visual abnormalities, particularly squints, and their damaging effect on educational attainment.

With respect to hearing, the overall position in relation to physical impairment is somewhat better. Cruickshank (1976), again, notes between 8 and 12 per cent cerebral palsied children with defective hearing in the total population, though it must be assumed that with increasing central nervous system damage and lowered IQ this figure will again rise. Hearing loss in spina bifida children is fortunately, as Anderson and Spain (1977) note, relatively rare, according to their figures affecting between 0.1 and 2.7 per cent.

In like manner we might anticipate progressive decreases in tactile sensitivity and the ability to use tactile information in the performance of a task with increasing impairment in these conditions. Lencione (1976) suggested that is the case with cerebral palsied individuals and that this will decrease their ability to gather information about the shape of objects on the basis of touch. Comparable loss of sensation in spina bifida is to be expected depending upon the site of the lesion in the spinal cord. Miller and Sethi (1971) have clearly shown that for some spina bifida children tactile sensation is indeed poor.

Further evidence indicates that the channelling and co-ordination of sensory information to produce controlled movements is also going to be impaired in cerebral palsied and spina bifida children, again with the qualification that there will be variation between the various sub-categories noted earlier. These studies have been experimental and have also employed standard tests of perceptual-motor function. Employing the Bender-Gestalt Test, an assessment involving the children in redrawing a variety of figures embodying various spatial relations, Cruickshank *et al.* (1976) found markedly deficient performance in cerebral palsied children and showed the relation of IQ and type of cerebral palsy to errors made. They also review studies suggesting that these children have special difficulties in differentiating figure from ground. Tew (1973) reports parallel work with children with myelomeningoceles who on average were 19 months poorer than nonhandicapped children on the Frostig Test of Visual Perception. In an experimental study with 7–10 children with spina bifida and hydrocephalus, Anderson and Plewis (1977) found these children 25 per cent slower than their nonhandicapped peers though there was overlap between the groups and the spina bifida children did make substantial progress during the course of the activity. When the task had to be carried out without them seeing what they were doing, there was no difference between the groups, suggesting that kinesthetic ability was not markedly affected in these spina bifida children's performance.

Findings of the sort we have noted must have relevance to the way

in which we encourage early development though they have not bee
undertaken or conceived within a developmental framework. The man
neurological anomalies that the various writers comment on as causin
the various deficits in the perceptual processes already exist from th
first days of life and will play their part in impeding development.

Gross Motor Development

There is a certain paradox in the fact that we have left so major
characteristic of many physically impaired children until almost the en
of this chapter. The disabling consequences of lack of bodily contro
in coping with the world are profound, and for many physically impaire
individuals constitute the essence of the handicapping outcome in late
life. Here, however, our focus is narrower as we intend illustrating som
of the more immediate developmental consequences for the very youn;
physically impaired child.

For many cerebral palsied, spina bifida and thalidomide-damage
children alike, immobility will constitute a direct threat to their inter
action with people and objects. In the case of spina bifida, *expecte*
mobility following spinal cord damage at various segmental levels is onl
actually observed in 50 per cent of the cases for whom walking woul
have been anticipated (Wallace 1973). In a study of cerebral palsie
children, Denhoff (1976) indicates that the average age for walking b
themselves was 32.9 months, though some cerebral palsied individual
will not walk or attain any form of mobility. Roskies comments on th
high motivation to be mobile of young thalidomide children in her study
By whatever means, if they were able, they crept or shuffled round th
floor to reach their mothers, in contrast to the cerebral palsied childre
in Shere and Kastenbaum's study who were totally immobile and depend
ent on their mother for contact with people and objects. Thus, lack o
mobility restricts those very motoric actions that permit the child to mov
into situations where schemes based on eye-hand and head movement
might evolve. Though as the report on sensorimotor development i
thalidomide-damaged children indicated, physical impairment does no
of itself preclude such development, in the case of children with gros
upper limb dysfunction a further major impediment is introduced
Wallace (1973) found that in spina bifida children inadequate mobilit
was associated with neurological abnormalities in upper limb function
Again, some cerebral palsied children are reported never to reach fo
objects, while for the majority a delay is found beyond the expecte

5–month level (Denhoff 1976). Detailed variations in these disabilities and their neurophysiological correlates are described by Melyn and Grossman (1976) for cerebral palsy and by Anderson and Spain (1977) for spina bifida. The impediments to interaction with the world caused by both upper and lower limb dysfunction are in fact even more far reaching than might be expected. The way in which development of a mature object concept can be affected has been elegantly shown by Wedell, Newman, Reid and Bradbury (1972). These authors took as their starting point Piaget's stress on the importance of motor activity in perceptual development. A group of cerebral palsied children and a group of nonhandicapped children were compared with respect to their judgements of size constancy — i.e. the ability to judge the size of an object despite the fact that at a distance its retinal image is reduced. The cerebral palsied children were typically poorer in size constancy than their nonimpaired peers, but of special interest was the relation between ability to make accurate judgements of size and the length of time for which these children had been independently mobile. Thus children who had been independently mobile for 4:0–6:2 years achieved a higher degree of size constancy than those who were not mobile or had only been mobile for a period of up to three years. This difference was not related to degree of brain damage, and the authors conclude:

> A disturbance in the development of size constancy is likely to handicap the child establishing a stable visual environment. An object would appear to expand or shrink as it approached or receded. When encountered on separate occasions at different distances, an object might not be recognised as the same. (p. 619)

Such effects would be anticipated on the basis of Held's work described in Chapter 3.

Thus immobility, and other aspects of gross movement impairment, will have cognitive and perceptual consequences of the sort not recognised by Shere and Kastenbaum's mothers with their fully understandable emphasis on motor improvement. In addition, immobility will have consequences for emotional development, and it is to these that we now turn.

Behavioural Consequences

In this concluding section we will focus more on our fourth group of physically impaired children, namely those who have experienced some degree of isolation or restriction, usually for benign medical reasons. We have already made some comment above on the linguistic and intellectual consequences of such restriction in studies of PKU and nonhandicapped children by Sibinga *et al.* (1968) and Sibinga and Friedman (1971) respectively. Here our emphasis is more on the behaviour disturbances that may ensue.

We are fortunate in dealing with this topic in having Prescott's (1976) valuable theoretical account of the consequences of 'somatosensory deprivation' described in Chapter 4. As we noted, Prescott draws on a wide literature in order to demonstrate his claim that 'sensory stimulation is like a nutrient and just as malnutrition adversely affects the developing brain so does sensory deprivation' (p. 68). Berkson's work with primates is cited to show that somatosensory deprivation contributes to disturbed behaviour in animals, while Adelson and Fraiberg's observation that congenitally blind children do not develop movement stereotypes provided they receive sufficient somatosensory stimulation is quoted. Studies from child development are noted as is Yarrow, Rubinstein and Pedersen's (1975) evidence on the primacy of somatosensory and vestibular stimulation over sight and hearing in nonhandicapped infants. Zubek's (1963) work on sensory deprivation in adults is also used as further evidence. On the basis of this and other evidence, Prescott suggests that an important determinant of a variety of behaviour disorders is somatosensory deprivation and that emotionally this can be a more fundamental cause of such disturbance than any specific handicap, sensory or physical. There is with respect to the consequence of hospitalisation evidence to support Prescott's position. Apart from the studies already noted, Douglas (1975) provided strong and unexpected evidence that one admission of more than a week's duration or repeated admissions before the age of 5 years are associated with an increased risk of behaviour disturbance (and indeed poor reading) in adolescence. Specifically, such children are more likely to have difficulties in classroom adjustment, become delinquent and have unstable career patterns. Quinton and Rutter (1976) found support for this position. While single admissions to hospital of a week or less did not lead in their study to psychiatric disturbance, repeated admissions are associated with such disturbance at Chronological Age 10:0 years. Though Quinton and Rutter point out that a firm causal link cannot be drawn, the fact of hospitalisation does contribute to disturbance in conjunction, they suggest, with other psychosocial factors. It is important to note that while taken in the complete framework of Prescott's theory these findings are quite consistent, they do not in themselves deal directly with the effects of somatosensory deprivation.

The wider psychosocial influences noted by both Douglas and Quinton and Rutter relate in part to stress experienced by the infant or young child. Douglas (1975) comments that: 'The children most vulnerable to early admission are those who are highly dependent on their mothers or who are under stress at home at the time of admission' (p. 476). Quinton and Rutter agree, suggesting that children from homes with psychosocial disadvantage are more subject to chronic stress. Prugh (1973) has provided a fuller developmental framework for considering the emotional effects of hospitalisation on children. Clearly physically handicapped children experiencing hospitalisation would also be vulnerable to similar influences. While, for example, thalidomide children were well able to form attachment to their mother and had assumedly experienced appropriate tactile and movement experiences, hospitalisation was again found to cause serious emotional disruptions.

In commenting on the outcome of socially enduced temporary physical impairment, we have introduced the possibility of further impairing events on the development of children who are already at risk through developmental and multiple impairments. While Prescott's theory is attractive and supported by substantial evidence, the complexities of the overall social situation must also be taken into account. In so far as Prescott is right, then the need for tactile and vestibular stimulation must be as relevant to the development of people who are seriously physically impaired and profoundly retarded as it is to nonhandicapped children. The parent's desire to maintain passivity in the child who is multiply handicapped reported by Shere and Kastenbaum may well lead to reduced somatosensory experience through lack of being held and carried as an activity in its own right. In the same way that those authors take the mothers to task for emphasising movement in its own right rather than with respect to its cognitive importance, so professionals should not neglect the influence of affective experience in their pursuit of cognitive enhancement.

References

Anderson, E.M. and Plewis, I. (1977) 'Impairment of Motor Skill in Children with Spina Bifida Cystica and Hydrocephalus: An Exploratory Study, *British Journal of Psychology, 68,* 61–70
Anderson, E.M. and Spain, B. (1977) *The Child with Spina Bifida*, Methuen, London
Black, P.D. (1980) 'Ocular Defects in Children with Cerebral Palsy', *British Medical Journal, 281,* 487–8

Cruickshank, W.M. (1976) 'The Problem and its Scope' in W.M. Cruickshank (ed.), *Cerebral Palsy: A Developmental Disability*, Syracuse Press, New York

Cruickshank, W.M., Hallahan, D.P. and Bice, H.V. (1976) 'Personality and Behavioural Characteristics' in W.M. Cruickshank (ed.), *Cerebral Palsy. A Developmental Disability*, Syracuse Press, New York

Denhoff, E. (1976) 'Medical Aspects' in W.M. Cruickshank (ed.), *Cerebral Palsy: A Developmental Disability*, Syracuse Press, New York

Douglas, J.W.B. (1975) 'Early Hospital Admissions and Later Disturbances of Behaviour and Learning', *Developmental Medicine and Child Neurology, 17*, 457–80

Eagle, R.S. (1985) 'Deprivation of Early Sensorimotor Experience and Cognition in the Severely Involved Cerebral Palsied Child', *Journal of Autism and Developmental Disorders, 15*, 269–83

Gouin Décarie, T. (1962) *Intelligence and Affectivity in Early Childhood* (trans by E. and L. Brandt), International Universities Press, New York

Gouin Décarie, T. (1969) 'A Study of the Mental and Emotional Development of the Thalidomide Child' in B.M. Foss (ed.), *Determinants of Infant Behaviour: Vol. 4*, Methuen, London

Lagergren, J. (1970) 'Motor Handicapped Children: A Study from a Swedish County', *Developmental Medicine and Child Neurology, 12*, 56–63

Lencione, R.M. (1976) 'The Development of Communications Skills' in W.M. Cruickshank (ed.), *Cerebral Palsy: A Developmental Disability*, Syracuse Press, New York

Lonton, A.P. (1976) 'Hand Preference in Children with Myelomeningocele', *Developmental Medicine and Child Neurology*, Supplement 37, 143–9

Lonton, A.P. (1977) 'Location of the Myelomeningocele and its Relationship to Subsequent Physical and Intellectual Abilities in Children with Myelomeningocele Associated with Hydrocephalus', *Zeitschrift fur Kinderchirurgie 22*, 510–19

Lonton, A.P. and Sklayne, K.D. (1980) 'The Relationship between Social Class and Educational, Psychological and Physical Aspects of Spina Bifida and Hydrocephalus', *Zeitschrift fur Kinderchirurgie, 31*, 369–75

Love, R. (1964) 'Oral Language Behavior of Cerebral Palsied Children', *Journal of Speech and Hearing Research, 7*, 349–59

Melcer, J.D. (1966) 'Sensory-motor Experience and Concept Formation in Early Childhood', unpublished doctoral dissertation, University of Texas

Melyn, M.A. and Grossman, H.J. (1976) 'Neurophysiological Correlates' in W.M. Cruickshank (ed.), *Cerebral Palsy: A Developmental Disability* Syracuse Press, New York

Miller, E. and Sethi, L. (1971) 'Tactile Matching in Children with Hydrocephalus', *Neuropaediatrica, 3*, 191–4

Perlstein, K.A. (1949) 'Medical Aspects of Cerebral Palsy', *Nervous Child, 8* 125–51

Prescott, J.W. (1976) 'Somatosensory Deprivation and its Relationship to the Blind' in Z.S. Jastrzembska (ed.), *The Effects of Blindness and Other Impairments on Early Development*, American Foundation for the Blind, New York

Prugh, D. (1973) 'Emotional Aspects of the Hospitalization of Children', *Child and Family, 12*, 19–35

Quinton, D. and Rutter, M. (1976) 'Early Hospital Admissions and Later Disturbances of Behaviour: An Attempted Replication of Douglas' Findings', *Developmental Medicine and Child Neurology, 18*, 447–59

Reynell, J. (1969) *Reynell Developmental Language Scale*, NFER, Slough

Roskies, E. (1972) *Abnormality and Normality: The Mothering of Thalidomide Children*, Cornell University Press, Ithaca and London

Shere, E. and Kastenbaum, R. (1966) 'Mother-child Interaction in Cerebral Palsy: Environmental and Psychosocial Obstacles to Cognitive Development', *Genetic Psychological Monographs, 73*, 255–335

Sibinga, M.S. and Friedman, C.J. (1971) 'Restraint and Speech', *Pediatrics, 48*, 116–22

Sibinga, M.S., Friedman, C.J., Steisel, I.M. and Sinnamon, H.M. (1968) 'The Effect of Immobilization and Sensory Restriction on Children with Phenylketonuria', *Pediatric Research, 2*, 371–7

Spain, B. (1974) 'Verbal Performance Ability in Pre-school Children with Spina Bifida', *Developmental Medicine and Child Neurology, 16*, 773–80

Tew, B.J. (1973) 'Spina Bifida and Hydrocephalus: Facts, Fallacies and Future', *Special Education, 62*, 26–31

Wallace, S.J. (1973) 'The Effect of Upper-limb Function on Mobility of Children with Myelomeningocele', *Developmental Medicine and Child Neurology, Supplement 29*, 84–91

Wedell, K., Newman, C.V., Reid, P. and Bradbury, I.R. (1972) 'An Exploratory Study of the Relationship between Size Constancy and Experience of Mobility in Cerebral Palsied Children', *Developmental Medicine and Child Neurology, 14*, 615–20

Yarrow, L.J., Rubenstein, J.L. and Pedersen, F.A. (1975) *Infant and Environment: Early Cognitive and Motivational Development*, Hemisphere-Halstead-Wiley, Washington, D.C. and New York

Zubek, J.P. (1963) 'Counteracting Effects of Physical Exercise Performed During Prolonged Perceptual Deprivation', *Science, 142*, 504–6

7 ASSESSING DEVELOPMENT IN PEOPLE WITH PROFOUND RETARDATION AND MULTIPLE IMPAIRMENT

In the preceding chapters we have described some aspects of development that are relevant to our understanding of people who are profoundly retarded and the way in which specific impairments influence the course of development. In the next chapter we relate this information to the group with whom we are concerned. In order to understand more fully the studies that have been undertaken with this group, in this chapter we will review some of the assessment procedures that have been employed, both those that have been published in their own right as tests, and also scales available in research studies but not necessarily subjected to careful and general standardisation.

The very fact that tests of specific aspects of cognitive functioning have been developed, shows a marked departure from the traditional ways of measuring intelligence in which an attempt was made to establish an overall measure, usually expressed as an Intelligence Quotient (IQ) or Developmental Quotient (DQ). A Mental Age (MA) equivalent was also employed based on the relation between rate of development as measured by IQ or DQ and the person's Chronological Age (CA) (for a full discussion see Berger and Yule 1986). The need to go beyond such assessments in developmental psychology in general and in mental retardation in particular was expressed many years ago by Inhelder in a book published in 1943, *The Diagnosis of Reasoning in the Mentally Retarded* (English translation, Inhelder 1968). In this she commented on the usefulness of intelligence testing for the rapid detection of 'mental anomalies', but the limitation of such an approach when it came to saying something about the nature of thought processes and any inadequacies that might exist. Her reasons for this statement still hold today and have been reiterated in various forms by many subsequent writers:

(i) IQ tests and their downward extension into infant developmental tests are essentially concerned with outcomes and products. Can the child achieve such and such a behaviour which we would typically expect from a child of that particular CA? Indeed, the very items of such tests are in large measure chosen because they reliably distinguish between children at different age levels. Such testing is not concerned with the cause of the behaviour, nor with the overall structure of the child's behaviour at a given time.

(ii) Psychometric tests tell us nothing about the stages of development. All we have is a simple series of increments that add to a continuously increasing score. Even if the idea of stages of development is not accepted, we must agree with Inhelder's related criticism that this total global score can be achieved in several ways. Hogg and Moss (1983), for example, have shown how young children with Down's Syndrome can achieve the same MA as nonhandicapped children despite performing more poorly on fine motor items by achieving a relatively higher score on certain aspects of language development.

(iii) Psychometric testing tells us nothing about the way in which behaviour is transformed at successive levels of mental development.

With respect to people who are retarded, and those who are profoundly so in particular, the value of psychometric testing is reduced further by the fact the tests have not been developed on, or standardised on, these particular groups of individuals. With those who are profoundly retarded and have additional impairments, this fact creates further difficulties. Testing such a person on an IQ test and finding an MA of 12 months will not have involved the same procedure, or mean the same thing, as for a nonhandicapped 12 month old. At the very best, all we have is an imperfect shorthand expression of the extent to which a person lags behind CA expectations. It is in this way that we have used IQs and MAs to describe groups in this book.

What Inhelder sought was a technique of assessment that would enable the operations of mental activity to be assessed by placing children in a situation in which it can be established whether retarded children are fixated at a lower operational stage than would be expected for their age. This entailed presenting a child with a variety of problems in which evidence of operational thought could be assessed. Questions and answers dependent upon the child's observations of the situation were used and the approach was essentially clinical or experimental, rather than standardised as in the case of psychometric tests. The tasks actually used by Inhelder are far more advanced than those with which we are concerned in this book, and indeed, she excludes from her study children who were severely or profoundly retarded. Thus her concern in Piagetian terms was with the later stages of intuitive thinking and with concrete operations.

The extension of Inhelder's approach to the functioning of children who are profoundly retarded and the sensorimotor stage of development came some years later with Woodward's (1959) important paper on the same topic. Here for the first time an attempt was made to present a consistent procedure for undertaking a developmental assessment in a Piagetian framework with children with profound retardation. Further studies by authors have on occasions also employed scales and test items devised by the author for the specific purpose of the study. Increasingly, however, Piagetian-based tests developed with nonhandicapped children have been extended to children with retardation, a similar extension to that which has occurred with many psychometric and infant development tests.

Dunst (1980) notes a number of differences between these Piagetian tests and traditional psychometric tests. In the latter, composition of the global score, MA, usually takes into account the highest item passed (the ceiling item) and the item before the first failure, i.e. the basal item. This is necessary because it is rare to find a distinct break in the person's performance where passes stop and failures begin, there usually being a grey area where failures occur but higher-level items are passed. In contrast, the Piagetian tests take the highest pass as representing the child's ceiling and actual level of development, the assumption being that the items form a rank order or ordinal scale in which a pass on an item assumes passes on all previous items. Second, Dunst points out that general administrative procedures for psychometric tests are much more rigid than for Piagetian testing. Taking their cue from Inhelder's flexible approach to Piagetian assessment, the authors of these tests vary material and context and utilise informal observations. Third, while psychometric tests yield Intelligence and Developmental Quotients, Piagetian tests do not, though, as Dunst points out, for any particular activity it is possible to establish an MA equivalent.

A more positive note with respect to IQ testing is sounded by Lunzer (1970) who considers the standardisation of the test situation may more adequately cue the child:

> In other words, such tests may be purer measures of intellectual power than Piaget tests themselves. Even granted this were so, (and it has not been proven), it is still possible that the very fact that the Piaget situations tap the spontaneous behaviour of the child renders them better instruments for educational diagnosis and prediction, for a measure of effective intelligence may be more informative than one of (relatively) 'pure' mental power. (pp. 54–5)

Piagetian scales that have been used with people who are profoundly retarded fall broadly into two categories: those that have been published as scales with something approaching standardisation and those appearing in experimental studies that have been developed for specific purposes. In reality, the distinction is often blurred, though it is with the more obviously standardised scales that we begin.

Sensorimotor Assessment

Uzgiris and Hunt's 'Ordinal Scales of Psychological Development'

These scales, which cover key areas of sensorimotor development, were devised (i) in response to shortcomings perceived by the authors in traditional psychometric tests; and (ii) to provide an instrument that would enable studies to be made of theoretical issues in child development. With respect to the former, Uzgiris and Hunt (1975) draw attention to the limitations of DQ and IQ testing that we noted above, particularly with respect to global measures that assume some general factor of intelligence or developmental status, and also with respect to measuring this status with reference to performance of a standardisation group at a given age. With regard to intention (ii), their concern with theoretical issues is set out in the first chapter of their book where they indicate the need for an instrument that will permit empirical testing of various theoretical positions.

While disregarding Piaget's stage placements and any link with CA, Uzgiris and Hunt draw heavily on Piaget's observations for the ordinal scales they propose. It is, however, the sequential nature of development in various sensorimotor domains that is their main concern, not the six stages we have described in Chapter 3. One important reason for this is that they argue that the Piagetian position is as yet unproven. That is, achievement of the same stage in different sensorimotor domains at the same time has not been demonstrated and, indeed, it would only be through the development of scales such as their own, that a test of this hypothesis could be achieved. As we saw in Chapter 3, and will consider again in the following chapter on development of people with profound retardation, such an assumption is, indeed, questionable. The Uzgiris-Hunt Scales, therefore, are independent of both CA and Piagetian stage placements.

Following studies in which naturally eliciting situations were established, items refined and reliability studies undertaken, ordinal scales for the following domains of development were produced:

I   Progress in visual pursuit and permanence of objects
II   Means for obtaining desired environmental events
III Imitation. I. Vocal; II. Gestural
IV Operational causality
V   Construction of object relations in space
VI Schemes for relating to objects

Highly satisfactory reliabilities, both inter-observer and test-retest, were established for most of the items on each of these scales. The scalability of the items within a scale was also considered. The term 'ordinal' in fact, refers to the other in which a child passes various items. For example, with respect to visual pursuit, consider the following items:

a   Does not visually follow an object
b   Follows object, but jerkily
c   Follows object through part of arc smoothly
d   Follows object through complete trajectory smoothly

We would expect the child's visual tracking to follow this order, i.e. passing (a), then (b), then (c) and (d). Statistical measures of the consistency with which items followed such an ordinal scale were highly satisfactory.

The authors conclude that their instrument does permit description of an infant's psychological development without having to refer to a standardised group of infants or to CA as in the case of DQ or IQ testing. In order to give a clear indication of the instrument, we will now illustrate further the development of Visual Pursuit and the Permanence of Objects.

Figure 7.1 reproduces Scale I from Uzgiris and Hunt (1975 pp. 206–9) completed for a child (LP) who is profoundly retarded and multiply impaired. As may be seen, there are 15 situations, starting with 'Following a Slowly Moving Object through a 180° Arc' (No. 1) to 'Finding Object Following a Series of Invisible Displacements by Searching in Reverse of the Order of Hiding' (No. 15). In each situation a range of possible behaviours is listed, with those asterisked indicating that the child has accomplished the skill. Again, taking Situation 1, a–c behaviours do not give evidence of the accomplishment of smooth tracking while 'd' does. The recording form permits repeated presentations, though the recommended number appears in parentheses after each situation description. As may be seen from the summary form in Figure 7.2, this child passed all situations up to and including Scale Step 9, with the exception of Scale Step 4. Her pass on No. 9, Finding an Object Following One Invisible Displacement, is then the highest item and this places her developmentally in this scale. A full description of the location of testing, choice of objects and administrative directions are also given for each situation.

In their original form the Uzgiris-Hunt Scales retain all the central distinctions between psychometric developmental testing and cognitive ordinal assessment that we have noted. Most importantly, they represent an attempt to assess a child's sensorimotor development within a Piagetian framework, eschewing not only derived measures of Mental Age but even stage placements. As we have seen, they did not envisage that their scales would be evolved or used in a direction that moved them towards more traditional approaches to assessment. Nevertheless, there has been real interest in applying these scales to a cognitive assessment of people who are retarded and in the use of the resulting information in developing intervention programmes.

Dunst's Clinical and Educational Manual for Use with the Uzgiris and Hunt Scales of Infant Development

Dunst (1980) has responded to this need by formalising the Uzgiris-Hunt Scales in such a way as to make them usable for assessment and intervention. Here we will summarise the procedure he advocates with respect to the former, i.e. assessment, and illustrate the outcome from some of our own assessments. His suggestions regarding the use of his material will be dealt with when we consider intervention and sensorimotor behaviour in Volume 2, Chapter 3.

Dunst retains the seven sensorimotor domains covered by the Uzgiris-Hunt Scales. The 73 items in the test are spread unevenly among these domains, and to them Dunst adds a further 53 experimental items which are designated with a Prefix 'E' in the various recording sheets. Thus, for Stage V, 'Object Permanence', the items in ascending order are 6, 7, E_6, 8 and 9. E_6 is here a Dunst addition, while the remainder are from the original Uzgiris-Hunt Scales. These items are administered in a semi-standardised fashion, but allowing for greater flexibility than would be acceptable in a standardised developmental test. Thus, the position of the child, suitable objects, directions for administration and critical responses are all described (Dunst 1980 Appendix B).

The information that these assessments yield can best be described by reference to the recording forms. Figure 7.3 shows the recording form for Visual Pursuit and the Permanence of Objects and has 21 items, the original Uzgiris-Hunt items and additional 'E' items provided by Dunst

Figure 7.1 Sample Examination Record Forms

SCALE I: THE DEVELOPMENT OF VISUAL PURSUIT AND THE PERMANENCE OF OBJECTS

Name: *L P*

Birthdate: *1 : 5 : 69*

Date of Examination: *14/15 : 3 : 83*

SITUATION	PRESENTATION (*Suggested number of presentations for each situation is indicated in parentheses*)						
	I	2	3	4	5	6	7
1. *Following a Slowly Moving Object through a 180° Arc* (3–4)							
a. Does not follow object	—	—	—	—	—	—	—
b. Follows jerkily through part of arc	—	—	—	—	—	—	—
c. Follows smoothly through part of arc	—	—	—	—	—	—	—
*d. Follows object smoothly through complete arc	✓	✓	✓	—	—	—	—
Other:	—	—	—	—	—	—	—
2. *Noticing the Disappearance of a Slowly Moving Object* (3–4)							
a. Does not follow to point of disappearance	—	—	—	—	—	—	—
b. Loses interest as soon as object disappears	—	—	—	—	—	—	—
*c. Lingers with glance on point of disappearance	✓	✓	✓	—	—	—	—
*d. Returns glance to starting point after several presentations	—	—	—	—	—	—	—
e. Searches around point of disappearance	—	—	—	—	—	—	—
Other:	—	—	—	—	—	—	—
3. *Finding an Object Which Is Partially Covered* (3)							
a. Loses interest	✓	—	—	—	—	—	—
b. Reacts to the loss, but does not obtain object	—	—	—	—	—	—	—
*c. Obtains the object	—	✓	✓	—	—	—	—
Other:	—	—	—	—	—	—	—
4. *Finding an Object Which Is Completely Covered* (3)							
a. Loses interest	✓	—	—	—	—	—	—

SCALE I (continued)

	PRESENTATION (Suggested number of presentations for each situation is indicated in parentheses)						
SITUATION	1	2	3	4	5	6	7
b. Reacts to loss, but does not obtain object	—	—	—	—	—	—	—
c. Pulls screen, but not enough to obtain object	—	—	—	—	—	—	—
*d. Pulls screen off and obtains object	—	✓	✓	—	—	—	—
Other:	—	—	—	—	—	—	—
5. *Finding an Object Completely Covered in Two Places* (2)							
a. Loses interest	—	—	—	—	—	—	—
b. Searches for object where it was previously found	—	—	—	—	—	—	—
c. Searches for object where it is last hidden	✓	✓	—	—	—	—	—
Other:	—	—	—	—	—	—	—
6. *Finding an Object Completely Covered in Two Places Alternately* (3–5)							
a. Becomes perplexed and loses interest	—	—	—	—	—	—	—
b. Searches haphazardly under one or both screens	—	—	—	—	—	—	—
*c. Searches correctly under each of the screens	✓	✓	✓	—	—	—	—
Other:	—	—	—	—	—	—	—
7. *Finding an Object Completely Covered in Three Places* (5–7)							
a. Loses interest	—	—	—	—	—	—	—
b. Searches haphazardly under some or all screens	—	—	—	—	—	—	—
*c. Searches directly under correct screen	✓	✓	✓	✓	✓	—	—
Other:	—	—	—	—	—	—	—
8. *Finding an Object after Successive Visible Displacements* (3–5)							
a. Does not follow successive hidings	✓	✓	✓	—	—	—	—
b. Searches only under the first screen	—	—	—	—	—	—	—
c. Searches under screen where object was previously found	—	—	—	—	—	—	—
d. Searches haphazardly under all screens	—	—	—	—	—	—	—
e. Searches in order of hiding	—	—	—	—	—	—	—

SCALE I (*continued*)

SITUATION	PRESENTATION *(Suggested number of presentations for each situation is indicated in parentheses)*						
	1	2	3	4	5	6	7
f. Searches directly under the last screen in path							
Other:							
9. *Finding an Object under Three Superimposed Screens* (2–3)							
a. Loses interest	✓						
b. Lifts one or two screens, but fails to find object							
*c. Removes all screens and obtains object		✓	✓				
Other:							
10. *Finding an Object Following One Invisible Displacement* (3)							
a. Loses interest							
b. Reacts to loss, does not search							
c. Searches only in the box							
*d. Checks the box and searches under the screen	✓						
*e. Searches under screen directly		✓	✓				
Other:							
11. *Finding an Object Following One Invisible Displacement with Two Screens* (2)							
a. Searches only in box							
b. Searches under screen where object was previously found							
*c. Searches directly under correct screen							
Other:	Loses interest						
12. *Finding an Object Following One Invisible Displacement with Two Screens Alternated* (3)							
a. Loses interest	✓						
b. Searches haphazardly under screens							
*c. Searches directly under correct screen							
Other:							
13. *Finding an Object Following One Invisible Displacement with Three Screens* (5–7)							
a. Loses interest	✓						
b. Searches haphazardly under all screens							

SCALE I (*continued*)

	PRESENTATION (Suggested number of presentations for each situation is indicated in parentheses)						
SITUATION	1	2	3	4	5	6	7
*c. Searches directly under correct screen	—	—	—	—	—	—	—
Other:	—	—	—	—	—	—	—
14. *Finding an Object Following a Series of Invisible Displacements* (4–6)							
a. Searches only in E's hand	*Loses interest*					—	—
b. Searches only under first one or two screens in the path	—	—	—	—	—	—	—
*c. Searches under all screens in the path in the order of hiding	—	—		—	—	—	—
*d. Searches directly under the last screen in the path	—	—	—	—	—	—	—
15. *Finding Object Following a Series of Invisible Displacements by Searching in Reverse of the Order of Hiding* (2)							
a. Searches only under last screen	*Loses interest*					—	
b. Searches haphazardly under all screens	—	—	—	—	—	—	—
*c. Searches systematically from the last screen back to the first	—	—	—	—	—	—	—
Other:	—	—	—	—	—	—	—

* Indicates that the child has accomplished the skill.
Source: Uzgiris, I. and Hunt, J.McV. (1975) *Assessment in Infancy: Ordinal Scales of Psychological Development,* University of Illinois Press, Chicago.

Figure 7.2: Scale I: The Development of Visual Pursuit and the Permanence of Objects

Infant Code Number: *L P*

Age: 13 yrs 10

Scale Step	Relevant Situation Number	Critical Infant Action	Infant Actions Observed (List situation by no. and response by letter)
1	1	d	1d
2	2	c	2c
3	3	c	3c
4	2	d	−
5	4	d	4d
6	6 (and 5)	6c (and 5c)*	5c + 6c
7	7	c	7c
8	9	c	9c
9	10	d or e	10d + e
10	11	c	
11	12	c	
12	13	c	
13	14	c	
14	14 and 15	14d plus 15c	

* Infant actions in situations 5 and 8 were not included in the scaling analysis. The scale step for which actions in situation 5 may be relevant is indicated in parentheses.

Source: Uzgiris, I. and Hunt, J. McV. (1975) *Assessment in Infancy: Ordinal Scales of Psychological Development,* University of Illinois Press, Chicago.

to create a finer progression through the series. In the second column, Estimated Developmental Age Placements (EDAs) are given, based on a variety of psychometric tests and experimental studies, and marking a clear departure from Uzgiris and Hunt's conception of the assessment procedure, though the possibility of such a procedure is considered by them (Uzgiris and Hunt 1975 pp. 18–19). The validity of these EDAs has been established by Dunst correlating them with a psychometric assessment of developmental level. Dunst cautions that the EDAs are not predictive and have no normative value. While the former claim is certainly the case, it is difficult not to see the introduction of EDAs in the assessment as anything other than a legitimate attempt to place the outcome of sensorimotor assessment within a normative framework.

In column 3 the appropriate stage placement is given, again an extension to Uzgiris and Hunt's procedure. In practical terms, Dunst's

Figure 7.3:

I: VISUAL PURSUIT AND THE PERMANENCE OF OBJECTS

Child's Name __L P__   Date of Birth __1 : 5 : 69__   Date of Test __14/15 : 3 : 83__

SCALE STEP	AGE PLACEMENT (Months)	DEVELOP-MENTAL STAGE	ELICITING CONTEXT	CRITICAL BEHAVIORS	CRITICAL ACTION CODE	SCORING 1	2	3	4	5	OBSERVATIONS
E₁	1	I	Visual Fixation	Fixates on object held 8 to 10 inches above the eyes	—	+	+	+			
1	2	II	Visual Tracking	Tracks object through a 180° arc	1d	+	+	+			
2	3	II	Visual Tracking	Lingers at point of object's disappearance—child in supine position or in an infant seat	2c	+	+	+			
E₂	4	III	Visible Displacement	Searches for object at point of disappearance—child seated on parent's lap	—	ι	ι	ι			
3	5	III	Visible Displacement	Secures partially hidden object	3c	ι	+	+			
4	6	III	Visual Tracking	Returns glance to position above the head after object moves out of visual field	2d	ι	ι	ι			
E₃	7	IV	Visual Tracking	Reverses searching for object in anticipation of reappearance—child seated on parent's lap	—						Not applicable
E₄	7	IV	Visible Displacement	Withdraws object held in hand following covering of hand and object with cloth	—						
5	8	IV	Visible Displacement	Secures object hidden under a single screen	4d		+	+			
E₅	9	IV	Visible Displacement	Secures object hidden with two screens (A & B)—hidden under A twice then B—searches under A only	5b	ι	ι				
6	9	V	Visible Displacement	Secures object hidden under one of two screens—hidden alternately	6c	+	+	+			
7	9	V	Visible Displacement	Secures object hidden under one of three screens—hidden alternately	7c	+	+	+	+	+	
E₆	10	V	Successive Visible Displacement	Secures object hidden through a series of successive visible displacements with three screens	8e	ι	ι	ι			
8	10	V	Superimposed Screens	Secures object under three superimposed screens	9c	ι	+	+			
9	13	V	Invisible Displacement	Secures object hidden with a single screen	10d 10e	+	+	+			
10	14	VI	Invisible Displacement	Secures object hidden with two screens (A & B)—hidden under A twice then B	11c	ι					
11	14	VI	Invisible Displacement	Secures object hidden under one of two screens—hidden alternately	12c	ι					
12	15	VI	Invisible Displacement	Secures object hidden under one of three screens—hidden alternately	13c	ι					
13	18	VI	Successive Invisible Displacement	Secures object hidden with three screens—object left under last screen—child searches along pathway	14c	ι					
E₇	22	VI	Successive Invisible Displacement	Secures object hidden with three screens—object left under last screen—child searches directly under last screen	14d	ι					
14	23	VI	Successive Invisible Displacement	Secures object hidden with three screens—object left under first screen—child searches in reverse order	15c	ι					

Source: Dunst, C.J. (1980) *Clinical and Educational Manual for Use with the Uzgiris and Hunt Scales of Infant Psychological Development*, PRO-ED, Inc., Austin, Tex.   Copyright©1980, University Park Press

decision to include stage placements is based on the need to establish a stage profile in which strengths and weaknesses in different areas can be indicated. The value of such an approach will be shown in Chapter 8, in which recurrent deficits in specific sensorimotor domains in group data point to areas requiring special remediation. From a theoretical point of view, Dunst hopes that this procedure will tell us what cognitive operations the child can perform in the various domains since equivalent stage placements are assumed to reflect equivalent cognitive operations.

Column 4 indicates the eliciting context, essentially a cue to the assessor as to the situation or behaviour of interest. In column 5 the behaviour required of the child to indicate that a given level of functioning has been achieved is noted. The number indicates the eliciting situation in which the behaviour is assessed and the letter refers to the critical behaviour which is described in the 'Critical Behaviours' column (5). These codes relate in general to the original Uzgiris-Hunt codes.

Critical behaviours are listed in column 6, and Dunst suggests that taken with the eliciting context information, a reasonable description of what is required in administration and scoring can be inferred, always assuming that the assessor is familiar with the background provided in the original Uzgiris-Hunt procedure. Provision is then made (column 7) for up to five assessments and a code for 'pass' on the critical item, 'pass following demonstration', 'critical behaviour in the course of emerging', and 'not manifest' is given (codes are not shown in Figure 7.3). Subsidiary codes for item omission, and other reports of behaviour and mistrials are given. In the final column space is provided for observations on the child's behaviour that are deemed of interest.

Dunst provides a detailed account of how the items should be administered and emphasises the need to be familiar with Uzgiris and Hunt's general and specific procedures. General indications on establishing rapport between infant and assessor, environmental considerations, order of presentation of scales and initial approach are given. More detailed suggestions on administering the seven individual scales are then offered. A summary form is also provided on which information from the seven individual scale administrations can be collated.

The form for producing a profile of a child's sensorimotor abilities is given here in Figure 7.4. The six sensorimotor stages are indicated on the left of the profile in Roman numerals I-VI. The profile is generated by simply ringing the scale step passed in each domain and joining these. As noted earlier, this allows a clear visual representation of the extent to which the child is performing consistently with respect to cognitive operations and the pattern of strengths and weaknesses exhibited.

Figure 7.4: Uzgiris and Hunt Scales of Infant Psychological Development

Child's Name	L P	Sex
Date of Birth	Date of Test	Age
Examiner		
Comments:		

Uzgiris and Hunt Scales of Infant Psychological Development
PROFILE OF ABILITIES FORM

STAGES OF DEVELOPMENT	Object Permanence	Means-Ends Abilities	Vocal Imitation	Gestural Imitation	Operational Causality	Spatial Relationships	Scheme Actions
VI	14 E_7 13 12 11 10	E_{19} E_{18} 13 E_{17} 12	9	9	7	11b E_{47}	E_{53} 10
V	$\textcircled{9}$ 8 E_6 7 6	$\textcircled{10}$ E_{12} 9 E_{11} 8	E_{14}, E_{15}, E_{16} 11 E_{13} E_{25} E_{24} 8	E_{33} E_{31}, E_{32} 8 E_{30} E_{28}, E_{29} 7	6 E_{37} 5 E_{36} E_{35}	11a 10 E_{46} $\textcircled{9}$ 8 E_{45}	9 E_{52} $\textcircled{8}$
IV	E_5 5 E_4 E_3	7 6 E_{10} 5	7b 7a 6 5b 5a	6 5 4b 4a	4c 4b 4a 6	E_{43}, E_{44} E_{41}, E_{42} 7 E_{39}, E_{40} 6	E_{51} 7 6
III	4 3 E_2	E_9 4 3 2	E_{23} 4c 4b 4a E_{22}	3 2 E_{27}	3c, 3d $\textcircled{3e}$ 3b 2	5 4	5 E_{50} 4 3
II	2 1	1	E_{21} 3 2b 2a 1	1b $\textcircled{1c}$	1	3 2 1	2 1 E_{49}
I	E_1	E_8	E_{20}	E_{26}	E_{14}	E_{38}	E_{48}

SENSORIMOTOR DOMAINS

Source: Dunst, C.J. (1980) *Clinical and Educational Manual for Use with the Uzgiris and Hunt Scales of Infant Psychological Development,* PRO-ED, Inc., Austin, Tex.

The applicability of this assessment to both nonhandicapped children and people who are retarded is clearly demonstrated by Dunst with illustrative profile data on children from both groups. Work by the authors has also shown the utility of the scales with children who are multiply impaired and profoundly retarded. Here, the passes for LP indicated in Figures 7.1 and 7.2 have been transcribed on Dunst's form in Figures 7.3 and 7.4.

The movement to develop Piagetian-based tests of sensorimotor functioning began towards the end of the 1950s and in the 1960s. At that time, the Uzgiris-Hunt Scale was one among several. Continued development, publication in 1975 and a growing volume of published research with both nonimpaired and intellectually impaired children has established the scale as the most readily available and best understood device for assessing sensorimotor development. It is possible that Dunst's attempt to move the instrument towards a more standardised traditional approach will further entrench use of the scale. Other instruments developed at that time have not become so prominent and have remained available through journal articles or mimeographed notes. These will be described here as they are mentioned in several chapters in this book, notably the following on the development of people who are profoundly retarded.

Woodward's Assessment of Sensorimotor Development

Woodward's (1959) approach to Piagetian assessment is of particular interest on at least two counts. First, this represented the first published attempt to extend Inhelder's work with more able retarded children downwards to those who are profoundly retarded. Second, the emphasis is essentially on a semi-structured play context from which inferences about the child's sensorimotor development could be made. She presented six problems, two each derived from Stages IV, V and VI. In Stage IV two object-behind-screen tasks were presented, one with a transparent and the other with an opaque screen. In Stage V retrieval of an object by pulling a support or pulling a piece of string attached to it were presented. In Stage VI retrieval of an object with a rake and reorienting object to draw it through bars was required. It is, of course, possible to observe Stages I-III behaviour within this context, for example, sucking one of the presented objects indicating Stage II. Though a flexible procedure for administration is described, Woodward gives details of presentation, and also an eliciting sequence which is the reverse of Piaget's grasping sequence: 'The toy was placed',

a   so that the child could see it and his hand together,
b   in his mouth,
c   touching his hand, and
d   in his palm. (p. 63)

As with the Uzgiris-Hunt Scales and others, Woodward's development of an assessment procedure was dictated by experimental considerations, and we will review her findings in the next chapter. Like Uzgiris and Hunt, she has been insistent on the fact that her approach is exploratory, and she has made no attempt to evolve it into a standardised technique. In making her approach more widely available later (Woodward 1967) she emphasised the nonstandardised nature of her approach and her intention not to formalise the procedure. Her reservations about such formalisation of her own and other scales have recently been reiterated (Woodward 1984), not only with respect to the nature of Piagetian assessment itself, but also in relation to the special problems of assessing children who are severely or profoundly retarded.

Gouin Décarie's Scale of Object Permanence

This scale was employed in the study of thalidomide children described in Chapter 6 (Gouin Décarie 1969), and reported fully in Gouin Décarie (1962). It consists mainly of visual-manual items and allows the assessor to locate the child in one of six sequential stages of the sensorimotor period. It also permits location at the start and end of each scale, e.g. Ia or Ib. In line with the application of ordinal scale tests of this sort, flexibility of administration permits assessment of children with additional impairments. Thus, in assessing thalidomide children, Gouin Décarie permitted children to move screens with mouth or toes.

The Corman-Escalona Scales of Sensorimotor Development

As with all other scales of sensorimotor development, those developed by Corman and Escalona (1969) began life with a specific experimental aim in view. The authors were beginning a longitudinal study of personality development and on the basis of Piaget's observations set about constructing three separate scales:

(i)   *Prehension.* This assesses development changes in hand use, from Stage II — Primary Circular Reactions — through to Stage III — co-ordination involving hand, eye and other modalities.

(ii) *Object Permanence.* This reflects development of the object concept in itself and the relation between action and object. It covers behaviour from Stage III (failure to search for a hidden object) through to Stage IV where the object is found after complex displacements.

(iii) *Spatial Relations*. Again, this covers from Stage III to Stage VI, i.e. from movement in space that is limited by the child's own range of movement to a fuller construction of the understanding of space in which the child can invent new routes and employ complex detours.

(The authors comment on future development of a causality scale.)

Data are reported showing a high degree of reliability in administering the scales, and general confirmation of the sequences described by Piaget. A longitudinal study shows almost perfect sequencing of the hypothesised stages by all children. For example, Child 1 on the Object Concept Scale achieves the various stages at the following months: III — 4 months, IV — 6.3 months, V — 8.7 months, VI — 19.7 months, completing all Stage VI items at 20.2 months.

In this publication, the authors indicate that a manual is available and two films dealing with the object concept and spatial relation scales were also made, though we have been unable to establish whether these are still available.

Other Piagetian Assessments of Sensorimotor Development

The major authors noted above are all insistent on the need for those undertaking Piagetian assessments to be well grounded in the theory underlying specific observations. Such a requirement is in marked contrast to standardised psychometric or developmental testing. Such is the relevance of the approach to assessment of people who are profoundly retarded that practitioners have increasingly developed and modified existing Piagetian instruments in order to make them more directly applicable in their own clinical or educational practice. One aspect of such relevance is the consideration of time, where abbreviated scales are more viable. Foxen (1977), for example, employed the Object Schemes Scale of the Uzgiris and Hunt Assessment as an observational procedure for training professionals in the assessment of people who are severely or profoundly retarded. Working in a teaching context, Coupe and Levy (1985) have developed the Object Schemes Scale specifically in relation to children and young people who are severely and profoundly retarded: 'The Object Related Scheme Assessment Procedure: A cognitive assessment for developmentally young children who may have additional physical or sensory handicaps'. The approach differs in that details are given of presentation to multiply impaired children and suggestions made for remedial activity. As yet no formal standardisation or evaluation of the approach has been attempted.

Preoperational Assessment

The general lack of research into the preoperational period is reflected in the dearth of assessment instruments compared with those generated by sensorimotor studies. The increasing differentiation of function that we have noted towards the end of the sensorimotor period becomes even more apparent during the preoperational period, and there is no comparable instrument to, say, the Uzgiris-Hunt Scales. Instead, various attempts to assess manipulative, symbolic or linguistic function can be noted, though the instruments that we describe here are mainly those that have been brought to bear on children with profound retardation. Clearly, many specialised instruments will be excluded from this review. For example, language assessment devices covering developments in the nonhandicapped child between 18 and 60 months are potentially relevant and fuller discussion of these will be found in Berger and Yule (1986) and Bryen and Gallagher (1983).

Cognition

Woodward has described changes in cognitive functioning as reflected in manipulative behaviour (Woodward 1972, 1983; Woodward and Hunt 1972). Here familiar tasks requiring matching to sample, nesting cups and arranging blocks are employed to assess the transitions in cognition from the later stages of the sensorimotor period through to the intuitive phase of the preoperational period. For Woodward, the interest is not in the simple achievement of nesting or matching but in the gradual elimination of inappropriate strategies as the child acquires mastery through increasingly complex mental operations.

One particular attraction of Woodward's approach is the familiarity and availability of the material employed which we note below:

Fitting Tasks
    (i)   Round hole pegboard with 10 holes arranged in pairs.
   (ii) Round hole pegboard with 9 holes grouped irregularly and one displaced from group.
 (iii) 12 rings of different size and colour for placement on a stick.

(iv) 4-item formboard with circle, cross, square and triangle.
(v) 5 'trees' with 5 sticks onto each of which beads could be fitted

Material for Spontaneous Handling
(i)   36 one-inch cubes in six colours.
(ii) 24 triangular pieces in six colours.
(iii) 27 items varying in colour, shape and size (cubes, triangles, rods, in three sizes and three colours).
(iv) 100 identical counters.

Induced Matching Tasks
Matching linear and circular arrays of cubes or beads on basis of colour, e.g. 9 cubes of different colours as standard, 8 matches to be selected from an array of 23 cubes and 12 different colours.

Spatial Order Tasks
Here matching requires location of beads on a rod, again involving the same standard and match numbers as in the induced matching task.

Positioning Task
Location of four cubes into a tray into which they fitted exactly if correctly positioned permitting observation of error correction and anticipation.

Any attempt to use Woodward's materials to assess cognition requires the same grounding in her conception of development as does use of sensorimotor tests in Piagetian theory. In addition, for most teachers some co-ordination with available rating scales would be feasible, for example, Gunstone's (1979) checklists, which cover several of the curriculum areas involved in use of Woodward's material.

Smith (1982) drew on Lunzer (1970), Woodward (1972) and Woodward and Hunt (1972) to develop an instrument for assessing preconceptual and intuitive development in the preoperational period. Though at present available only in her PhD thesis, 'A Study of Mental Growth in Young Severely Subnormal Children', this development does illustrate the way in which assessment procedures of this sort can be developed into a usable instrument. Detailed procedures for presenting tasks and standardised recording forms are presented in Appendices B and C (pp. 294–306) of her thesis, with response coding in Appendix D (pp. 307–17).

Smith's developmental areas are comparable to those of Woodward in a number of respects. She includes:

A1 Classification: (i) Sorting by colour or shape
                              (ii) Sorting into piles where colour or shape can be used as an attribute

A2 Seriation: (i) Stacking of cups
                              (ii) Seriation of wooden rods (scoring based on Lunzer 1970)

A3 Number: (i) Copying models with given number of blocks
                              (ii) Number matching and conservation of number (again based on Lunzer)

A4 Spatial Relations: (i) Spontaneous arrangement of blocks
                              (ii) Copy of models with varying horizontal and vertical arrangements

Of particular interest is the emphasis placed by Smith on the strategies employed to achieve the various outcomes rather than a simple pass-fail approach. In adopting this approach Smith again draws on Woodward (1972) and Woodward and Hunt (1972). To illustrate more fully the procedure we will follow through one example, the use of stacking cups to assess the ability to seriate and the strategies employed.

CUPS: (2 trials). Materials 12 stacking cylindrical cups. Present the cups already stacked. Say 'Let's take them apart' and encourage the child to help. Place cups singly on the base with the largest in front of the child and the others to the right or left. Say 'Put the cups back in there' indicating the largest cup.

A coding system has been derived from Woodward which records each move the child makes in the sequence of stacking the cups. If the child is not successful on the first trial demonstrate and give a second trial.

CORRECT CUP (largest from array) put in nest.

STRATEGIES WHEN OTHER THAN LARGEST IS PLACED:

(1) The placed cup is consecutive in size but a larger one has been omitted earlier;
(2) A cup of the wrong size (not the largest in the array) is held inside the top of the last cup nested, and then returned to the collection, without being dropped in;
(3) A cup of the wrong size is dropped into the last one nested, and

then removed and returned to the collection.

OBSTRUCTION SITUATION:

(4) The obstructed cup is taken off the nest and the obstructing cup(s) removed, the obstructed cup is then placed in the nest. Strategy 4 may result in restoration of the sequence or may be abortive in that too few or too many cups are removed and the cup placed in the nest is not the next consecutive one. The different outcomes are recorded in brackets thus:

    4 () Result of strategy 4 was that the cup placed in the nest was not the next consecutive one. If the child removed the obstructing cup as he approached the nest, i.e. he anticipated the obstruction, record this in brackets as (ant) after the outcome, e.g. 4() or 4(x)(ant);

(5) The obstruction is taken off the nest and the obstructing cup removed; both are returned to the collection of unnested cups;

(6) The obstructed cup is taken off and placed underneath the main nest, then returned to the collection, or nested, if it is bigger than the main nest;

(7) The obstructed cup is taken off and placed successively on cups not nested until it goes on;

(8) The obstructed cup is taken off and returned to the collection of unnested cups;

(9) No action, the obstructed cup is left where it is. (Smith 1982 pp. 297–8)

An appropriate recording form is presented on p. 305 of Smith (1982) permitting recording on each of the two recommended trials. Both success and strategy are covered as well as whether several separate nests were made or other uses to which cups were put. Computer coding of these responses is also described (p. 314). Some other tasks are included in the preoperational assessment form in Appendix B, namely use of pegboards, rings on stick and formboards. Three- or four-point scales were developed for rating the relation between strategy sophistication and degree of success.

Smith describes three main levels of functioning, 'non-operational', 'transitional' and 'operational', the latter implying the ability to use some degree of cognition prior to the response rather than just an action strategy. Strategy hierarchies were determined for most tasks. By considering achievement of strategy scores across qualitatively different tasks, some statement of stage congruence can be made and what Smith calls a 'rough and ready' (p. 95) estimate of organisation of cognition made. On this basis groups of items constituting preoperational sub-stages are derived.

Smith emphasises that in administering the assessment, allowance must be made for attention, mood, fatigue and motor problems. Nevertheless, the items achieved good scalability and construct validity when considered in relation to the children's special education category and the extent to which the instrument predicts language and social skills. Reliability, however, proved difficult to assess in conventional statistical terms.

Assessment was undertaken of a number of other measures of language, symbolic functioning, self-help, number work and motor abilities. The children assessed were between CA 7 and 13 years. Significant correlations between all these measures, including cognition, were found, with the exception of expressive language. Smith presents her results separately in five groups: I No specific pathology; II Down's Syndrome; III Specific medical diagnosis; IV Trauma; V Arrested development. For average assessment results there are no dramatic improvements across the years although steady progress was noted. Between 11 and 12 years significant improvements were found in cognition, representational drawing and ability to copy forms.

Assessing Symbolic Functions

We described in some detail in Chapter 3 the relation between symbolic function and language, with special reference to the work of Lowe (1975). Her approach has been extended to work with children who are retarded and in Chapter 8 we will describe some of the relevant studies. From these emerged her Symbolic Play Test (Lowe and Costello 1976). These authors describe the need for such a test:

> The presumed close, though probably complex, relationship between non-verbal semantic functions (particularly the ability to use symbols in any form) and the development of verbal language prompted the development of a diagnostic tool that would aim at evaluating the language potential of children who for some reason have failed to develop receptive or expressive language. (p. 5)

Such a test, while being language-free and therefore a kind of performance test, '. . . should explore the child's ability to appreciate semantic rather than spatial relationships, his early concepts, and his ability to deal with symbols in their simplest form to express his own experience and phantasies' (p. 5).

The test is aimed at children who are developmentally in the 12–36 months range, and involves spontaneous play with minature objects derived from Lowe's (1975) study. It is not intended to replace other existing tests for children in this period, but to complement them and provide a comparison with other areas of development. Thus, at its simplest, it is directed at finding whether language development and symbolic function are proceeding in the expected way, or whether discrepancies exist. For example, is there a discrepancy between language development and symbolic function with the latter lagging behind the former in such a way that we might be led to search for sensory or environmental factors that may have retarded language development?

Four situations are presented:

I   (a) large doll, sitting;
    (b) add saucer, spoon, cup;
    (c) add brush, comb.
II   bed, pillow, blanket, small girl doll.
III chair, table, table cloth, fork, small boy doll, knife, plate.
IV trailer, tractor, man, logs in random positions.

These were selected in order that:

(a) the toys in a situation should lend themselves to meaningful interrelationships;
(b) have spontaneous appeal to both sexes;
(c) should appeal to children of different backgrounds; and should permit:
(d) short administration time (10–15 minutes);
(e) simple administration;
(f) administration independent of verbal comprehension and expression;
(g) scoring based on direct observation.

The scalability of the types of play within the situations was found to be good, i.e. if the child showed a given level of play on one item, he or she would also have 'passed' on earlier items. Reliability was also acceptable, and validity was assessed in relation to the child's present and future performance in expressive language. While correlations between Play Test score and present language tended to be low, much higher correlations were found between the score and language development at a later date. Lowe and Costello (1976) comment: 'Moreover there is a tendency for the correlations to rise as the time interval increases, which argues that there may be a time-lag before complexity of thought is manifest in speech' (p. 14).

Detailed descriptions of administration are given (p. 20) with the emphasis on encouraging spontaneous play. A detailed scoring guide is included (pp. 30–3). This may be illustrated from Situation I activity, 'Feeds, combs or brushes self or other person'. Here the criteria for a positive (+) or negative (−) score are given thus:

+   'drinks' from cup;
     'eats' from spoon;
     feeds or offers food to person present.

+   also, if brush is clearly used as cloth, or toothbrush e.g. dipped
     in the cup and moved to an fro in the mouth;
−   indiscriminant mouthing, e.g. if cup and spoon
     are in wrong position;
     puts brush in mouth;
     puts brush in cup. (p. 30)

A scoring sheet permitting further observations is also provided (pp. 34–5). In addition to the score, an age equivalent can also be derived (cf. Dunst's Mental Age Equivalent).

In the experimental literature on symbolic play a variety of other, often comparable, approaches are employed. One of the most elaborate is that of Nicholich (1977) who selected her toys on the basis of a list used by Sinclair (1970). Here 30 toys are presented in a bucket with a similar configuration on each occasion. The child is observed playing with the toys and a transcription of play and transitions between play made. The judgement as to placement of the child at a given level is essentially a clinical one. The stages of play as defined by Piaget (1962) and Nicholich's levels, criteria and examples are given in Table 7.1.

Table 7.1: Sequence of Symbolic Levels According to Piaget and as Applied in Research by Nicholich

Piaget (1962)		Nicolich Levels and Criteria	Examples
Sensorimotor Period			
Prior to Stage VI	(1)	Presymbolic Scheme: The child shows understanding of object use or meaning by brief recognitory gestures. No pretending. Properties of present object are the Stimulus. Child appears serious rather than playful.	The child picks up a comb, touches it to his hair, drops it. The child picks up the telephone receiver, puts it into ritual conversation position, sets it aside. The child gives the mop a swish on the floor.
Stage VI	(2)	Auto-symbolic Scheme: The child pretends at self-related activities. Pretending Symbolism is directly involved with the child's body. Child appears playful, seems aware of pretending.	The child simulates drinking from a toy baby bottle. The child eats from an empty spoon. The child closes his eyes, pretending to sleep.

Symbolic
Stage I

(3) Single Scheme Symbolic Games
Child extends symbolism beyond his own actions by:

Type I A Assimilative

A. Including other actors or receivers of action, such as doll or mother.

Child feeds mother or doll (A).
Child grooms mother or doll (A).

Type I B Imitative

B. Pretending at activities of other people or objects such as dogs, trucks, trains, etc.

Child pretends to read a book (B).
Child pretends to mop floor (B).
Child moves a block or toy car with appropriate sounds of vehicle (B).

These distinctions are not made by Piaget

(4) Combinatorial Symbolic Games

4.1 Single Scheme Combinations: One pretend scheme is related to several actors or receivers of action.

Child combs own, then mother's hair.
Child drinks from the bottle, feeds doll from bottle. (4.1)
Child puts an empty cup to mother's mouth, then experimenter, and self. (4.1)

4.2 Multi-scheme combinations: Several schemes are related to one another in sequence.

Child holds phone to ear, dials.
Child kisses doll, puts it to bed, puts spoon to its mouth. (4.2)
Child stirs in the pot, feeds doll, pours food into dish. (4.2)

Table 7.1: Continued

Piaget (1962)	Nicolich Levels and Criteria	Examples
	(5) Planned Symbolic Games: Child indicates verbally or non-verbally that pretend acts are planned before being executed.	
	5.1 Planned Single Scheme Symbolic Acts Transitional Type: Activities from levels 2–3 that are planned.	Child finds the iron, sets it down, searches for the cloth, tossing aside several objects. When cloth is found, she irons it. (5.1)
		Child picks up play screw-driver, says 'tooth-brush' and makes the motion of toothbrushing. (5.1)
Type II A	Type A Symbolic identification of one object with another	
Type II B	Type B Symbolic identification of the child's body with some other person or object	Child picks up the bottle, says 'baby', then feeds the doll and covers it with a cloth. (5.2)
Type III A	5.2 Combinations with Planned Elements: These are constructed of activities from Levels 2–5.1, but always include some planned element. They tend towards realistic scenes.	Child puts play foods in a pot, stirs them. Then says 'soup' or 'Mommy' before feeding the mother. She waits, then says 'more' offering the spoon to the mother. (5.2)

Source: Nicholich (1977).

Both Lowe's (1975) and Nicholich's (1977) procedures were employed
in Riguet, Taylor, Benaroya and Klein's (1981) study of symbolic play
in Down's Syndrome, autistic and nonhandicapped children. In this the
following material was employed, some with modelled actions by the
adult and some without:

Toy Group 1 (session 1):
—Modelling toys— plush monkey (2215 cm) with plastic spoon 10
cm) or Popsicle stick.
—Actions modelled— monkey made to hold spoon/stick in paw and
bring accessory to its mouth, tilting it as if sipping liquid from it.
—Transfer toys— baby doll (34 cm) with plastic cup (ht. 2.6 cm/diam.
3 cm) or pill container (ht. 5 cm/diam. 2.5 cm).

Toy Group 2 (session 1):
—Modelling toys— pink panther (47 cm) with whisk broom (15.5
cm) or rectangular cardboard piece (18 cm x 10 cm).
—Actions modelled— frog made to use folded cloth to scrub with
circular motions both sides of its face and back of neck.
—Transfer toys— cloth and vinyl monkey (37 cm) with toothbrush
(13 cm) or wood dowel (13 cm).

Toy Group 4 (session 2):
—Modelling toys— stiff vinyl doll (17 cm) with wooden cart (15 x
12 cm) or plastic container (12 x 10 cm).
—Action modelled— doll made to push cart/container across the table,
its raised arms against cart/container, its feet tapped up and down
('walking') as moved along the table.
—Transfer toys— plush baboon (30 cm) with small dictionary (8 cm
x 5 cm) or corrugated cardboard (16 cm x 11 cm) folded with a V
shape.

The actual assessment which permitted a comparison of modelled and
unmodelled play involved a relatively complex sequence as follows:

Initial Free-Play Period (4 min).
—Display— all playthings to be used in the session: 4 animate toys,
2 realistic accessories, and 2 substitute objects.

*Structured Play Period (Toy Group 1, Session 1; Toy Group 3, Session
2).*
—Trial 1— transfer baseline (1 min).

—Display— transfer toy and assigned accessory plaything.
—Trial 2— modelling baseline (1 min).
—Display— modelling toy and assigned accessory plaything.

Modelling (Untimed).
—Display— modelling toys used in Trial 2. Experimenter models symbolic play saying 'Look what the (toy) is doing!'
—Trial 3— modelling test (1 min).
—Display— modelling toys used in Trial 2.
—Trial 4— transfer test (1 min).
—Display— transfer toys used in Trial 1.

Structured Play Period (Toy Group 2, Session 1; Toy Group 4, Session 2).
—Trials 1–4— repetition of sequence of first structured play period.

Final Free-Play Period (4 min).
—Display— re-presentation of all playthings used in the session.

Play was rated with respect to actual play, stereotyped activity and off-task behaviour. The highest level of play was recorded even if it only occurred once. Where play was observed it was rated as follows:

1. motor;
2. transitional;
3. symbolic;
4. animation or non-animated sequence;
5. animated sequence.

Measures of 'symbolic fluency' and imitation were also taken. 'Symbolic fluency' was assessed for each child by determining the number of different substitute symbolic uses of the objects, such as 'using the pill container as a cup to give the toy a drink . . .' (p. 444). Imitation was scored on a six-point scale:

0. none;
1. possible imitation of action by child;
2. clear imitation of action;
3. attempt to animate toy by having it hold the object or accessory, followed by the child imitating the action himself;
4. child assigns independent action to the toy, making it perform

a reasonable imitation of the action;

5. imitation of animation and action as shown in 4, then variation or elaboration of the animation sequence.

Standardised observations have also been made by Wing, Gould, Yeates and Brierly (1977) of children who were retarded employing Sheridan's (1969) observational procedure of play as a means of assessing symbolic representation. Sheridan developed her procedure as a paediatric screening tool for preschool children to assist in the differential diagnosis of delayed and disordered language development. The aim was to evolve a nonverbal task and as with other techniques reviewed used a range of functional and play materials. Two tests were employed, a common objects test and a miniature toy test.

Common Objects Test. Applicable from 12 months and employing life-size cup and spoon, baby's brush and comb, small hand mirror and three toys, a ball, doll and car. These are presented one by one. Spontaneous reactions are recorded and whether the child's manipulations indicate comprehension of the objects' function was noted.

Miniature Objects Test. Applicable from 21 months and employing 20 toys all under 2.5 inches. They include dolls, domestic animals, household objects and transport. Again, these were presented one by one and encouragement only given when needed. Ability to understand spoken instructions noted, particularly prepositions — on, under, behind, in front of and between.

Sheridan points out that the assessment can generate a great deal of information on the child's alertness, understanding, hearing, speech, language development, interpersonal relationships and social competence. In addition, eye-hand co-ordination, manipulative ability, concentration and distractibility can be assessed. Assessment is essentially clinical and numerical scores cannot be derived from the procedure as described by Sheridan. Observations are recorded descriptively.

Conclusion. From a practical point of view, Lowe and Costello's Play Test offers an ideal instrument for use with people who are profoundly retarded and who have sufficient motor control to use the items. Where older individuals are involved, it may be desirable to use age-appropriate objects or objects directly related to their more immediate interests. Play Test is short and relatively easy to score. The more detailed procedures we have described suggest ways in which teachers could explore further the individual's symbolic abilities in a relatively informal and enjoyable situation.

What do these Cognitive Tests tells us about Intelligence?

The way in which the assessment instruments described here have been employed to illuminate the development of people with profound retard-ation will be described in the following chapter. Here we will return briefly to our starting point in which we compared tests of specific cognitive function with psychometric tests. Even among proponents of Piagetian-derived assessment there is agreement that psychometric tests have value in diagnosing marked deviations from normative develop-ment. To this should be added the reservation that such a diagnosis will only be convincing with people who are multiply impaired where sufficient care is taken to ensure that responses available to the person are permitted and indeed engineered by the tester where required. Similarly, the more selective assessment of particular areas of cognition linked at least in part to a wider theory of development has special advantages in both 'placing' the child developmentally and developing appropriate educational strategies as we shall see in Volume 2. It should be noted, however, that relations *do* exist between the two types of assess-ment. Though we have found no studies concentrating exclusively on people who are profoundly retarded, both Wachs (1970) and DeVries (1974) found significant correlations between standardised measures of IQ and Piagetian-based assessment. DeVries (1974) concluded that:

> This evidence indicates that intelligence as defined by Stanford-Binet mental age overlaps to a moderate degree with Piagetian intelligence but that they are not identical. Therefore, the theoretical differences between Piagetian and Psychometric intelligence do seem to corres-pond to real differences in cognitive measurement. (p. 750)

Similarly, with Down's Syndrome children McCune-Nicholich and Hill (1981) found significant correlations between symbolic development as assessed through play and psychometrically assessed mental age.

The function of psychometric testing and specific tests of cognitive development can therefore be regarded as related and complementary. While the following chapter is concerned mainly with cognition and what such tests tell us about people who are profoundly retarded, we also draw on psychometric information where it assists in describing those studied or trends in their general development.

Assessment of Language and Communication

In Chapter 3 we showed how cognitive, social and linguistic factors contributed to the development of language and communication. The type of assessment described in the preceding sections clearly contributes to an understanding of the first of these, and, as we shall see, a number of studies have explored the relation between language and cognition using them. Direct formal and informal assessments of language and communication are reviewed by Bryen and Gallagher (1983), and of course many of the assessment instruments reviewed in the opening chapter of Volume 2, 'Beyond Developmental Assessment', are concerned with this area.

Some development has been made in assessing the social or pragmatic function of language as it develops and has been employed in studies reviewed in Chapters 3 and 8. These techniques, as with those concerned with early cognitive assessment, have derived from specific experimental studies, notably those of Bates and her colleagues (see Chapter 3). Snyder (1978) evolved two scales concerned with declarative and imperative performatives. Observation of these communicative acts is carried out in the context of play. These simple play situations were devised to elicit imperatives, either gestural or vocal, by putting objects out of reach, or of sufficient interest to encourage the child to produce declaratives. Greenwald and Leonard (1979) have used the scales with both nonhandicapped and Down's Syndrome children and present the scoring in the following way:

Performative/Score		*Behavioral Description*
(a) Imperative	1.	Child looks at adult, or Child looks at, extends arm towards object;
	2.	Child looks at and fusses at adult, or extends arm towards object, vocalizes and/or points to objects;
	3.	Child points to and/or reaches for object, then looks at adult, or Child points to and/or reaches for object, then looks at adult's hand;
	4.	Child performs act to get adult's attention first, then points to and/or reaches for object;
	5.	Child uses linguistic symbol to indicate desire for object.

(b) Declarative
1. Child uses direct manipulation to get adult's attention;
2. Child uses showing off to get adult's attention;
3. Child uses showing, giving, and/or pointing to object to get adult attention to it;
4. Child uses pointing and vocalizing to get attention to an object;
5. Child uses word to get adult to attend to object. (p. 229)

Developed as a more formal assessment battery, Kiernan and Reid's (1983a,b) Preverbal Communication Schedule (PVC) Manual encompasses a much wider range of skills necessary to enter initial speech or nonverbal communication programmes. Here the emphasis is again on the use of language, i.e. its communicative, pragmatic function. There are 195 items consisting of 28 sections each of five or six items. The sections concerned with precommunicative behaviour are: 1: Needs and preferences; 2: Vision and looking; 3: Control of hands and arms; 4: Use of visual cues; 5: Social interaction without communication; 12: Giving; 14: Hearing and listening; 15: Development of sounds; 16: Control of speech musculature; 17: Consistent use of noise; 18: Expression of emotion (noncommunicative); and 19: Music and singing. The authors comment that: 'These assessments provide background information in terms of which preverbal communication can be understood' (p. 5). This aspect of the assessment also provides an aid to programme planning.

An intermediate level of assessment between precommunicative and communicative behaviour is offered by sections 6: Motor imitation, and 20: Vocal imitation. Communication through nonverbal means is assessed by items concerned with communication through 7: Pictures and objects; 8: Whole body actions; 9: Gesture; 10: Manipulation; 11: Pointing; 13: Looking; 21: Use of sounds; 22: Expression of emotion (communicative); 23: Manipulation of emotion; 24: Understanding of nonvocal communication; 25: Understanding of vocalisation and speech; 26: Understanding of emotion; 27: Communication through symbols, signs, speech; and 28: Meanings communicated.

Scoring on the items is simply by a judgement of 'Usually', 'Rarely' or 'Never'. The items are grouped into six social function categories: I. Seeking attention; II. Need satisfaction; III. Simple negation;

IV. Positive interaction; V. Negative interaction; VI. Shared attention.

The use of the Preverbal Communication Scale itself (Kiernan and Reid 1983b) is explicitly to facilitate programme planning and we will comment further on this in Chapters 1 and 4 in Volume 2. The scale does not directly assess cognition, but the authors recommend that assessments derived from the scales should be taken in conjunction with the Uzgiris and Hunt Scales of Ordinal Development and the Symbolic Play Test described above, as well as with criterion referenced tests of the kind described in Chapter 1 of Volume 2.

The approaches to the assessment of language and communication can be employed in almost any context through direct observation of the individual. Brinker and Goldbart (1979) have also incorporated similar items on pragmatic aspects of communication into a wider observational scheme for studying language and social communication in young children and have applied it in a setting in which such children were integrated with more able, retarded and nonhandicapped children. Similarly, Carney, Clobuciar, Corley, Wilcox, Bigler, Fleisher, Pany and Turner (1977) offer an analysis of social interactions in people with severe and profound mental handicap that includes a skill chart for assessing behaviour in this area. The lower limits of this chart readily encompass individuals who are profoundly retarded as is illustrated in the following examples:

I   Reacts to others:
- A. Reacts to being touched by others
- B. Turns towards an adult speaker who calls name
- C. Turns towards a peer speaker who calls name
- D. Turns towards a person who enters room
- E. Watches the movement of others
- F. Establishes and maintains eye contact
.
.
- I. Follows simple commands

II   Reacts to objects:
- A Turns in direction of noise
.
.
.
.
- D Looks at and tracks moving object

III   Seeks attention

IV   Interacts with objects

V   Demonstrates concept of self

VI   Interacts with others:
  A. Receives interaction
    1   Returns hug
    2   Gives smile
    3   Gives object to other who has requested it
      .
      .
      .
      .
    9   Discriminates appropriate time, place situation before responding
  B. Initiates interaction
      .
      .
      .
  C. Sustaining interactions
      .
      .
      .
      .
      .
  D. Terminates interactions

Specific criteria for scoring are given, e.g. for IA above,

Reacts to being touched by others
    1. When other touches or pats person does not push person away, tense muscles or pull body away
    2. When tickled, touched or patted by person
        — turns face to person
        — turns face towards person and looks at them
        — turns face and establishes at least 2 second eye contact.

These assessments are also intended to suggest sequentially organised teaching objectives and this aspect of the authors' approach is dealt with in Chapter 4 of Volume 2.

Conclusion

In this chapter, we have described assessment approaches to early development that have in general been shown to be of relevance to people with profound retardation. They occupy a place somewhere between traditional developmental assessment and tailor-made assessment tools devised with the curriculum in mind. With this information we can now proceed to a review of developmental research with people who are profoundly retarded.

References

Berger, M. and Yule, W. (1986) 'Psychometric Assessment' in J. Hogg and N.V. Raynes (eds.), *Assessment in Mental Handicap: A Guide to Tests, Batteries and Checklists,* Croom Helm, London

Brinker, R.P. and Goldbart, J. (1979) 'The Problem of Reliability in the Study of Early Communication Skills', *British Journal of Psychology, 72,* 27–41

Bryen, D.N. and Gallagher, D. (1983) 'Assessment of Language and Communication' in K.D. Paget and B.A. Bracken (eds.), *The Psychological Assessment of Preschool Children,* Grune and Stratton, London

Carney, I., Clobuciar, G., Corley, E., Wilcox, B., Bigler, J., Fleisher, L., Pany D. and Turner, P. (1977) 'Social Interaction in Severely Handicapped Students: Training Basic Social Skills and Social Acceptability' in B. Wilcox, F. Kohl and T. Vogelsberg (eds.), *The Severely and Profoundly Handicapped Child: Proceedings from the 1977 Statewide Institute for Educators of the Severely and Profoundly Handicapped,* Specialized Educational Services, Illinois

Corman, H.H. and Escalona, S.K. (1969) 'Stages of Sensorimotor Development: A Replication Study', *Merrill-Palmer Quarterly, 15,* 351–61

Coupe, J. and Levy, D. (1985) 'The Object Related Scheme Assessment Procedure: A Cognitive Assessment for Developmentally Young Children who may have Additional Physical or Sensory Handicaps', *Journal of the British Institute of Mental Handicap, 13,* 22–4

DeVries, R. (1974) 'Relationships among Piagetian, IQ and Achievement Assessments', *Child Development, 45,* 746–56

Dunst, C.J. (1980) *Clinical and Educational Manual for Use with the Uzgiris and Hunt Scales of Infant Psychological Development,* PRO-ED, Inc., Austin, Tex.

Foxen, T. (1977) 'Observation as Assessment in the ESN(S) Child', unpublished but manuscript available, Hester Adrian Research Centre, University of Manchester, Manchester

Gouin Décarie, T. (1962) *Intelligence and Affectivity in Early Childhood,*

International University Press, New York

Gouin Décarie, T. (1969) 'A Study of Mental and Emotional Development of the Thalidomide Child' in B.F. Foss (ed.), *Determinants of Infant Behaviour: Vol. 4,* Methuen, London

Greenwald, C.A. and Leonard, L.B. (1979) 'Communicative and Sensorimotor Development of Down's Syndrome Children', *American Journal of Mental Deficiency, 84,* 296–303

Gunstone, C. (1979) 'Checklists used at Anson House Preschool Project', Research Paper, Dr Barnado's Publications, Barkingside

Hogg, J. and Moss, S. (1983) 'Prehensile Development in Down's Syndrome and Non-handicapped Preschool Children', *British Journal of Developmental Psychology, 1,* 189–204

Inhelder, B. (1968) *The Diagnosis of Reasoning in the Mentally Retarded,* Day, New York

Kiernan, C. and Reid, B. (1983a) 'Preverbal Communication Schedule (PVC) Manual' 2nd edn, unpublished but manuscript available, Thomas Coram Research Unit, London

Kiernan, C. and Reid, B. (1983b) 'Preverbal Communication Schedule (PVC)', 6th edn, unpublished but manuscript available, Thomas Coram Research Unit, London

Lowe, M. (1975) 'Trends in the Development of Representational Play', *Journal of Child Psychology and Psychiatry, 16,* 33–47

Lowe, M. and Costello, A.J. (1976) *Manual for the Symbolic Play Test: Experimental Edition,* NFER, Windsor

Lunzer, E.A. (1970) 'Construction of a Standardised Battery of Piagetian Tests to Assess the Development of Effective Intelligence', *Research in Education, 3,* 53–72

McCune-Nicholich, L. and Hill, P. (1981) 'A Comparison of Psychometric and Piagetian Assessments of Symbolic Functioning in Down's Syndrome Children' in M.P. Friedman, J.P. Das and N. O'Connor (eds.), *Intelligence and Learning: NATO Conference Series III: Human Factors, Vol. 14,* Plenum, London

Nicholich, L.M. (1977) 'Beyond Sensorimotor Intelligence: Assessment of Symbolic Maturity through Analysis of Pretend Play', *Merrill-Palmer Quarterly, 23,* 89–101

Piaget, J. (1962) *Play, Dreams and Imitation in Childhood,* W.W. Norton, New York

Riguet, C.B., Taylor, N.D., Benaroya, S. and Klein, L.S. (1981) 'Symbolic Play in Autistic, Down's and Normal Children of Equivalent Mental Age', *Journal of Autism and Developmental Disorders, 11,* 439–48

Sheridan, M.D. (1969) 'Playthings in the Development of Language', *Health Trends, 1,* 7–10

Sinclair, H. (1970) 'The Transition from Sensorimotor Behavior to Symbolic Activity', *Interchange, 1,* 119–25

Smith, B. (1982) 'A Study of Mental Growth in Young Severely Subnormal Children', unpublished Ph.D. thesis, University of Birmingham, Birmingham

Snyder, L. (1978) 'Communicative and Cognitive Abilities and Disabilities in the Sensorimotor Period', *Merrill-Palmer Quarterly, 24,* 161–80

Uzgiris, I. and Hunt, J.McV. (1975) *Assessment in Infancy: Ordinal Scales of*

Psychological Development, University of Illinois Press, Chicago

Wachs, T.D. (1970) 'Report on the Utility of a Piaget-Based Infant Scale with Older Retarded Children', *Developmental Psychology*, 2, 449

Wing, L., Gould, J., Yeates, S.R. and Brierly, L.M. (1977) 'Symbolic Play in Severely Mentally Retarded and in Autistic Children', *Journal of Child Psychology and Psychiatry*, 18, 167–78

Woodward, W.M. (1959) 'The Behaviour of Idiots Interpreted by Piaget's Theory of Sensorimotor Development', *British Journal of Educational Psychology*, 29, 60–71

Woodward, W.M. (1967) 'Notes on Techniques Devised for the Assessment of Severely Subnormal and Young Normal Children on the Basis of Piaget's Observations and Interpretation of Sensorimotor Development', University College Swansea, Swansea

Woodward, W.M. (1972) 'Problem-solving Strategies of Young Children', *Journal of Child Psychology and Psychiatry*, 13, 11–24

Woodward, W.M. (1983) 'The Development of Thinking in Young Children: 'The Problem of Analysis', *International Journal of Behavioral Development*, 6, 441–60

Woodward, W.M. (1984) personal communication

Woodward, W.M. and Hunt, M.R. (1972) 'Explanatory Studies of Early Cognitive Development', *British Journal of Educational Psychology*, 42, 248–59

8 THE DEVELOPMENT OF PEOPLE WITH PROFOUND RETARDATION AND MULTIPLE IMPAIRMENT

In previous chapters we have presented a general picture of early child development that an increasing number of workers in this field consider highly relevant to our understanding of people with mental retardation. We have also given some indication of the way in which specific types of impairment will influence early development and have suggested that knowledge about these influences is important for understanding the development of people with intellectual retardation and multiple impairments. It might be hoped that at this stage we can bring these two areas together — early child development and the effect of sensory and physical impairment — in the context of studies of people with profound retardation. Such an expectation can only be met in a limited way for the simple reason that directly relevant studies are few. Though research in mental retardation has continually extended into the range of profound retardation, most studies of development still concern themselves with more able children in the severe to mild retardation range. In addition, where such studies are undertaken with people with profound retardation, care is often exercised to exclude children with major physical and sensory impairments. Nevertheless, those studies that have been carried out highlight the importance of developmental assessment with very low functioning children, young people and adults, and offer clear pointers as to content and method in teaching. Our review will therefore concentrate on profound retardation and explore the effects of additional handicaps where possible. Occasionally we will allow ourselves a sortie upwards and consider more able people who are retarded. We will always give their details so that it is clear what level of functioning they exhibit in order that observations can be related by readers to their own pupils' and clients' abilities.

We have attempted broadly to follow the general outline of Chapter 3 with respect to *areas* of development, taking as our starting point sensorimotor development and moving on to its relation to the development of communication and self-help skills. We then consider preconceptual development, play, and motor development. In later sections we look at the effect of specific impairments and some observations on behaviour disorders in the context of development. Our parallel with Chapter 3 is not exact, for available studies of profound retardation do not themselves cover anywhere near the ground encompassed in the general child development literature.

Sensorimotor Development

We have seen earlier (Chapter 3) that Piaget distinguishes several domains of development that progressively advance during the first 18 months of the nonimpaired child's life. We have also seen (Chapter 7) that in the United Kingdom and the United States of America at least, the complex and unstandardised method of 'critical exploration' of Piaget and his colleagues has given way to the development of more standardised assessment procedures directed, in the case of the Uzgiris and Hunt Scales, to the development of: the object concept; spatial understanding; causality; vocal and gestural imitation; means-end behaviour; and action schemes to objects.

The development of such approaches to sensorimotor development has not only given practitioners and researchers the opportunity to undertake with people who are retarded developmentally relevant assessments that go beyond psychometric assessment, but also permits tests of some central aspects of Piaget's own theory. We commented on some such tests with nonhandicapped children in the previous chapter, and these issues also provide a useful basis for reporting on the development of people who are profoundly retarded. The remainder of this section, then, is organised around some of these principal issues.

The Similar Sequence Hypothesis

Piaget describes an orderly progression both within and across developmental domains and this is reflected in the scaling of the various tests derived from his theory. Indeed, one of the essential requirements of such a test is that passes on items follow a clear and reliable rank order with children succeeding at progressively more advanced items as they get older. While this is to be expected with nonimpaired children, is it also to be anticipated with those who are retarded? Some authors have suggested that it is, and refer to this as the 'similar sequence hypothesis': 'The *similar sequence hypothesis* holds that retarded and nonretarded persons traverse the same stages of cognitive development in the same order, differing only in the rate at which they progress and in the ultimate development ceiling they attain' (Weisz and Zigler 1979 p. 831). As these authors go on to note, such a view comes directly from the Piagetian idea that cognitive-development sequences are rooted logically in the way in which a normal nervous system and the environment interact: 'If retarded and nonretarded children were to differ in their sequence of development, then universality could hardly be claimed for the Piagetian account' (Weisz and Zigler 1979, p. 832).

You may have already noticed that such a view reflects the *developmental,* rather than the *difference,* position described in Chapter 2. It is a view which in its strong form applies not only to people who are retarded but who are delayed as a result of a disadvantaging environment, but also to those delayed through organic brain damage or abnormalities. Support for the similar sequence hypothesis has come from a number of studies.

While Piaget's colleague, Inhelder, was the first to apply both Piagetian theory and methods to the study of intellectual development in children who are retarded, her concern was in the main with older and more able retarded children. With respect to the development of people who are retarded in the sensorimotor period, Woodward (1959) must be regarded as the prime innovator in such applications. Not only did she undertake the first sensorimotor assessments of children with profound retardation, but she also advanced important ideas on the relation between development and stereotyped behaviour to which we shall return.

The children studied by Woodward lived in a large mental handicap hospital and fell into two age groups, Chronological Age (CA) 7–9 years and 14–16 years. These were divided into Group A and Group B. Group A failed to reach a basal level of 2 years on the Terman-Merrill Intelligence Scale, but had no motor or sensory disabilities, and all but 12 could walk unaided. Group B children were added as they were admitted to the hospital. Despite the absence of obvious sensory and physical impairments, it is clear from her classification of aetiologies that most of the children would be expected to have brain damage or abnormality as the groups contained microcephalic, spina bifida and epileptic children. In addition, it is almost certainly the case that some sensory impairments will have escaped notice given the absence of adequate screening procedures for such children at that time. Her very varied group, therefore, does contain children who were not only profoundly retarded, but also multiply impaired.

Using her own Piagetian-based procedures, Woodward focused on the development of the object concept, and also observed grip and manipulation of objects (to be discussed later) as well as problem-solving abilities. Her observations were made in a play context with suitable material. The highest pass on the object concept items was used to determine the child's stage placement within Stages IV, V or VI. In terms of the similar sequence hypothesis, it is noteworthy that 59/65 children did indeed pass all items prior to their highest success, i.e. they were tending to show the same ordinal sequence as would be expected for nonhandicapped children.

Rogers (1977) pursued this question in more detail employing the Corman and Escalona (1969) Scales as well as her own to assess object permanence, spatial concepts, causality and imitation (vocal and gestural combined). Her group was not dissimilar to Woodward's in that it consisted of residents of an institution, CA 6–14, IQ below 20 and average Mental Age (MA) less than 24 months. Employing more thorough statistical analyses than Woodward, Rogers also found sequences of development in these areas that followed the normal progression.

The only major discrepancy from Piagetian theory found, and one of some interest, related to the items in Rogers's imitation series. She writes that:

Piaget suggests that both visible and invisible (facial) imitation skills are present during stage IV, but this was clearly not supported in this study. Only one-third of the subjects who passed stage IVb [Imitates new sounds, movements, e.g. a novel sound or movement such as thumb tapping] imitations (and most passed only motor imitations at this level) were able to pass stage IVa [Invisible movements, e.g. rater opens mouth and puts out tongue] imitations. It may be that advanced imitation skills are more dependent upon appropriate models and social responses than other sensorimotor skills, and that among imitation skills the facial imitations (like vocal imitations in that they require imitation of behaviours which the subject cannot see himself perform) are extremely dependent upon positive, responsive models. (p. 841)

She suggests that it is a lack of models in institutional environments that, as well as causing general deficits, cause a specific deficit in imitation. Indeed, no children passed Rogers's level VI imitation task, i.e. immediate *exact* imitations of novel sounds and movements, IVb only having required an approximate imitation. As we shall see in the ensuing discussion of congruence between developmental stages, deficits in imitation present themselves frequently, with obvious implications for teaching strategies.

In the light of Woodward's and Rogers's studies we can conclude that developmentally, children who are profoundly retarded, usually with evidence of brain pathology, and probably in many cases with some sensory and/or motor impairment, *do* support the similar sequence hypothesis, i.e. they do tend to pass items within the various developmental domains in the same sequence. Weisz and Zigler (1979) see such findings as offering unexpectedly strong support for the hypothesis. Nevertheless, following the normal sequence *within* domains does not mean that children achieve equivalent stages in them at the same time, as we saw in reviewing studies with nonhandicapped children. With respect to retarded children we can consider this question of *stage congruence* again starting with the work of Woodward and Rogers.

Stage Congruence

Using only a restricted number of domains, Woodward (1959) suggested that the degree of congruence between stages was as high as 87 per cent, a figure not borne out in either Rogers's research or several subsequent studies. Rogers worked out the percentage of occasions on which the children's highest stage placements were the same, e.g. when Stage V was achieved for both object permanence *and* spatiality. Perfect agreement would, of course, yield 100 per cent for each of the possible pairs of domains. In reality the range was from 10 per cent (between imitation and spatiality) to 57.5 per cent between spatiality and causality, the average being around 30 per cent. Again, imitation seems to stand out on its own bearing less relation to the other scales. Object permanence and spatiality tended to bear higher relations to her domains than did imitation. Rogers suggests that closer links between object permanence, spatiality and causality skills are related to Piaget's position that they all develop from action with objects.

Subsequent studies have attempted to define the degree of stage congruence and the relation between different domains through complex statistical analyses. Dunst, Brassell and Rheingrover (1981), like Woodward, considered a very varied group of retarded toddlers, but unlike Woodward included three developmental age groups: MA 3–8 months, 8–12 months and 12–18 months. Their intention was to consider not only the degree of stage congruence but also its changing composition during the sensorimotor period. The children ranged from those with Down's Syndrome through to those with motor dysfunction (including cerebral palsy), and with micro- or hydrocephaly, all being assessed on the seven scales of the Uzgiris-Hunt Test.

First, with respect to stage congruence, Dunst *et al.* (1981) supported Rogers in finding a marked asynchrony in development across domains and suggest that again the Piagetian position is not supported.

Nevertheless, they do point out that there is a very real structure to infant intelligence as revealed in their analysis of the seven scales. In the 3–8 month and 8–12 month groups the following clusters of scales emerged:

3–8 months:	I	Spatial relations + object schemes
	II	Means-ends + operational causality + object permanence
	III	Verbal + gestural imitation
8–12 months:	I	Spatial relations + object schemes
	II	Object permanence + means-ends
	III	Gestural imitation + operational causality
	IV	Verbal imitation

With the exception of some change in relations between operational causality and gestural imitation, a clear and enduring structure is apparent. For the oldest group other differences can be seen:

12–18 months:	I	Means-ends + object schemes + operational causality
	II	Object permanence + spatial relations
	III	Verbal + gestural imitation

We will comment further on the significance of these various clusters, but it is interesting to add details of one further study by two of these authors (Dunst and Rheingrover 1983). This was undertaken not with a varied group of retarded children but with aetiologically similar Down's Syndrome children. In carrying out this study the authors were attempting to deal with their own criticism of their previous work that varied characteristics of children might artificially produce the clusters of domains noted. Though in no way profoundly retarded and multiply impaired, these children fell well within the *developmental* range which we are concerned with here. A group attending a centre-based intervention programme had an average MA of 9 and CA of 13 months, while a home-based group was of the same MA with a CA just over 15 months. Results differed slightly for these two groups and varied across different analyses: here we will report them only in so far as they bear on the earlier study.

First, as with the previous mixed-aetiology group, there was no general stage congruence as would be expected from a Piagetian position.

In the first analysis two broad organisational patterns emerged for both groups:

I   Vocal and gestural imitation
II   Differentiated sensorimotor actions, i.e. the other five Uzgiris-Hunt Scales

In a subsequent analysis this pattern was repeated for the centre group though Causality was found to be related to Vocal and Gestural Imitation. Dunst and Rheingrover (1983) suggest that this grouping of Imitation scales and Causality may be regarded as a 'Modification of behaviours based on social interactions' cluster in contrast to the 'Differentiated sensorimotor actions' cluster noted above. Both these clusters were also found in the home group though vocal imitation separated off into a third cluster and object permanence plus means-ends into a fourth, the last cluster being labelled by the authors, 'problem solving'. They speculate that the greater congruence in the centre group might arise from intervention, perhaps leading to more consistent all-round development.

In relation to our present concern, it is clear that this study with Down's Syndrome children confirms the overall outcome of the earlier report with children of diverse aetiologies. Dunst and Rheingrover (1983) point particularly not only to the absence of stage congruence, but also to the fact that marked similarities exist in developmental structure between the previous 8–12 month groups and the home-based children in this study. This pattern appears more variable than that in nonhandicapped children, but a direct comparison would be needed to confirm this.

In both Dunst studies, imitation lagged behind the other sensorimotor abilities, in line with Rogers's finding. Her suggestion that this might result from institutional deprivation, however, is not supported as all children were living at home, as were 15/45 children in MacPherson and Butterworth's (1981) study. Here children who were severely and profoundly retarded were assessed on the Uzgiris-Hunt Scales and a marked deficit in imitation, particularly gestural imitation, noted relative to other scales and to nonhandicapped children. When children were grouped into the six sensorimotor stages and compared with a nonhandicapped sample not only was a marked unevenness in the profiles of the seven scales seen relative to the nonhandicapped group, but also the deficit in imitation was found. Throughout Stages II-VI, performance was poorest on Gestural Imitation, and from Stages IV-VI the next poorest was Vocal Imitation. The authors describe the progress of imitation across the stages:

Stage II:	Similar profiles for nonhandicapped and handicapped with gestural imitation not observable in either.
Stage III:	Nonhandicapped infants beginning to develop imitation skills but not yet apparent in children who are profoundly retarded.
Stage IV:	Gestural and verbal imitation markedly low relative to other scales in the group which was profoundly retarded but means-ends and object schemes relatively high and equivalent to nonhandicapped group.
Stage V:	Those who were profoundly retarded begin to show evidence of imitation, both vocal and gestural.
Stage VI:	The ability to imitate both gesturally and vocally, though both falling far below other sensorimotor achievements of the group with profound retardation and are well below imitation in the nonhandicapped group.

Most of the studies we have reviewed have found deficits in imitative ability in young retarded children, a finding confirmed for vocal imitation in Kiernan and Reid's (1983) study of preverbal communication. The lack of stage congruence of imitation with other abilities has suggested that this represents a distinct ability underlain by processes different from those underpinning other areas of sensorimotor development. MacPherson and Butterworth (1981) pursue the possibility that this fact involves some revision of Piaget's constructionist view of imitation. Their results, which suggest a serious impairment in the processes underlying imitation in people who are profoundly retarded, might be accounted for by recent theories of imitation which suggest the ability may be innate, and may depend upon detecting sensorimotor equivalences through an active matching process. 'According to this revised view, a deficit in imitation could be a result of inability to detect such an abstract sensorimotor correspondence, perhaps as a consequence of brain damage' (p. 9). They also go on to suggest that such impairment could in turn delay language acquisition.

Stability and Change

Observations by teachers and parents of individual people who are profoundly retarded are often sensitive to slow and barely perceptible developmental changes. In this section we consider such change within the framework of sensorimotor development we have described.

That change does occur in this group *as* a group (leaving aside for the present individual progress) has been shown in two psychometric studies by Fisher and Zeaman (1970) and Silverstein (1979). Here, a technique was used that enabled the growth curve for IQ, as measured on the Stanford-Binet Scale of Intelligence, to be determined for residents who were retarded living in a large hospital from infancy to old age. In the former study, MA continued growing for up to 15 years, after which it flattened and remained stable until about 60 years of age. Then, it tended to taper off. This pattern is quite clear in borderline, mild, moderate and severe retardation groups (see Chapter 1 for definitions), with the initial rise obviously being steeper the more advanced the group. The pattern is less clear for the group with profound retardation. A cursory glance at Fisher and Zeaman's graph (Figure 8, p. 163) gives the impression of almost a straight line after the first few years. Closer inspection, however, shows that again the most rapid period of growth is from infancy to the early teens, and that after 60 years MA begins to decline. Silverstein's results confirm this general picture, the only exception being that the higher-ability groups had a longer growing season, i.e. took longer to reach their peak MA than did lower-ability groups.

While MA reflects the growing attainment of adaptive skills, IQ expresses the *rate* of development. Here, for all groups this declines rapidly until about 15–20 years, i.e. the growth in MA progressively slows up. MA then remains relatively stable until around 60 years after which it again begins to drop off. This pattern can be seen as clearly for residents with profound retardation as for higher-ability groups (Fisher and Zeaman 1970 Figure 13). Diagnostic category does not predict changes in IQ, i.e. individuals with profound retardation with epilepsy or cranial anomolies show the same IQ pattern as those without a clear aetiology.

These findings, then, indicate that people with profound retardation show similar, if less clearly accentuated patterns of general intellectual change though at a very much lower level than their more able peers. They tell us little, however, about the nature of this intellectual growth and it must be emphasised that many of those in the study will have spent much of their life in a highly deprived institution without systematic teaching or opportunities for intellectual growth. For a clearer account of the nature of the developmental changes in people who are by definition rarely going to go beyond the preoperational stage, we need to consider the qualitative changes that occur in sensorimotor development.

It was also Silverstein who addressed this question. Silverstein, Brownlee, Hubbell and McLain (1981) considered the stability of the object permanence and spatial relation scale of Corman and Escalona's (1969) Piagetian Scales over a period of one year in which three assessments were made. These findings were taken to indicate that there was a high stability in performance when environmental conditions were constant, as they were in the hospital setting in which the tests were undertaken. In a second study, Silverstein, Pearson, Colbert, Cordeiro, Marwin and Nakaji (1982) comment on the earlier finding that 'alternatively, and with equal justification, we might have said that the subjects showed little evidence of cognitive development over the one-year period' (p. 347). In this second study, therefore, they administered the same scale to many of the same young people to seek evidence of further development in the five years following the earlier work.

Seventy-one of the original group remained, all originally under 18 years of age. Now their average CA was 19.62 years and their mean IQ 19.65. They were thus clearly profoundly retarded though with at least partial vision, ambulation and arm-hand use. Their main diagnosis was 'gross brain disease-postnatal'. Significant correlations between the earlier assessment of five years ago and the present assessments were found with both object permanence and spatial ability appearing quite stable. Change, however, was significant but small, less than 2 points on average on each scale. This indicates continuing development over the 5-year period, but what of development in individuals?

While 30 young people gained on the object permanence scale, a further 30 slipped back — a nonsignificant difference overall on this scale. In the case of the spatial scale, 44 gained and 25 lost, a just-significant improvement overall. While optimistically we can use these findings to point to sensorimotor development in many individuals who are profoundly retarded, multiply impaired and brain damaged, they also confirm the apparent slowness and at times nonexistence of change. At the very least, it can be said that these findings were, as with the studies of IQ, gathered against a background of total lack of educational and training intervention, and must give a very conservative estimate of potential change. The authors comment that in the five years intervening between the studies, the young people:

. . . had not participated in any special programs designed to promote their cognitive development. We can only speculate about the possible effects of such programs had they been instituted. Nevertheless, the evidence we have obtained that the cognitive development of some individuals who are severely and profoundly retarded continues into early adulthood may justify more concerted efforts to sustain and enhance such developments. (p. 349)

It might also be added, though no information is given on this point, that these young people would already have experienced some institutionalisation even before the first study, with possible cumulative, detrimental effects.

A further longitudinal study by Wohlhueter and Sindberg (1975) bears directly on this question, for here the children, though in an institution, were considerably younger, 1 to 6 years of age. Included in the sample were children with profound retardation as well as those who were severely or moderately mentally retarded. These authors assessed the development of object permanence monthly for a period of up to 18 months. Only children who did not reach for objects or who had already achieved the object concept were excluded. The criterion of success was that on two successive monthly assessments the child would make deductions about the object conceiving of it as stable, permanent and predictable (Gouin Décarie's 1969, Stage VIb). While children with severe and moderate retardation were more successful in achieving Stage VIb, three who were profoundly retarded did reach criterion. Other children showed upwards progress without reaching this stage, though again a smaller proportion of children with profound retardation than those who were able showed such progress.

Of special interest in this study, and of particular relevance to profound retardation, are the patterns of development that emerged: (i) plateau — i.e. little change over most of the assessments; (ii) variable — i.e. monthly variation with equal likelihood of up and down movement; (iii) upwards — i.e. despite short plateau and occasional reversals. Nine children came in the plateau group, and all were under 4 years at the time of the assessments. All but one were profoundly retarded. Ten children were variable, fluctuating over three or four sub-stages generally in the middle of the scale. Most were over 5 years of age and were severely retarded, six children being considered profoundly retarded. Ten children showed upward movement, seven of whom were profoundly retarded. It is interesting to note that the children who were profoundly retarded exhibited the three patterns equally.

What then might differentiate the children with respect to these patterns if classification fails to do so? The authors examined medical and electroencephalogram records and observe:

> The majority of the variable group were found to have EEG abnormalities, especially dysrhythmias or a history of seizures. Among the plateau subjects, diagnoses of cat-cry syndrome and pre or post natal anoxia or evidence of substantial cerebral atrophy were most common. Down's Syndrome and/or findings suggesting relatively mild brain damage were most frequent in the upward group. Among the criterion subjects, diagnoses of hydrocephaly (arrested) or of multiple congenital anomalies accounted for one-half of the cases; and findings suggested only diffuse, mild cortical damage, or none at all, in a majority of cases. (p. 516)

Thus, a close look at developmental patterns in relation to diagnostic category shows category to be a more relevant variable in understanding intellectual growth than was the case for predicting IQ.

Nevertheless, some children who were profoundly retarded did show measurable change in attainment of the object concept, particularly when beyond a CA of 3 years. In part, Wohlhueter and Sindberg suggest, improving motor ability might contribute to such development. Indeed, re-evaluation of some children initially classified as profoundly retarded led to their reclassification as severely or moderately retarded.

There can be little doubt that the potential usefulness of Piagetian-based tests is fully realised in the light of the studies we have just reviewed. Though deviations from a strict Piagetian position may have been discerned, the basic sequences and structure of sensorimotor development can be defined with a majority of the most profoundly retarded of people. Indeed, even the lack of stage congruence, possibly also the case with nonimpaired children, can be seen as having useful implications. It enables us to determine relative strengths and weaknesses in the child's competence, and even points towards the existence of quite distinct mechanisms and processes underlying different aspects of early cognitive development such as imitative ability.

The Emergence of Language

Play

The feasibility of using the various symbolic play tests we have described with mentally retarded children in general has by now been well demonstrated. Lowe (1975) comments on the clinical use of her own test with such children, and suggests that changes in symbolic play are linked to MA rather than CA changes. McCune-Nicholich and Hill (1981), with Down's Syndrome children of MA 12–26 months, showed the applicability of Nicholich's (1977) symbolic play scale with these children as well as suggesting that symbolic play and object permanence are related to productive language at the one- and at the two-word levels. Riguet, Taylor, Benaroya and Klein (1981) also show the use of such scales with autistic children falling in or at the margin of profound retardation. Nevertheless, there is not a body of studies comparable to that on sensorimotor development, on play in profoundly retarded people generally.

A study by Whittacker (1980) points the way in this area. He assessed a group of children with profound retardation in an institution using Lowe and Costello's Symbolic Play Test. Whittacker compares the age at which Lowe's children typically passed an item with the age at which 50 per cent of the profoundly retarded children passed that item. While the latter, by this comparison, did pass some items at the same developmental age as the nonhandicapped children, in most instances they were found to pass items substantially later than their nonhandicapped peers. In some cases this difference was quite great; for example, 'Relates knife/fork to plate' was passed at 15 months by Lowe's children and by 50 per cent of Whittacker's children at 30 months. If we bear in mind Lowe's observation that symbolic play is dependent upon a growing understanding of relations in the real world, this finding is particularly surprising. Does the late acquisition of symbolic play in this area by children with profound retardation reflect a lack of experience in this crucial self-help area arising from an institutional experience in which active self-feeding was neither taught nor encouraged? In an area where inevitably these children would have experienced appropriate relations, i.e. between person, bed, blanket and pillow, a reasonably close concordance between the nonhandicapped and the developmentally similar children with profound retardation exists. Nevertheless, the sequence of passes for the two groups *is* broadly similar, suggesting that, as with sensorimotor stages, children with profound retardation do follow the expected progression of symbolic play and (working backwards) the mastery or practice play of the sensorimotor period.

In one other interesting respect the children in Whittacker's study differ from those in Lowe's. The latter showed a shift from self-directed to doll-directed play, i.e. the child would start combing his or her own hair and would then, around 21 months, begin to show a decrease in this activity and an increase in play directed to the doll. This was not found in the children with profound retardation observed, though it is possible that this was because the children had been specifically selected to have no speech or to be at the one-word level.

Lowe (1975) had suggested that the shift from self- to doll-directed play came about at the same time as the emergence of the two-word utterances, a linguistic level reached by no children in Whittacker's sample. Indirectly, Whittacker's finding could be taken as support for this position. Certainly further studies on the relation between expressive language and symbolic play would be welcome, as they would with respect to symbolic play and comprehension. With respect to comprehension, Wing, Gould, Yeates and Brierly (1973) note that there were children in their study who, though showing comprehension of language, exhibited no symbolic play.

It has already proved impossible to separate our discussion of early sensorimotor development from the early development of communication, since the growth of imitation has already figured large in our account. Deficits in imitation, it has been suggested, will lead to langauge delay. What, though, of other cognitive influences on language development of the sort considered by Bates and others and reviewed in Chapter 3? We shall shortly turn to this question in the context of profound retardation. It is necessary first, however, to consider other early processes that have been implicated in language acquisition prior to the important advances that have been found to be associated with movement into Stage VI of sensorimotor development.

Auditory Discrimination

First, given the high prevalence of hearing impairment in people with profound retardation noted in Chapter 1, and the obviously detrimental effect of such impairment on the development of communication (Chapter 5), it must be anticipated that the language development of many will be adversely affected through hearing impairment. This raises important questions regarding the assessment of hearing in such children which are dealt with in Chapter 1 of Volume 2 and from such assessments come considerations for the type of communication programme with which we deal in Chapter 4 of Volume 2. Second, in the absence of serious hearing impairment, we must ask whether the highly selective reactions of nonhandicapped children to speech sounds and other forms of auditory input can be established, and it is to this question we shall first turn.

Many important questions have been answered and raised with respect to this issue by Glenn and Cunningham (1984) in a series of carefully designed studies of auditory responses in children who are profoundly

retarded and multiply impaired. Since these studies also are significan
for considerations of basic learning and sensorimotor teaching, we shal
return to her findings with respect to these issues in Chapter 9. Glenn
employed a device developed by Friedlander (1968) and known as
PLAYTEST. PLAYTEST has been employed with many different groups
of children including nonhandicapped, moderately retarded and language
disordered children. One of the most relevant applications prior to
Glenn's study was that undertaken by Cyrulik-Jacobs, Shapira and Jones
(1975) with cerebral palsied children whose average age was 20 months
but who in gross motor functioning were at an 8-month level. The
relevance to this group of PLAYTEST can be seen from these authors'
description of the device. It consists of two separate sound sources. Either
source can be switched on by a simple motor response by the child, i.e.
simply touching the box. Thus, if the two sounds coming from the sources
are different, e.g. speech and a monotone, the child can display a
preference by selecting which he or she prefers by a simple action.
Likewise, the tester can establish different preferences by choice of different contrasted pairs of sounds. Thus: 'The system will presumably allow
scrutiny of a wide range of acoustic and linguistic variables either known
or suspected to be critical factors of auditory perception and processing'
(p. 186). In this study, the feasibility of the technique was shown by
establishing that the length of time the child chose to listen to one sound
rather than another (relative response duration) was quite clear, most
children preferring to listen to music rather than a constant hum. What,
then, of the use of such a technique with children also physically impaired
but more markedly retarded than those in Cyrulik-Jacobs *et al.*'s report?

All children that Glenn studied were below a 12-months developmental
level. In her first study, three out of five children were considered profoundly retarded and multiply impaired: Child 1 was MA 4.5 months
and CA 8.4 years; Child 2, MA 7.2 months and CA 4.9 years; Child
3, MA 3.0 months and CA 3.0 years: These children will be clearly
recognised as falling within the group with whom we are concerned in
this book. Two further children, regarded by Glenn as severely retarded,
were also included, these having MAs and CAs respectively of: Child
4, 8.0 months and 3.2 years, and Child 5, 9.5 months and 2.1 years.
These children were all assessed with PLAYTEST with various contrasted sounds:

1. *Sesame Street* song vs Tone
2. Familar nursery rhyme vs Nonsense rhyme
3. Mother or teacher talking to a baby vs Talking to an adult

4. Second *Sesame Street* song vs No sound

The children with profound retardation learnt that by touching the sound-producing boxes it was indeed possible to elicit sounds from them. They showed, however, no preference for one sound over another. The children with less retardation did show distinct and expected preferences comparable to Down's Syndrome and nonhandicapped children of a comparable MA, i.e. 8–9 months.

Two explanations for the failure of the children with profound retardation to show a preference were suggested. One was that they were of a lower development age than those who did show preferences, and the other that they were unable to make spatial discriminations between the two boxes. In her second study, therefore, Glenn considered children who were profoundly retarded and multiply impaired but of a higher developmental level. The three children with profound retardation involved were on average of MA 9.2 months and here all showed some measure of clear preferences. Conversely, nonhandicapped children below this level were found not to exhibit preference for one sound over another, but by MA 9.5 months did do so. Glenn suggests that critical to this development is some advance in the child's understanding of the relation between objects in space.

Glenn goes on to describe application of the technique with children who were more profoundly retarded and/or multiply impaired, children typical of those occupying special needs classes and units. She also describes how modifications to the assessment procedure were employed to promote or give the opportunity to express auditory preferences. These manipulations will be described in relation to learning processes in the following chapter and in relation to intervention in Chapter 3, Volume 2. With respect to the nature of the auditory discriminations, and hence to language development, Glenn concludes that the children who were profoundly retarded followed a similar pattern as did those who were severely, moderately and nonhandicapped. Thus, rhythmical, familiar speech stimuli elicit more responding than do simple tones, bells, etc. It is clear, then, that many children with profound retardation in Sensorimotor Stage IV and onwards are sensitive to speech input, providing, of course, that their hearing is relatively unimpaired. While this provides an important input necessary for learning one's native language, it will be evident from our earlier summary on language development (Chapter 3) that other cognitive developments occurring in the sensorimotor period are also necessary prerequisites for language learning, particularly developments in and beyond Sensorimotor Stages V and VI.

Language and Cognition

It is again Woodward who first gave detailed consideration to this link in people who are retarded. Woodward and Stern (1963) describe this relation with special reference to development of the object concept permitting symbolic function and leading to the emergence of spoken language. While children with gross medical conditions were excluded from her sample (i.e. those with cerebral palsy, hydrocephalus or visual or auditory deficit likely of themselves to retard development), the majority were virtually all profoundly retarded and functioning below a 2-year level.

Using her own scales, Woodward (1959) assessed sensorimotor development and related it to a scale assessing the development of speech. She noted a wide range of speech at all stages of sensorimotor development, but found meaningful and relevant word combinations and short sentences occurred only in the speech of some Stage VI children. It was also noted that none of the children at Stages III and IV, nor the majority at Stage V, understood spoken words (though some of the latter did respond to communicative gestures). However, all children at Stage VI showed evidence of verbal comprehension and differences between these and Stage V children emerged in all aspects of comprehension.

Despite this intriguing confirmation of the link between cognitive development and language in children with profound retardation, it was over ten years before more detailed analyses were made using the newer assessment instruments that had developed in the intervening period. Most notably, Kahn (1975) related four scales of the Uzigiris-Hunt assessment procedure to two groups of children who were profoundly retarded, one an expressive language group (vocabulary of 10+ words), and a nonlanguage group lacking any expressive vocabulary. The scales he employed were: visual pursuit and permanence of objects; development of means for achieving desired environmental events; development of causality; development of imitation. Children were classified as Stage VI or Stage V and below. Significant correlations were found between all four scales and the development of expressive language. Interestingly, the highest correlation was between imitation and expressive language while the lowest, in contrast to Bates's position, was the means-end scale and language. Most of the children with expressive language had reached Stage VI on all four scales, and the lowest performance was Stage VI on two scales. None of the children in the nonlanguage group reached Stage VI on all four scales though a minority did achieve that stage on two scales. As with Woodward and Stern's study, then, the expected relation between cognition and language emerged, though not perfectly.

Nevertheless, Kahn does conclude by arguing that his results support the Piagetian position on mental representation as the basis for acquisition of expressive language, and spells out the implications for language teaching. Information from the training studies he undertook do indeed strengthen his conclusion, but these we will leave until Chapter 4 of Volume 2 when language programming is discussed.

Other studies offer further support for Kahn's findings. Cappuzzi (1979) considered young people who were institutionalised and profoundly retarded (ambulant, and without major sensory impairment). She divided her sample into a receptive plus expressive group, and a receptive only group. Again, the presence of receptive language was found to be most significantly related to the Uzgiris and Hunt imitation scales (both gestural and vocal), with object permanence showing the next closest link. All other scales were also significantly related with the exception of means-end behaviour. There is, here, a strong parallel to Kahn's (1975) finding, and in a subsequent study of a variety of adaptive behaviours Kahn (1983), himself, found object permanence, verbal and gestural imitation the best predictors of expressive and receptive language in children who were severely and profoundly retarded. While the reliable effect of imitation (here gestural) again emerged as an important predictor of communicative ability, so did means-end behaviour and spatial development.

There does, then, appear to be a close link between early cognitive development and the emergence of spoken language — perhaps mediated by the development of symbolic abilities. It also appears that the ability to represent words and actions through imitation is particularly critical, and that object permanence also plays an important part. It seems unlikely, however, that any of the areas defined in, for example, the Uzgiris-Hunt assessment scales, can safely be ignored. To anticipate our discussion of teaching in this area, Cappuzzi (1979) makes the point that:

> Educational plans . . . should be designed to stimulate the total sensori-motor cognitive abilities of the individual. Procedures designed to stimulate the development of all areas of sensorimotor functioning may well provide the basis of a communication plan for the institutionalised profoundly retarded individual (p. 7278a)

Such a conclusion need not be restricted simply to institutionalised individuals, of course. In addition, such a position does not preclude a special emphasis on areas where obvious deficits exist which might relate to special weaknesses in development — most obviously the link between deficient imitation and language delay.

Where discrepancies between stage placement and expected develop ment on language do occur, what are we to conclude? First, of course the position advocated by Bates is not one of simple prerequisites in cogni tion leading automatically to language acquisition. Impairments in socia interactions could also contribute, and as we shall see, such impairment are indeed likely in many children who are multiply handicapped.

Social Interaction

Again, it is Woodward who has pointed the way to accounting for suc discrepancies, though no work has subsequently been carried out explor ing her observations. In the study we noted (Woodward and Stern 1963) she reports that, in several of the cases where Stage V and VI childre: were markedly behind in language, severe behaviour disorders wer exhibited. When such children were removed from the analysis then th correlation between stage attained and language development increase substantially.

The study of social factors in the development of communication i individuals who are profoundly retarded and multiply impaired has however, barely begun. It is clear that if significant disruption to parent child communication can be seen with far more able children who ar moderately retarded, such as those with Down's Syndrome, then thi interaction will be even more impaired in children of much lowe intellectual ability with additional impairments. We have already see how specific sensory handicaps impair communication in nonretarde children (Chapters 4 and 5) and such influences will undoubtedly pla their part in those who are profoundly retarded with these impairments The problem will be particularly exacerbated, too, by severe physica impairment.

Some indication of the form this may take can be gained by reconsider ing a study we reviewed in Chapter 6 by Shere and Kastenbaum (1966) The focus of this study, it will be remembered, was on physical impair ment, the children being cerebral palsied. They were not classified wit respect to degree of retardation but with a CA range of 2.6 to 4.8 year and MAs of 0.7 months to 2 years 6 months it is likely that som approached the level of ability and degree of retardation we are concerne with.

Central to the description of the interactions between mother and chil was that play was essentially ignored, the need to overcome the physica handicap *per se* being the critical concern. Objects, therefore, did no provide items for joint attention, exchange, etc., the interactions describe by Bruner as central to the social construction of communication, bu were essentially incentives to movement. This is just what Shere and Kastenbaum mean when they refer to the way in which the organic affliction was not only disabling in its own right, but also inhibited the emergence of an interaction pattern that fosters psychological growth. Clearly other forms of impairment, visual and auditory, would accentuate this state of affairs. Bruner's (1975a, b) scaffold would remain incomplete, and even assuming other areas of cognitive growth reached the required level, the development of communication would be seriously impaired.

It can be seen from the above that slow development of communication in people who are profoundly retarded and multiply impaired is likely to be accounted for through all the elements that have been suggested to be necessary for language development — social, cognitive and linguistic. For any given child the balance of these factors will vary, and it will only be through assessment and observation that we will have any opportunity to enhance communication skills. It is to these issues that we shall return in Chapter 4 of Volume 2.

Cognition and Adaptive Behaviour

Important though language development and its antecedents are, the concern of those working with people with profound retardation extends beyond this specific area. Two studies have explored how early adaptive behaviour is underpinned by specific cognitive advances (Wachs and DeRemer 1978 and Kahn 1983). They explored this question in the same way that the link between cognition and language has been considered, i.e. by correlating performance on the Uzigiris-Hunt Scales with measures of adaptive behaviour. Again, however, this link was anticipated in Woodward and Stern's (1963) study with specific reference to self-feeding. Here children were classified as being at Sensorimotor Stage III, IV, V or VI. This placement was then cross-tabulated with three aspects of self-feeding: (i) *Does not drink from cup.* No Stage VI children were thus classified, while all Stage III, 70 per cent of Stage IV and 24 per cent of Stage V could not drink from a cup; *Drinks if cup held.* Again no Stage VI children came into this category, nor any at Stage III. All who did were either Stage IV or V; *Helps to hold cup.* The majority here were Stage V, with a small proportion of Stage VI requiring such assistance (6 per cent). No Stage III or IV children were able to use a cup even with help; *Hold cup without help.* Again no Stage III or IV children were able to drink independently, while 31 per cent of Stage V children were able to and 94 per cent of Stage VI children could

206 Development with Profound Retardation and Multiple Impairmen

drink from a cup independently. (ii) *Use of fingers for feeding.* All Stage VI children fed themselves with their fingers, and this was also note for some children in Stage IV and a substantial number at Stage V. N Stage III children fed themselves with their fingers. (iii) *Spoon use.* The majority of Stage VI children could use a spoon without spilling the food and most of those who could not do so did use a spoon though with som spillage. Only 24 per cent of Stage VI children could not use a spoon In contrast, most Stage V children and all Stage III and Stage IV coul not use a spoon. Indeed, only 20 per cent of Stage V children used a spoon, most spilling food from it.

As with language, Stage VI seems closely related to the self-help skil of self-feeding. Stage V appears to be the traditional stage and give that none of these children could use spoon or cup at Stage IV, this has clear implications for the cognitive prerequisites of self-feeding and appropriate training programmes to which we will return in Chapter 6 of Volume 2.

The more recent studies noted above adopt a more global approach than did Woodward relating, as we noted, performance of sensorimotor scales to standardised measures of adaptive behaviour and language (the latter discussed above). Both Wachs and DeRemer's (1978) and Kahn's (1983) studies agree in allotting the development of the object concept a place of special importance in the development of adaptive behaviour. They part company in that the former emphasises spatial development as of special importance and the latter emphasised vocal and gestural imitation. Given the relevance of Kahn's group to our present concerns (the CA was average 6.25 years and MA 15.8 months) we will consider his findings further without attempting to account for this discrepancy. This is also appropriate because again the importance of imitation skills emerges. Kahn notes that vocal imitation is a good predictor of how socialised the child is. In the scale used, socialisation is assessed through items dealing with co-operation, interaction and group activities. Thus, the ability to imitate would enable an individual to co-operate within a group and adopt its norms by being able to produce observed and accepted models of behaviour and language. Similarly, Kahn suggests: '. . . it is not surprising that object permanence, which involves the understanding of what happened to an object or person when out of sight, is relevant to social behaviour' (p. 75). However, Kahn does express surprise that means-end behaviour does not predict socialisation. It would be expected that the ability to manipulate the environment would permit greater control of events and enhance social adjustment.

Vocal imitation was a good predictor of independent functioning. Kahn suggests that since imitation is the prime Piagetian example of accommodation, and since the acquisition of independent functioning requires individuals to adapt to the environment — a form of accommodation — the link makes sense. He emphasises, however, the central importance of object permanence to adaptive functioning, giving as it does unity and stability to mental activities.

While it is certainly the case that such analyses are somewhat abstract, the cognition-behaviour links determined by Woodward and Stern do offer more to the teacher by way of a practical rationale for intervention, and we must hope for more studies of that sort in future. Nevertheless, the more complex statistical predictions from sensorimotor to adaptive behaviour scales do point up the continuity of cognitive development and overt forms of competence. Convenient though it may be to distinguish 'cognitive' from 'social' development, they are inextricably linked and interdependent.

Motor Development

Motor impairment in many people who are profoundly retarded and multiply impaired is to be expected either through direct central nervous system damage leading to cerebral palsy or spina bifida, or through less direct causes such as damage to the visual system. The consequences of such impairments for development have already been described in Chapters 4–6. They will clearly accentuate the slower development of individuals already at risk for profound retardation. Here we will not rereview this information, but will consider a small number of studies that place motor development in the wider context of cognitive development and its impairment.

It is inherent in the Piagetian view of development that self-initiated movement is one critical factor in the development of understanding of the world. Physical impairment will at best impede sensorimotor development and at worst prevent it. Combinations of fine and gross movement are involved in all aspects of the development of domains described in the various tests of sensorimotor functioning, and we saw in Chapter 6 in Wedell, Newman, Reid and Bradbury's (1972) study of cerebral palsied children how subtle these effects could be, with perceptual constancy directly affected by lack of self-initiated ambulation. Similarly, we saw in Shere and Kastenbaum's (1966) report on how social interactions with physically impaired children could further and unwittingly affect development.

Similar effects on the person with profound retardation and multiple impairments must also be anticipated. Though 92 per cent of people who are profoundly retarded will walk if their condition is not accompanied by obvious neurological dysfunctions, only 11 per cent of those who also have cerebral palsy will also do so, and these much later in childhood (Shapiro, Accardo and Capute 1979). For these authors, failure to walk is not essentially bound up with slow cognitive development, but with neurological causes that underlie both retardation and gross motor development delay. Nevertheless, even when cerebral palsied, hydrocephalic and sensorily impaired children are excluded, as in Woodward and Stern's (1963) study, locomotor development is delayed. Here children who were retarded and in the sensorimotor period (CA 11 months-8 years 7 months, Mean 4.85 years) were studied, some of whom were almost certainly profoundly retarded within our present definition. Throughout the sensorimotor period, however, improving locomotion was found.

Development of gross motor skills in retarded children can undoubtedly be directly influenced by environmental factors. Wilkins, Brown and Wolf (1980) report on a group of *Cri-du-chat* Syndrome children, a condition which was once considered to be associated with ability in the upper reaches of the profound retardation range. In these studies, however, the children who were raised at home were typically ambulant in contrast to reports on *cri-du-chat* Syndrome children raised in institutions. Indeed, few of the children in this study fell into the expected category of profound retardation.

Fine Motor and Manipulative Development

Much of what needs to be said about early manipulative development has indirectly been covered in our earlier discussion of sensorimotor development. In one of these studies, however, Woodward (1959) focused more directly on both grasping and on Circular Reactions, each in relation to problem-solving. Ability to solve problems was assessed through items directly reflecting obvious sensorimotor achievement, i.e. retrieving objects from behind a transparent screen, then an opaque screen, gaining an object through pulling the object on which it has been placed, by a piece of string and with a small rake, and finally getting a long object through bars by reorientating the object through 90°.

Grasping of objects was also observed first as a spontaneous behaviour directed towards a toy, after which, if the child did not grasp, it was placed where both hand and object could be seen by the child. Failing this, the object was put to the child's mouth, then touching the hand, then in the palm (i.e. the reverse of Piaget's grasping sequence). The actual manipulations were also recorded in terms of Circular Reactions. Primary Circular Reactions of Sensorimotor Stage II were: hand regard, watching hand movement, clasping hands and rubbing them together, playing with the fingers and opening and closing the hand. The Secondary Circular Reactions of Stage III were simple, repetitive actions such as banging or shaking, while Stage IV Secondary Reactions involved turning an object round and examining it or repeatedly dropping the object. Tertiary Circular Reactions of Stage V included spinning or rolling objects and experimental banging on different surfaces or dropping an object from different heights and watching it fall. Children were also classified as showing no manipulations, or other types of manipulation.

The correspondence anticipated was not here as high as expected. Nine children who grasped an object on sight did not show Stage III Secondary Circular Reaction and all 35 per cent of children showed less complex Circular Reactions than expected. Nevertheless, none of the children who only grasped objects when tactily stimulated by them manipulated them except to look at them or suck the object as would be expected from Piaget's own observations. Nor was there as high a relation between problem-solving and manipulation when considered in relation to the stage of Circular Reactions.

Woodward suggests two possible explanations for this result. First, in this developmental respect it is possible that children who are profoundly retarded do not conform to the Piagetian structure. Second, it may be that they have the ability to execute various Circular Reactions but fail to demonstrate them. Woodward suggests that such a failure may result from behavioural disturbances or because such manipulations are inherently less motivating than problem-solving activities where an actual object is found. The possibilty of such a motivation deficit is suggested by children who did not grasp immediately but did so after some time.

Among these children were three who took up to 30 minutes to grasp, then went on to demonstrate the Piagetian sequence prior to co-ordinating vision and grasping. Was this really the first time the child displayed this behaviour or was it, more likely, a recapitulation of an already developed behaviour? If this was the case, why the lapse? Woodward suggests that if earlier learning's permanence results in stable learning because it is built on rather than replaced, then perhaps in children who are profoundly retarded slow development leads to a failure to utilise early learnt behaviour and hence it extinguishes, i.e. declines, because of lack of reinforcement.

In this study Woodward does not deal with manipulation at Sensorimotor Stage VI because no Circular Reactions are described for this stage. That children who are profoundly retarded do show manipulation characteristic of this stage is shown by this and other studies in which that stage, and indeed beyond is achieved. While Woodward and Stern (1963) excluded from their study children who were obviously multiply impaired, it is likely that some were profoundly retarded. Children classified as Sensorimotor Stage VI did perform differently on a range of manipulative tasks consisting of a four brick tower, three figure form board presented in two orientations, pegboards, a block bridge, bead threading, the Seguin formboard and so on. Those at Stage VI passed two or more of these items in contrast with those below Stage VI where no child passed any item.

Beyond Stage VI it would be anticipated that some children who are profoundly retarded will show advances in manipulative behaviour characteristic of the preconceptual phase of the preoperational period developments described in Chapter 3. We have not found, however, any study exclusively concerned with manipulative development in such children in this sub-stage, let alone those with additional impairments. It is likely that some children in Woodward's work would fall into these categories and did show such developments. However, a report by Smith and Philips (1981) of the full range of Educationally Subnormal (Severe) (ESN(S)) children in Birmingham at the time of the study suggests that such developments will at best be extremely slow. These authors note that on Piagetian-based cognitive scales half of the younger children (7 to 11 years) are at the beginning of the preconceptual period while half the older ones (12 and 13 years) are at the end of this period preceding the achievement of some intuitive operational concepts. When it is borne in mind that very few of these children were profoundly retarded, and that by definition they would function at lower levels and develop more slowly than average, then the limits of their preoperational attainments will be apparent not only in manipulation, but in symbolic and communicative abilities as well.

Profound Retardation and Multiple Impairments

Much of the developmental evidence we have summarised so far is taken from studies in which people who are profoundly retarded but without major physical or sensory impairments are reported. Nevertheless, it is clear from a close reading of the description of those involved that many did have some measure of additional impairment and in a number of instances brain damage or pathology existed. Given this, then the application of the developmental framework described to many people who are profoundly retarded and multiply impaired is appropriate and potentially useful.

In the light of our reviews of sensory and physical impairment in Chapters 4–6, however, it is to be expected that additional impairments will compound the degree of developmental delay further in a range of specific functions. It might also be expected that the behavioural and emotional consequences of additional impairments will be detrimental, as will be the consequences of specific forms of brain damage. In the remainder of this chapter we will address ourselves to two aspects of these questions, i.e. the relation of profound retardation and additional impairments on the one hand, and the disruption of developmental patterns through abnormal brain function.

Profound Retardation and Additional Impairments

We have come across only one report that has attempted systematically to link profound retardation with two major forms of impairment — visual and physical. We will therefore present this information in a little detail as it illustrates many of the problems that we raised in Chapter 2 with respect to the common causes of impairment, their interaction and the influence of the environment on children with such impairments. In addition, Van Dijk (1982) has undertaken an important study of children who are rubella damaged with additional hearing and/or visual impairments. In this study the presence or absence of visual impairment as a consequence of bi-lateral cataracts enable Van Dijk to consider the developmental effect of such impairment when added to hearing impairment.

Warburg (1983) studied a large group of children who were retarded with specific reference to visual and physical impairment. He noted that while the prevalence of visual impairment in children who were retarded is 5 per cent as against 0.02 per cent in nonhandicapped children, it is as high as 30 per cent in those with profound retardation. Warburg provides evidence that brain damage may be a common cause of visual impairment and retardation. In comparing children who were variously profoundly and severely retarded vs mildly and moderately retarded, Warburg found that almost all with cerebral blindness were in the former group as examinations of their eyes indicated no ocular impairment. Of these children, 80 per cent were permanently seated or recumbent as a result of severe motor impairment. In these instances, brain damage was considered to be the common cause of motor and visual impairments. Of children with visual impairment due to optic atrophy, 85 per cent were profoundly or severely retarded, 70 per cent of whom were unable to walk. Again a common causation of the multiple impairments and retardation through extensive brain damage is suggested. Where visual impairment occurred because of defects of the eyes themselves, children who were profoundly and severely retarded were again in a majority, though much less markedly so than in the case of cerebral blindness and optical atrophy. Here, however, the position with respect to ambulation was reversed, as more children blind from this cause walked than lay or sat.

In this last instance, where common brain damage is not implicated, we might infer that people who are profoundly retarded with visual impairment not arising from central neural damage affecting motor functioning will follow a comparable course to the children with visual impairment described in Chapter 4. Thus, we saw that visual impairment could lead to delayed mobility in intellectually nonhandicapped children. Warburg's study suggests that those with profound retardation with visual impairment will follow the same path given neuromuscular readiness and absence of motor impairment.

Warburg's results also confirm that many other additional impairments seen in the person with visual impairment and profound retardation will be associated with generalised brain damage. Epilepsy, spasticity or hearing impairments are all more frequently concomitants of profound retardation where the person is cerebrally blind or has optic atrophy than in those with ocular disorders.

One outstanding problem that we cannot resolve from these results is the cause of failure to develop ambulation in 37 per cent of children who are profoundly and severely retarded whose blindness was ocular. Does this failure reflect developmental factors of the sort described by Fraiberg (1968) or might there also be specific damage to the motor centres of the brain? In reality the answer to this question is possibly 'both', and for any given child clinical examination might go some way to resolving the question.

The term 'visual impairment' implies, of course, variations in the extent of sightedness, and again differences exist within the retarded population. Warburg shows that among the population of children who were profoundly, severely and moderately retarded, the first of these predominate by a large majority in the categories of 'no light perception' and 'perception to light only'. There, numbers are appreciably reduced in the partially sighted category where moderately retarded children predominate. Warburg presents evidence suggesting that where residual vision exists (perception of light) development can benefit and be enhanced over the years to a greater extent than is the case for children with no light perception. This raises the possibility that incidence of profound retardation decreases over the childhood years as development is enhanced through the use of residual vision, a possibility that would, however, require further exploration in relation to mortality rates and the assessability of children from birth onwards.

Van Dijk's study of children damaged by the rubella virus with additional hearing impairment and/or visual impairments was not concerned exclusively with children who were retarded. A proportion of the children studied, however, would fall within the definition employed in this book, some of whom are, of course, profoundly retarded and multiply impaired as a result of rubella damage. The full sample of children were initially assessed on a variety of tests without reference to whether they were visually impaired or not. These assessments embraced their physical status, independent walking, mother-infant relationships, stereotyped behaviour (discussed later in this chapter), general development, fine motor behaviour, imitation of simple gestures and invisible imitation, eurythmia, finger location and speech performance.

Many of the children in Van Dijk's sample were retarded in both growth and motor development. In addition, he argues, against a background of feeding difficulties, sleep problems and possible hospitalisation, disruption of mother-infant bond can also be anticipated:

> Because the physical condition of many rubella children is so vulnerable they are often very sensitive to environmental stimulation. Very young rubella babies often arch themselves away from the mother and this can lead to frustration on her part. The pleasure of effective interaction between the child and the environment, including the mother, is lacking. Even in the motivated mother this may cause feelings of resentment. This impoverished situation is worsened when the child is blind or is being deprived of visual stimulation because of the growing density of the cataract(s). (p. 55)

While about 20 per cent of Van Dijk's sample were developing normally, the majority were considered not to be developing normally or to have possible developmental problems. While about 25 per cent showed delays to spoken language, 10 per cent of the sample were substantially delayed in personal-social development and fine and gross motor skill. The ability to plan motor actions was also considerably delayed. With the children who were over 3 years, Van Dijk employed a test of learning aptitude developed for deaf children (the Hiskey-Nebraska Test). In line with other studies, the children who could be tested performed above average. It must be assumed that most of the children who were severely or profoundly retarded were not testable using this approach.

With respect to the cognitive skill of imitation, a large group performed well on the test employed (75 per cent) though a number with CA over 3 years failed to reach the appropriate level. Imitation of complex gestures involving quick movements presented great difficulties to a major group of children, perhaps because of the perceptual motor nature of the task. Van Dijk considers that this might result from overdependence on visual feedback while executing the movements, rather than, presumably, development of preprogrammed movement (see Chapter 3). Execution of rhythmic movements and transfer from visual to motor patterns and vice versa also presented difficulties for a substantial number of children.

As might be anticipated given both hearing impairment and the presence of retardation in some children, verbal communication was markedly affected. While half the sample consisted of 'talking' children, only four of these used normal sentences. In the other half of the sample speech did not play a role in spontaneous interactions, though some did have some appropriate verbal behaviour. Nevertheless, nearly 40 per cent of those who did not communicate verbally in spontaneous interactions had no means of communication at all, the remainder using gestures and signs. Similarly, articulation was poor in many of the children.

The summary above describes the findings on rubella-damaged children who were hearing impaired. This group can be further considered by contrasting those with bi-lateral cataracts with those lacking this additional impairment. Again, we will leave observations on stereotyped behaviour until later in this chapter. Ninety-five per cent of children with cataracts were found to be developmentally delayed. For children without cataracts, this figure was 20 per cent. Van Dijk summarises the findings further, noting that:

A rubella child with (removed) bi-lateral cataracts has been infected early in pregnancy and this has a prolonged influence on his physical and neurological development. The early behaviour of these children is governed by several types of stereotyped behaviour which have a negative influence on the child's interaction with his environment. The aetiology of these behaviour patterns can be seen as a combination of neurological, environmental and sensory deprivation factors. Because of these factors motor-, social and cognitive development is very delayed. The combination and mutual influence of all these variables results in a typical syndrome which is unique to the hearing impaired rubella child with bi-lateral cataracts. (p. 141)

While Van Dijk's study may not tease out the specific influences that lead to delayed development, it clearly shows the way in which damage to the central nervous system, the depriving consequences of sensory impairment and the impact of the child's behaviour on the environment interact to delay and distort the progress that we anticipate in the absence of these factors.

Brain Damage and Developmental Sequences

There is now evidence that the normal course of development in people who are profoundly retarded can be disrupted through underlying pathological conditions. Woodward (1959) found that 75 per cent of children whose manipulative behaviour lagged behind their ability to solve problems and their level of object permanence were also emotionally unstable and/or epileptic. Both Woodward (1959) and Wohlhueter and Sindberg (1975) comment on the variability of epileptic children across assessments and the absence of a constant upwards developmental progression. The latter observe that: 'The majority of the variable group were found to have EEG abnormalities, especially dysrhythmias or a history of seizures' (p. 516). Woodward (1959) herself links the variability to lethargy associated with nearness to onset of a fit or drug treatment rather than permanent loss of a developmental gain.

Woodward (1979) also comments on disruption to developmental consistency in different areas with a less obviously dramatic cause. She reports an unpublished study in which children with moderate to profound retardation not exhibiting severe disturbances were considered. She looked for the correspondence between problem-solving success and complexity of manipulative behaviour: 'None of 21 socially responsive children, who, for example, smiled readily, were discrepant, compared to 17 per cent of 53 slightly unresponsive ones, 47 per cent of 15 definitely unresponsive children, and 61 per cent of 23 withdrawn or distressed children' (p. 183). Woodward suggests that motivational factors may differ between these children with respect to engaging in the tasks in the two areas used for assessment. As she noted, this is of critical importance not only in making the assessment but also in how education proceeds. This introduces the concept of motivation into our consideration of development, and we shall return to this link in our next chapter.

The Development of Behaviour Disorders

As noted above, many people with profound retardation and multiple impairments will also exhibit behaviour problems. Unlike the foregoing account of the development of positive sensorimotor, motor and communicative behaviour, we lack any direct studies of the way in which such problems develop in this group. The best that we can do is to examine some of the suggested causes, noting at the outset that these may all contribute to the development of a behaviour problem in any given case.

Behaviour disorders should be viewed in the same ecological context as that described in Chapter 3, i.e. as the outcome of the interaction between the person and his or her environment. With respect to the person who is profoundly retarded and multiply impaired, these two elements, the developmental delay on the one hand, and the sensory or physical disabilities on the other, constitute two important elements that the individual brings to the situation that can lead to such interactions being distorted resulting in a behaviour problem. A third element may also make its contribution as recent research suggests the possibility that in some cases there is a biological disposition towards developing behaviour disorders.

The relation between early development and behavioural disorders is a particularly interesting one in the context of the present chapter for at least two reasons. First, many of the repetitive and stereotyped behaviours that we associate with some children who are profoundly retarded are not unlike the practice or mastery play and other sensorimotor interaction of the first year of life. Do they differ in function and character in this population? Second, if such behaviours are abnormal, what is their relation to the normal pattern of early development? Do they simply overlay it, or do they positively disrupt it?

Woodward (1959), whose innovatory Piagetian assessments we have referred to several times, also proposed the possibility that much of the activity of children who are profoundly retarded which is regarded as abnormal was simply the exercise of sensorimotor activity appropriate to their developmental age. Hand regard, that we have seen in Chapter 3 to be a scheme involved in the development of visually directed reaching at around 5 months of age, may look strange in a physically advanced person who is profoundly retarded because it is the persistence of an early infant behaviour, suggests Woodward. Similarly, hand movements acquired as appropriate schemes when holding an object, e.g. shaking a rattle, may persist over long periods of time and again appear incongruous. Resolution of the question of MA appropriate vs abnormal behaviour can only take place for a given person through careful developmental assessment of the kind we have described.

The developmental contribution can be further illustrated through two examples: one the prolongation of a normal infant behaviour as a result of the slow development noted above; the other through omission of a crucial stage of child development. The former example is taken from the literature on self-injurious behaviour (SIB) where the person hits, bites or otherwise damages himself or herself. Murphy (1985) summarises the hypothesis that certain forms of SIB such as head banging simply consistute a normal behaviour from infancy which is prolonged because of the slow pace of development, i.e. such behaviour is seen in many nonhandicapped infants and is unproblematical as it disappears as the child grows older. Given marked differences in the severity of 'normal' head banging and that seen in people who are retarded, Murphy herself is unconvinced by this argument.

The critical period argument may be taken from the literature on feeding problems. Jones (1982) suggests that a possible cause of eating disorders is the failure to introduce a child to solid food at the critical period at which he or she should be learning to chew, i.e. during the second half of the first year of life in nonhandicapped children. He cites studies indicating that failure to wean the child from a bottle or prolonged dependence on soft foods has frequently been a factor in the abnormal eating behaviour of children who are retarded. Again, specific ecological influences are suggested such as the reluctance of such children to accept a change from liquid foods and the unwillingness of parents and caregivers to cope with problems arising from this transition.

Superimposed on slow development are the many sensory and physical impairments present in this group. We have gone to some length earlier to show how these can affect development. Reference to Chapter 4 shows how the evolution of behaviour disorders has been investigated and some of the conclusions that have been drawn. Stereotyped behaviour, such as hand waving or body rocking, are associated with visual impairment. Van Dijk's work, described above, shows a strong association between holding the hands before the eyes and light gazing and the presence of bi-lateral cataracts in contrast to the behaviour of rubella-damaged children who do *not* have cataracts. It has been suggested that such activities may have a dual function, i.e. to increase stimulation when this is at a low level and to reduce stimulation if this is excessive. It was also pointed out that visual impairment in itself may not be the entire cause of such behaviour. The lack of mobility that can stem from lack of vision could in itself lead to behaviour disorders involving repetitive bodily movement. Given the high probability of visual impairment in people who are profoundly retarded (Chapter 1), then it is not surprising that they, like their peers who are not retarded, often exhibit stereotypic behaviour.

Similar arguments can be extended to the genesis of behaviour problems arising from physical impairment. We saw in Chapter 6 how both limited periods of immobility and more protracted immobilisation has consequences for the emotional and behavioural development of children who are otherwise not handicapped. The high probability of physical impairment among people with profound retardation will likewise dispose them to emotional and behavioural disorders.

While both visual and physical impairments can and do disrupt the development of communication, hearing impairment is the condition par excellence with this outcome. As we saw in Chapter 5, under some conditions deaf children will develop behaviour problems attributable to their problems of communication. Where there is profound retardation that in itself leads to slow development of communicative skills, the problem of additional hearing impairment will be exacerbated. Under such conditions attempts to communicate may be through inappropriate forms of behaviour that because of their disruptiveness do succeed in gaining attention.

In viewing a behaviour disorder as the outcome of an interaction between individual and environment, we are, of course, pointing to specific patterns of learning involving mechanisms such as reinforcement and punishment that will be more fully discussed in the next chapter. From this perspective, a behaviour problem is a learned behaviour and hence can be ameliorated through the application of these same processes in the context of behavioural programmes. Nevertheless, recent reviews suggest that a given behaviour problem may in different individuals have quite different causes. It may in one case be maintained by positive reinforcement as when attention seeking leads to social reinforcement, while in another, negative reinforcement may be the effective consequence, as when the behaviour leads to the termination of unwanted demands through a person withdrawing. Yet again, the reinforcement may be intrinsic to the person, as in the case of sensory reinforcement maintaining the behaviour. This state of affairs points to the needs for careful analysis of what is controlling undesirable behaviour in an individual, a topic dealt with in Chapter 2 of Volume 2.

We will also see in that chapter that behaviour modification programmes have been effective in many instances, thus supporting a learning-based view of behaviour disorders. The point has been made, however, that this only shows that the behaviour can be *unlearnt*. It does not conclusively prove that the original behaviour was acquired in the same way.

While brain abnormalities in people who are profoundly retarded and multiply impaired are associated with both their developmental delay *and* their additional impairments, it has also been suggested that certain specific aspects of brain dysfunction can dispose an individual to behaviour disorders. This suggestion comes from the fact that certain syndromes seem to be associated with specific forms of behaviour problems. The best documented of these is the association between SIB and Lesch-Nyhan's Syndrome (a sex-linked genetic disorder occurring in males and resulting in inability to metabolise the chemical purine as the result of an enzyme deficiency). Other characteristics described by Cataldo and Harris (1982) include mental handicap, writhing movements of the limbs (athetosis) and an excess of uric acid in the blood. Individuals with Lesch-Nyhan's Syndrome severely mutilate themselves by biting their fingers, tongue and lips. There have also been reports of head banging and eye gouging in those exhibiting the syndrome.

Several hypotheses have been advanced to account for the occurrence of SIB in those with Lesch-Nyhan's Syndrome. One is that the enzyme deficiency affects substances in the brain responsible for its normal functioning — specifically lowering the level of one of the substances responsible for neural transmission, serotin. Animal studies have shown that too low a level of serotin has been shown to increase aggressive behaviour. For the person with Lesch-Nyhan's Syndrome, retarded and physically handicapped as he will be, *self*-aggression will be the most readily available response. Administration of drugs increasing serotin level have been shown to produce a marked decrease in self-biting though this has only been short-lived. SIB in people with Lesch-Nyhan's Syndrome has also been shown to be influenced by the environment, pointing towards an interaction between biological factors, behaviour and the environment.

In their review Cataldo and Harris (1982) conclude that consideration of Lesch-Nyhan's Syndrome and others such as the Cornelia de Lange Syndrome, account only for a very small percentage of SIB in people who are retarded. In addition, specific brain mechanisms or processes responsible for SIB have not yet been identified.

Conclusion

The movement towards viewing even the most impaired of people within the framework of development derived from nonimpaired children seems amply justified. Not only can they be assessed within the framework, but in many respects these people show a remarkably similar, though extremely prolonged, pattern of development to their nonimpaired peers. Additional sensory and physical impairments in the people who are profoundly retarded also appear to have similar effects as on nonretarded children, though here we have only very limited evidence to go on. It is also clear, however, that extensive brain damage, epilepsy and failures of social development can disrupt sequences of development and may preclude further advances in a given area. This state of affairs, however, should not be seen as a limitation to the applicability of the developmental frame of reference, but a pointer to psychological, social or medical remediation that places the child more firmly within the context.

References

Bates, E. (1976) *Language and Context: The Acquisition of Pragmatics*, Academic Press, London

Bruner, J.S. (1975a) 'From Communication to Language: A Psychological Perspective', *Cognition, 3*, 255–87

Bruner, J.S. (1975b) 'The Ontogenesis of Speech Acts', *Journal of Child Language, 2*, 1–19

Capuzzi, L.E. (1979) 'Communication and Cognition in the Institutionalized Profoundly Retarded', unpublished doctorial dissertation, Temple University, Philadelphia

Cataldo, M.F. and Harris, J. (1982) 'The Biological Basis for Self-Injury', *Analysis and Intervention in Developmental Disabilities, 2*, 21–39

Corman, H.H. and Escalona, S.K. (1969) 'Stages of Sensorimotor Development: A Replication Study', *Merrill-Palmer Quarterly, 15*, 351–61

Cyrulik-Jacobs, A., Shapira, Y. and Jones, M. (1975) 'Automatic Operant Response Procedure (Play Test) for the Study of Auditory Perception of Neurologically Impaired Infants', *Developmental Medicine and Child Neurology, 17*, 186–97

Dunst, C.J., Brassell, W.R. and Rheingrover, R.M. (1981) 'Structural and Organisational Features of Sensorimotor Intelligence among Retarded Infants and Toddlers', *British Journal of Educational Psychology, 51*, 133–43

Dunst, C.J. and Rheingrover, R.M. (1983) 'Structural Characteristics of Sensorimotor Development among Down's Syndrome Infants', *Journal of Mental Deficiency Research, 27*, 11–22

Fisher, M.A. and Zeaman, D. (1970) 'Growth and Decline of Retardate Intelligence' in N.R. Ellis (ed.), *International Review of Research in Mental Retardation: Vol. 4*, Academic Press, London

Fraiberg, S. (1968) 'Parallel and Divergent Patterns in Blind and Sighted Infants', *Psychoanalytic Study of the Child, 23*, 264–300

Friedlander, B.Z. (1968) 'Effect of Speaker Identity, Voice Inflection, Vocabulary, and Message Redundancy of Infants' Selection of Vocal Reinforcement', *Journal of Experimental Child Psychology, 6*, 443–59

Glenn, S.M. and Cunningham, C.C. (1984) 'Selective Auditory Preference and the Use of Automated Equipment by Severely and Profoundly Multiply Handicapped Children', *Journal of Mental Deficiency Research, 28,* 281–96

Gouin Décarie, T. (1969) 'A Study of Mental and Emotional Development of the Thalidomide Child' in B.M. Foss (ed.), *Determinants of Infant Behaviour: Vol. 4,* Methuen, London

Jones, T.W. (1982) 'Treatment of Behavior-related Eating Problems in Retarded Students: A Review of the Literature' in J.H. Hollis and C.E. Meyers (eds.), *Life-threatening Behavior: Analysis and Intervention,* Monograph of the American Association of Mental Deficiency, No. 5, American Association on Mental Deficiency, Washington, D.C.

Kahn, J.V. (1975) 'Relationship of Piaget's Sensorimotor Period to Language Acquisition of Profoundly Retarded Children', *American Journal of Mental Deficiency, 79,* 640–3

Kahn, J.V. (1983) 'Sensorimotor Period and Adaptive Behavior Development of Severely and Profoundly Mentally Retarded Children', *American Journal of Mental Deficiency, 88,* 69–75

Kiernan, C. and Reid, B. (1983) 'Pre-verbal Communication Schedule (PVC) Manual', 2nd edn, unpublished but manuscript available, Thomas Coram Research Unit, London

Lowe, M. (1975) 'Trends in the Development of Representational Play', *Journal of Child Psychology and Psychiatry, 16,* 33–47

McCune-Nicholich, L. and Hill, P. (1981) 'A Comparison of Psychometric and Piagetian Assessments of Symbolic Functioning in Down's Syndrome Children' in M.P. Friedman, J.P. Das and N. O'Connor (eds.), *Intelligence and Learning: NATO Conference Series III: Human Factors, Vol. 14,* Plenum, London

MacPherson, F.D. and Butterworth, G.E. (1981) 'Application of a Piagetian Infant Development Scale to the Assessment of Profound Mentally Handicapped Children', paper presented to the Annual Conference, Developmental Psychology Section, British Psychological Society, Manchester, September 1981

Murphy, G. (1985) 'Self-injurious Behaviour in the Mentally Handicapped: An Update', *Association for Child Psychology and Psychiatry Newsletter, 7,* 2–11

Nicholich, L.M. (1977) 'Beyond Sensorimotor Intelligence: Assessment of Symbolic Maturity through Analysis of Pretend Play', *Merrill-Palmer Quarterly, 23,* 89–101

Riguet, C.B., Taylor, N.D., Benaroya, S. and Klein, L.S. (1981) 'Symbolic Play in Autistic, Down's and Normal Children of Equivalent Mental Age', *Journal of Autism and Developmental Disorders, 11,* 439–48

Rogers, S.J. (1977) 'Characteristics of Cognitive Development of Profoundly Retarded Children', *Child Development, 48,* 837–43

Shapiro, B., Accardo, P. and Capute, A. (1979) 'Factors Affecting Walking in a Profoundly Retarded Population', *Developmental Medicine and Child Neurology, 21,* 369–73

Shere, E. and Kastenbaum, R. (1966) 'Mother-child Interaction in Cerebral Palsy: Environmental and Psychosocial Obstacles to Cognitive Development', *Genetic Psychology Monographs, 73,* 255–335

Silverstein, A.B. (1979) 'Mental Growth from Six to Sixty in Institutionalized Mentally Retarded Sample', *Psychological Reports, 45,* 643–6

Silverstein, A.B., Brownlee, L., Hubbell, M. and McLain, R.E. (1981) 'Stability of Two Piagetian Scales with Severely and Profoundly Retarded Children', *Educational and Psychological Measurement, 41*, 263–5

Silverstein, A.B., Pearson, L.B., Colbert, B.A., Cordeiro, W.J., Marwin, J.L. and Nakaji, M.J. (1982) 'Cognitive Development of Severely and Profoundly Mentally Retarded Individuals', *American Journal of Mental Deficiency, 87*, 347–50

Smith, B. and Philips, C.J. (1981) 'Age-related Progress among Children with Severe Learning Difficulties', *Developmental Medicine and Child Neurology, 23*, 465–76

Van Dijk, J. (1982) *Rubella Handicapped Children: The Effects of Bi-lateral Cataract and/or Hearing Impairment on Behaviour and Learning*, Swets and Zeitlinger, BV

Wachs, T.D. and DeRemer, P. (1978) 'Adaptive Behavior and Uzgiris-Hunt Scale Performance of Young Developmentally Delayed Children', *American Journal of Mental Deficiency, 83*, 171–6

Warburg, M. (1983) 'Why are Blind and Severely Visually Impaired Children with Mental Retardation much more Retarded than the Sighted Children?', *Acta Ophthalmologica, Supplement, 157*, 72–81

Wedell, K., Newman, C.V., Reid, P. and Bradbury, I.R. (1972) 'An Exploratory Study of the Relationship between Size Constancy and Experience of Mobility in Cerebral Palsied Children', *Developmental Medicine and Child Neurology, 14*, 615–20

Weisz, J.R. and Zigler, E. (1979) 'Cognitive Development in Retarded and Nonretarded Persons: Piagetian Tests of the Similar Sequence Hypothesis', *Psychological Bulletin, 86*, 831–51

Whittacker, C.A. (1980) 'A Note on Developmental Trends in the Symbolic Play of Hospitalized Profoundly Retarded Children', *Journal of Child Psychology and Psychiatry, 21*, 253–61

Wilkins, L.E., Brown, J.A. and Wolf, B. (1980) 'Psychomotor Development in 65 Home-reared Children with *Cri-du-Chat* Syndrome', *Journal of Pediatrics, 97*, 401–5

Wing, L., Gould, J., Yeates, S.R. and Brierly, L.M. (1973) 'Symbolic Play in Severely Mentally Retarded and in Autistic Children', *Journal of Child Psychology and Psychiatry, 18*, 167–78

Wohlhueter, M.J. and Sindberg, R.M. (1975) 'Longitudinal Development of Object Permanence in Mentally Retarded Children: An Exploratory Study', *American Journal of Mental Deficiency, 79*, 513–18

Woodward, W.M. (1959) 'The Behaviour of Idiots Interpreted by Piaget's Theory of Sensorimotor Development', *British Journal of Educational Psychology, 29*, 60–71

Woodward, M.W. (1979) 'Piaget's Theory and the Study of Mental Retardation' in N.R. Ellis (ed.), *Handbook of Mental Deficiency Research*, 2nd edn, Lawrence Erlbaum, Hillsdale, N.J.

Woodward, M.W. and Stern, D.J. (1963) 'Developmental Patterns of Severely Subnormal Children', *British Journal of Educational Psychology, 33*, 10–21

9 DEVELOPMENT AND LEARNING

General Introduction

In the preceding chapters we have emphasised various concepts involved in theories of child development and their relevance to an understanding of people who are profoundly retarded and multiply impaired. Only in passing have such terms as 'generalisation' and 'reinforcement' been used, words we associate with many of the teaching techniques that have become increasingly applied in special education classrooms and training settings. These concepts are rarely employed in child development studies as they originate from a distinctly different tradition of psychology, namely learning theory.

In the present chapter we shall look first at some of the general features and concepts of learning theory that *have* been applied to an understanding of child development in general and to retarded development in particular. We shall then review some of the studies that have been undertaken within such a framework with those who are profoundly retarded and multiply impaired. Finally, we shall consider why learning-based approaches have so rarely been adopted in the type of developmental theory we have summarised in Chapter 3, and suggest that the total separation of developmental theory and learning-based accounts is (i) probably theoretically unnecessary, and (ii) can stand in the way of developing educational programmes in special education.

Learning-based Approaches to Retardation

In 1966 Bijou published a general account of such an approach entitled 'A Functional Analysis of Retarded Development'. He began this account by anticipating the present reaction against use of the term 'mental', as in *mental* handicap or *mental* retardation, and suggested instead that it would be more appropriate to adopt a behavioural term, i.e. developmental retardation. Developmental retardation, he suggests, should be considered as a delay arising not from hypothetical concepts such as 'defective intelligence' or 'clinically inferred brain damage', but from the point of view that '. . . a retarded individual is one who has a limited repertoire of behavior shaped by events that constitute his history' (p. 2).

As implied in this statement, the underlying view is that development is regarded as the outcome of the interaction between a person and his or her environment. This interaction can be described with a range of concepts derived from learning theory in which the person's observable responses are seen to be the outcome of specific stimulus conditions that precede and follow a behaviour, and the influence of the behaviour on the environment itself.

> For the so-called normal individual the succession of effective environmental events in development are more or less typical for his culture. The opportunities for him to interact with social and physical events have been within normal limits; his biological structure and physiological functioning are adequate and are maturing at the usual rates. For the retarded individual social, physical and biological conditions of development deviate in the direction of slowing down the pace of successive interactional exchanges — the more extreme the curtailments, the more extreme the retardation. (p. 2)

It will be seen that Bijou's view does not deny the influence of biological damage that is found with profound retardation, still less with the effect of the additional sensory and physical impairments associated with the condition. What he does argue is that we analyse how specific aspects of such impairment influence the individual's interaction with his or her own environment and lead to delayed development. The approach to determining what is happening in these interactions is referred to as 'functional analysis'. At its simplest this entails analysis of the stimulus conditions under which a behaviour develops and is maintained and the relation between these conditions, the behaviour and its consequences. Two types of learning may be considered when undertaking a functional analysis. Since the studies involving people who are profoundly retarded which we describe later involve both types, we will briefly describe them here before adding a little more of Bijou's account of the functional analysis of retarded development.

Respondent learning, also called classical or Pavlovian conditioning, builds ultimately upon reflexive or involuntary responses. At its simplest, respondent conditioning is based on an event known as the unconditioned stimulus (US) which elicits an unconditioned response (UR). For example, stimulation from the nipple or a feeding bottle will elicit sucking in a young infant, the touch of the nipple being the unconditioned stimulus leading to the unconditional response of sucking. In time, a variety of other stimuli present immediately before and during contact with the nipple come to elicit sucking. A situation such as this, i.e. the natural feeding context, is simplified in experimental studies. Here the initially neutral stimulus is usually some clear event like the sound of a buzzer for one second before placing the feeding bottle nipple in the infant's mouth, this tone continuing for several seconds afterwards. This neutral event, the buzzer, is referred to as the conditioned stimulus (CS). After several pairings the child will come to suck on hearing the conditioned stimulus in the absence of contact with the nipple. This is referred to as the conditioned response (CR). Outside the laboratory there may be a whole host of conditioned responses in the one situation. Thus, proprioceptive feedback, i.e. the infant's bodily sensation of position and movement in space, tactile stimulation from the adult's hold and various odours may all come to function as conditioned stimuli. A variety of other conditioned responses in addition to sucking have also been studied in young infant's including some specific reflexes (e.g. the Babkin reflex, unconditioned mouth opening in response to pressure on the palm), respiration, heart rate, motility, head turning and eye movements (Siqueland 1970). We can assume that these and other conditionable responses provide part of the foundations on which instrumental learning can build.

Instrumental conditioning, also referred to as operant or voluntary learning, is in contrast not dependent upon a stimulus *eliciting* a response, i.e. the US-UR relation, but on a response by the organism producing a consequence which in turn alters the future probability of that response. If that probability increases, then the consequence is regarded as reinforcing. If the consequence involves a specific event that leads to a lowering of the probability of future occurrence of the response, then that consequence is technically known as punishment. We will return to this definition when we consider behaviour disorders in Chapter 7 of Volume 2. If a piece of behaviour has been learnt and maintained by positive reinforcement which is then withdrawn, the behaviour will decline or *extinguish*. Note, in contrast to behaviour declining when it is punished, in the case of extinction there is no specific event or consequence of the behaviour, only the absence of previously occurring reinforcement.

An instrumental response and its consequence do not take place in a vacuum. The response will occur to observable stimuli sometimes referred to as 'discriminant stimuli'. This antecedent-behaviour-consequence chain conveniently gives the A-B-C pattern of instrumental responding. We shall describe more fully the nature of antecedent and consequent events in instrumental learning in the context of both studies dealt with later in this chapter and where relevant in our discussion of intervention in Volume 2. When developed as a model of teaching and training the attempt to establish a given A-B-C event has led to numerous additional training techniques and again these are defined or described where relevant.

To return, then, to the issue of functional analysis, this approach is concerned with accounting for changes in behaviour through an analysis of the stimuli and responses determining the behaviour and by employing the concepts of respondent and instrumental learning. We can functionally analyse any given piece of behaviour whether occurring spontaneously or as the product of a specific teaching intervention. Indeed these two approaches often follow each other when we observe a piece of behaviour and try to alter it. Functional analysis can also be applied to developmental changes of the kind described in Chapter 3, Bijou (1976) having reinterpreted much of developmental psychology from a learning theory viewpoint. For an example of short-term functional analysis, the reader is referred to Iwata, Dorsey, Slifer, Bauman and Richman's (1982) analysis of the factors influencing self-injurious behaviour by people with profound retardation which we describe fully in Chapter 7 of Volume 2.

An extension to developmental effects is clearly more complex than such short-term analyses, but Bijou and Baer (1966) have argued that:

> The concepts of operant and respondent conditioning can be more than mere operational handles on which to hang environmentally controlled behaviour. Owing to their number and scope, they can yield an account of the development of the human child's motor, perceptual, linguistic, intellectual, emotional, social and motivational repertoires. (p. 720)

With this observation of the functional analysis of non-retarded development, we can return to Bijou's (1966) account of the functional analysis of retarded behaviour.

Bijou goes on to describe very general influences that might retard development on the basis of more general information from other studies. Thus, he points first to the variety of studies on institutional rearing of children in which developmental delay is subsequently found. This he explains in part as the result of lean, or inconsistent, reinforcement of the child, particularly with reference to speech and social stimuli. Second, he notes how withholding of reinforcement (extinction) or non-contingent reinforcement (i.e. reinforcement not consequent on a specific behaviour) might restrict exploratory activities. Third, physical restrictions may decrease the opportunity for a child to produce responses that can be reinforced. In this category, too, would be physical restriction of the child, again leading to an absence of the production of reinforcible responses. Fourth, he notes how inconsistent or too severe punishment might serve to distort or prevent development. Fifth, it is possible that the appearance of a child, or his or her behaviour, might produce such negative responses in others that interactions are curtailed and the opportunity for learning limited.

Bijou's account gives a general picture of the influences that may retard development rather than a detailed account of how such factors influence development in children identifiably at risk for delayed development such as those with Down's Syndrome or neurologically identified brain damage. Between these two extremes are true functional analyses of retarded behaviour in which we can observe changes in behaviour over relatively limited periods of time, usually in intervention studies. Consideration of these is left until the relevant chapters in Volume 2.

The distinction that we have drawn between respondent and instrumental learning has been one that has not readily been accepted by all learning theorists. However, recent analyses of what occurs in learning situations have led to the conclusion that the distinction is a valid one and that two different learning processes do exist (Mackintosh 1983 Chapter 2). Mackintosh points out, however, that in any given learning situation, both types of learning process may occur and interact. If we return to our baby feeding, then while the initial elicitation of sucking may be to an unconditioned stimulus (the nipple) leading to sucking being elicited, i.e. respondent learning, the sucking response will gradually be produced voluntarily and reinforced by the consequence of milk in the mouth, i.e. instrumental learning. This instrumental response will be more efficient and economical, enabling the baby to control the flow of milk into the mouth. In reality, the situation will be even more complex because a number of stimuli will be present, i.e. proprioceptive, visual, possibly auditory stimuli, and a number of behaviours will co-occur, some under respondent and some under instrumental control, e.g. sucking, postural adjustments, vocalising.

The study of such interactions between processes has increased in recent years, though extension of such work to retarded people is generally lacking. We can only point to one study in which an attempt has been made to link respondent and instrumental learning in children who are profoundly retarded and we describe this below. Mackintosh makes two further points regarding the two types of learning that should be noted here. First, he suggests that Skinner, the founding father of operant psychology, had overemphasised the importance of instrumental learning at the expense of respondent learning. It may be seen from the simple example of breast feeding given above that both might be critical in the development of learned behaviour in the developmentally immature child. Second, any given response might be respondent or instrumental. Again, in the example of a baby sucking, this behaviour might be respondent or instrumental depending on the kind of learning involved. Nevertheless, it is equally the case that at one extreme there will be responses that are essentially respondent and at the other those that are essentially instrumental.

In general, it has proved quite feasible to extend the study of these learning processes to more able people who are retarded, i.e. those with severe or moderate retardation (Hogg 1976), or to put it another way, these basic learning processes appear to operate in a similar way with most retarded people as they do with individuals who are not retarded. What, then, of the way in which such processes function in people who are profoundly retarded and multiply impaired?

Learning Processes in People who are Profoundly Retarded

Respondent Learning

Unfortunately there is only very limited evidence on this topic. Franks (1964) notes that in large measure both respondent learning and extinction follow a broadly similar course in individuals who are retarded and *without* evidence of neurological damage. Where this is present, however, respondent learning is impaired, and when it comes to people who are profoundly retarded Franks pessimistically observes: 'There is apparently fair agreement that congenital idiots form conditioned responses with great difficulty if at all' (p. 156). In a later study, Hogg, Remington and Foxen (1979) attempted to condition an eye blink to a tone in five children who were profoundly retarded and multiply impaired. Here they were a little more successful. All five children were brain damaged, three of them being hydrocephalic, two with valves fitted and one without. One child was described as microcephalic and one was undiagnosed. Over several sessions, a tone was paired with a puff of air to the eye and then the extent to which the tone alone elicited eye blinking evaluated. An extinction phase was also employed in which the pairing of CS and US was terminated. The children were between 4 and 9 years of age with global developmental ages of 22, 4, 2, 2, and 0 *weeks* as assessed on the Bayley Scale of Mental Development. For the first two children, i.e. the most advanced developmentally, a normal pattern of conditioning was noted and clear extinction of the response observed for the first child. Both children were hydrocephalic, one with a valve and one without. The three remaining children did not show evidence of respondent learning.

In this study the authors suggested that care should be taken before concluding that the child who failed to learn a CR are described as 'unconditionable'. It is possible that a CS other than a tone, or different responses other than an eye blink, might lead us to conclude that other respondent learning associations can be formed. Nevertheless, given how basic eye blink conditioning is, and how readily it can be achieved even in individuals who are severely retarded (Hardwick and Lobb 1982), and bearing in mind Franks's observation, it must remain a possibility that perhaps for some people who are among the most profoundly retarded and multiply impaired, respondent learning is not possible.

Instrumental Learning

The literature is more substantial with respect to instrumental learning in individuals who are profoundly retarded. In considering this work, we will enter into some detail for two reasons. First, some of the basic concepts of operant psychology that are useful in work with this group can meaningfully be illustrated through a description of these studies. For example, different reinforcement schedules and their effects can be considered without entering into an unrelated technical account of all types of schedule. Second, at the level of functioning with which we are concerned there is no clear-cut dividing line between the experimental studies we describe and the early phases of a curriculum for people who are multiply impaired. The success of some of these studies has given encouragement to both teachers and psychologists in their work and we shall return to this work in Chapter 3 of Volume 2 where we discuss intervention and early cognitive development.

Any account of instrumental learning in individuals who are profoundly retarded and multiply impaired inevitably begins with a report by Fuller (1949), the first systematic attempt to study learning in this ability range. His brief note with the unfortunate title of 'Operant Conditioning of a Vegetative Human Organism' described his work with an 18 year old male in an institution. The description will be familiar to all those who work with such people. The young man lay on his back and could not roll over. He could open his mouth, blink and move his arms, head and shoulder to a limited extent. He was never seen to move his trunk or legs. Occasionally he vocalised. Using a sugar milk solution as a reinforcer, Fuller demonstrated operant conditioning of arm raising. The target behaviour, that is, the final teaching objective, was movement of the right arm to a nearly vertical position. Only this response was reinforced, movements not reaching the criterion for the target behaviour and more generalised attempts to lift head and arms not being reinforced. When the target behaviour was achieved, no more sugar-milk was given. The rate at which the behaviour declined and eventually returned to its original level, i.e. withdrawal of the reinforcer led to extinction of the learned behaviour.

Though Fuller's demonstration was successful, Piper and MacKinnon (1969) employed a more progressive approach with a similar young person. Here a girl of 15 years of age was also taught to raise her arm. She was '. . . able to move all four limbs as well as move her head from side to side. Vertical movements of the limbs were infrequent and she did not lift her head'. The reinforcement was again a fluid but this time delivered via a cannula through a stomach fistula. In contrast to Fuller's approach, a full arm movement was not required for reinforcement to occur in the first stages. Here lesser movements were reinforced, i.e. the technique of *successive approximations*:

Step 1.   She was reinforced whenever she raised her entire forearm more than two inches.

Step 2.   She was reinforced whenever she raised her entire arm and whenever forearm raises approximately to a vertical position.

Step 3.   She was reinforced whenever she raised her entire arm. Vertical raises of the forearm were reinforced at a progressively smaller probability as Step 3 progressed.

Step 4.   Only raises of the entire arm were reinforced.

Step 5.   She was reinforced whenever she raised her entire arm four inches or more.

Step 6.   She was reinforced whenever she raised her entire arm eight inches or more. (p. 628)

The criterion or target behaviour was that Step 6 behaviour should occur on 16 occasions within a 30-minute period of three consecutive days.

Piper and MacKinnon show how through the shaping procedure of successive approximations the height of the arm raise increased during the period of learning and how Step 4 behaviour was reached after 15 days and subsequently shaped up through Step 5 to criterion. They also describe a loss of learning that will be familiar to those working with individuals who are profoundly retarded and multiply impaired. On the fifth day of Step 5 the girl became ill and began to lose the learned response. On recovery, however, this was re-established after a further three days of learning. An event such as illness constitutes a 'setting condition', i.e. a condition that affects a wide range of learned responses. Tiredness or fatigue constitute other familiar setting conditions that can affect behaviour in this way.

Between these two important demonstrations of learning capabilities in people who are profoundly retarded and multiply impaired came a series of studies by Rice and his colleagues. While Fuller's and Piper and MacKinnon's studies showed normal operant learning using food as reinforcement, Rice and McDaniel (1966) first drew attention to the lack of effectiveness of food for some people with profound retardation and the occurrence of what they refer to as 'spontaneous extinction'. This led them to comment that: 'The population proves to be an abnormal one in an operant sense' (Rice, McDaniel, Stallings and Gatz 1967 p. 449). In this paper they studied two children of CA 6 years and MA about 6 months. The first child was profoundly retarded as the result of a metabolic defect but had neuromuscular impairment. The second was also profoundly retarded and spastic as a result of prolonged perinatal anoxia. A variety of reinforcers were employed but the main choice for the first child fell on moving pictures available as a consequence of pulling a ring. The inital operant level was nil and shaping through successive approximations was employed. As in Fuller's study, an excess of movement was at first noted, but this became more refined as a discrete downwards pull on the ring occurred. While a variety of films acted as reinforcers (including *The Adventures of Captain Grief*!), the effective aspect of the films could not be determined. They could be shown backwards or forwards or sound and vision could be desynchronised. Only when classical music was substituted for the sound track did any change in response occur. The child '. . . threw away the ring and pitched a tantrum which lasted for several minutes' (p. 454). However, far from reflecting any lack of good taste, this appeared to be a reaction to novelty that did not occur in subsequent sessions.

A high level of responding was also established for ring pulls that led to presentation of slide pictures. Clear preferences were noted for Venus de Milo over Diane the Huntress and scenes from the Yellowstone National Park got short shrift. However, responding to the slides declined and was only reinstated when moving pictures were reintroduced.

For the first child then, many features of instrumental learning were observed. The second child, physically as well as intellectually impaired, only had to touch the ring to be reinforced. This was achieved idiosyncratically with him lying prone on the bed and reaching backwards and touching the ring with his elbow or upper arm. Following an extensive search for reinforcers, ice cream was chosen. Initially all responses were reinforced, i.e. continuous reinforcement was employed (CRF Schedule). Later, every third response was reinforced, i.e. a Fixed Ratio 3 (FR3) Schedule. This initially produced a decrease in responding but subsequently a transition to reinforcing every fifteenth response was successfully made (Fixed Ratio 15 — FR15). Extreme variations in the rate of responding, i.e. the number of responses per minute, were noted and long gaps between responses (inter response times or IRTs) of up to 10 minutes were observed. It is suggested that these may result from bouts of *petit-mal* disrupting responding, a link to Woodward's (1979) suggestion regarding the disrupting effect of epilepsy on development. After 96 sessions in a seven-month period, responding began to decline. It might be thought that this resulted from satiation, i.e. excessive exposure to the reinforcer. If this were the case, then introduction of a novel reinforcer would be expected to re-establish responding. This was not the case and Rice *et al.* regard this as a demonstration of spontaneous extinction.

In a third and final paper, Rice (1968) observes that in a variety of respects some people who are profoundly retarded and multiply impaired are 'operantly abnormal'. Such abnormality can be quantitative or qualitative. Thus the problem of finding reinforcers and long IRTs differentiate those who are profoundly impaired from more able individuals, but responding does still occur under reinforcement control. Spontaneous extinction, however, is seen as a qualitative difference not observable in more able people. However, Rice's scientific analysis inevitably spills over into considerations that show the educational implications of even 'simple' instrumental learning in these people. Despite the difficulties Rice reports, he suggests the axiom 'Does not is not equal to cannot' (Rice 1968 p. 300). As shown in our discussion of respondent learning, it is never possible to determine finally that a child is inherently unreinforcible and incapable of instrumental learning.

There is also a limit to how far Rice's observations can be generalised across the whole range of people who are profoundly retarded and multiply impaired. Remington, Foxen and Hogg (1977), for example, did not find spontaneous extinction in any of the three out of four children (all profoundly retarded and multiply impaired) who learnt a simple operant response of moving a suspended ball in any direction in order to receive auditory reinforcement. A fourth child, however, failed to learn the response though no alternative reinforcers were employed. The actual reinforcers were:

(i) nursery rhymes, spoken and sung;
(ii) Central American drum music;
(iii) country blues.

Once responding was established on CRF, it was possible, as in Rice's work with visual reinforcers, to move on to FR schedules. In the present case some deterioration in responding was noted when this was done. Using this technique it was also possible to evaluate the children's preference by alternating two different reinforcers for periods of time and establishing whether one produced a higher rate of responding than the other. For the fourth child, however, it was not found possible to establish the simple instrumental response with the use of any of these auditory reinforcers.

Haskett and Hollar (1978) studied the reinforcing effect of both music and illumination on operant learning in four children who were profoundly retarded and physically impaired. While the CAs of these young people varied from 9:6 to 17:5 years, none had an MA in excess of 6.5 months or an IQ greater than 10. Operant learning was readily established in all four children. Haskett and Hollar tested out the children's ability to discriminate whether the reinforcement was resulting from their own behaviour. Thus, they compared responding when reinforcement occurred as a result of the child's response and when it was given in a way that was unrelated to his or her responding. In the latter situation responding decreased for three of the children, showing the child did discriminate the two conditions. These authors also looked at what may be felt to be an omission in operant studies of this kind, i.e. the emotional and other behaviours shown during the learning sessions. They also measured vocalising, stereotyped behaviour and smiling. Though there was no rigid association between these collateral behaviours and the learning conditions, links were found. For example, two children smiled when the various conditions changed from one to another, an effect they describe as 'contingency recognition'.

Lever pressing was also employed by Bailey and Meyerson (1969) with a 7 year old child who was profoundly retarded, nonambulant, blind and partially deaf, also lacking speech and self-help skills. Here vibration was employed as a reinforcer. From a low rate of responding when lever pressing did not produce reinforcement (baseline assessment), responding rose when reinforcement was available to 1,000 plus

responses per day, with a range of 700–2,000. When reinforcement wa
withdrawn, responding extinguished.

There is, of course, no reason why the instrumental response shoul
be restricted to movement of the upper limbs, though the adaptive conse
quences of teaching a person to interact with the world through han
use are obvious. However, with multiple impairments the developmen
of other bodily movements can also be of adaptive value as we shall se
in Chapter 3 of Volume 2 on intervention. Hill (1980) describes a stud
in which head control as well as arm movements were reinforced in
child who was nonambulant and multiply impaired. Contingent reinforce
ment consisted of presentation of cartoons. This occured when the chil
held his head up and maintained downward pressure with his arms o
a lever. As a consequence he exhibited increasing head control and
high rate of level pressing. It is interesting to note in this study that raisin
the head is a natural response with respect to observing the cartoon. Thi
point was also made in study by Hogg (1983) in which head turning wa
reinforced in a boy who had spastic quadriplegia and was profoundl
retarded (CA 9:7 years, highest mental item passed 2.6 months, highes
motor item 0.1 month). A variety of social and sensory reinforcers wer
employed but only visual reinforcement, the natural outcome of hea
turning, was effective. This study will be described in more detail i
Chapter 3 of Volume 2 where we discuss teaching of simple responses

A study of an even more basic response, blinking, is reported b
Brownfield and Keehn (1966) and illustrates the point made earlier tha
many behaviours may develop through either respondent or instrumenta
conditioning. Here two children who were profoundly retarded and wit
trisomy-18 (CA 4:11 and 2:8 years respectively, both IQs = 10) wer
studied. Blinking was reinforced with food on a CRF schedule
Significant increases in blinking were established and extinction occurre
when food was withdrawn.

In the studies described so far we have seen a range of reinforcer
employed, from food to sensory experiences of visual, auditory or tactil
nature. Lovett (1986) adopted a novel approach to establishing whethe
four children with profound retardation and multiple impairments coul
discriminate the conditions under which availability of reinforcemen
could be discriminated. In CA these children ranged from 6:9 to 13:
years with MAs between 2.0 and 3.5 months. The apparatus was
modified go-cart powered by battery and microelectronically operated
When an ultrasonic sound beam emitted across the car was broken, th
car would move on a predetermined circular course or follow a prelai
line on the floor.

The children, all of whom were physically impaired, were strapped in the car. By raising an arm or a leg, the beam was broken and the car put into motion for 10 seconds. Lovett shows that movement was an effective reinforcer leading the children reliably to break the beam and operate the car. By playing music when reinforcement was available, i.e. when breaking of the beam would result in movement, but not playing music when the same would fail to move the car, then reversing this state of affairs (no music=reinforcement available; music=no reinforcement available), Lovett showed the children could learn to discriminate when reinforcement was and was not available. He showed that children with profound retardation and multiple impairments can make discriminations regarding availability of reinforcement at a developmental age below 3 months. The study is also important in showing the potential of the new microelectronics in teaching this particular group of people with profound retardation.

A further step in increasing the complexity of the conditions with which people have to cope in an operant learning situation is to associate the availability of reinforcement with objects with different stimulus characteristics. These differences may relate to the spatial position of the objects, or to some feature of them such as colour, texture, size, shape or smell. Glenn and Cunningham (1984) employed both situations using Friedlander's (1968) PLAYTEST with children who were profoundly retarded and multiply impaired (see also Cyrulik-Jacobs, Shapira and Jones 1975; Friedlander, McCarthy and Soforenko 1967; Friedlander, Wetstone and McPeek 1974). The details of this study were given in the preceding chapter, but we will re-examine it here from the standpoint of the increasing complexity of learning in children who are profoundly retarded as they develop through the sensorimotor period.

The first child considered by Glenn and Cunningham was CA 8:4 years and MA 4.5, with athetoid cerebral palsy. A second child was CA 4:9 years and MA 4.5 months, similarly physically impaired. A third child (CA 3:0 years, MA3 months) was blind and retarded from prenatal viral infection. In the choice situation no child showed any preference between selected pairs of auditory stimuli nor between nursery rhymes vs no auditory stimulus. The first and second child, however, showed strong position biases, responding to left or right consistently. The authors comment that the children were, therefore, not aware that responses to the two boxes produced different feedback. The boxes were, therefore, made discriminably different, red and yellow vs brown and white stripe and green. The first child did then show a consistent preference. (The second was not tested because of illness.) Two further children did show

consistent preferences without the additional visual cues. One child wa
CA 3:2 years and MA 8.0 months with arhinencephaly, and the secon
was 2:1 years and MA 9.5 months, damaged by neonatal meningitis
The first two children described had shown high rates of simpl
instrumental responding but did not show differentiated responding i
the uncued two-choice situation. The second two children did demonstrat
discriminated responding and a developmental explanation is offered
Only at 8 to 9 months developmental age does discriminated respondin
begin to emerge, a finding in line with other work on both more abl
retarded children and nonretarded children. To establish further whethe
developmental level *per se* was the best predictor of discriminate
preference and that profound impairment in itself was not a bar to thi
behaviour, four more children with profound retardation and additiona
impairments were considered. One of these had spastic diplegia wit
scoliosis (CA 12:3 years and MA 6.0 months); one had Fahr's Syndrom
(CA 5:3 years and MA 20.0 months); a third was damaged throug
trauma and was partially sighted (CA 8:9 years and MA 16 months)
while a fourth had been damaged through neonatal meningitis and wa
blind (CA 7:6 years and MA 5.5 months). A fifth was CA 11:3 year
and developmental assessment was not possible. The first four childre
showed a preference for an auditory stimulus vs no auditory stimulu
and between certain contrasted auditory stimuli, thus showing th
relevance of development level to discriminated performance. The fift
child, in contrast, did not show prolonged responding to the equipmen
or preferential responding.

A third study broadly confirmed the results of the first two phase
of the investigation and also provided confirmation of Rice's finding o
long inter-response intervals. Again, for children not initially showin
consistent choice, enhancing the visual discriminability between the boxe
enabled the children to demonstrate preference.

Glenn and Cunningham's study points to two important features relate
to developmental trends in instrumental responding and sensorimoto
development. First, there is a developmental progression from 'simple
instrumental responding around 3 months to responding on the basis o
discriminant stimuli such as colour, pattern, etc., through to 'true' spatia
discrimination at around 9 months. Second, that though their procedur
was concerned with auditory preferences, it could in a sense be turne
round and used to teach spatial concepts by shaping the child to respon
on the basis of spatial information. Again, we will take this point u
when we consider intervention to increase sensorimotor teaching i
Chapter 3 of Volume 2.

It is clearly desirable to go beyond consideration of simple respondent and instrumental learning with people who are profoundly retarded.
It has been suggested that such training successes '. . . have often
involved limited behaviour in restricted settings, observed for short
durations of time with little follow-up or information on the durability
of behaviour' (Ellis, Deacon, Harris, Poor, Angers, Diorio, Watkins,
Boyd and Cavalier 1982 p. 187). These authors raise questions regarding learning, memory and the transfer of learning in individuals who
are retarded, including groups they describe as 'high profound' (CA 26.1
years and IQ 12.1) and 'low profound' (CA 26.9 and IQ 8.0). None,
however, had gross visual or auditory impairment. The task employed
involved learning and relearning three successive discrimination tasks
in which a choice between one of two stimuli was reinforced. Thus
transfer of learning from one task to the next could be assessed as could
memory for the correct response a month later. All the high profound
group learnt all three tasks as did half of the low profound group. When
the task had to be relearnt, the low profound group performed more
poorly than the high profound group. In neither of these groups was there
much evidence of transfer from one task to another, a failure also noted
in the severely retarded group studied.

In discrimination studies of this sort, two phases of learning can be
distinguished. In the first the person learns to make the actual instrumental
response required but does so at chance level picking the reinforced
stimulus as often as the one which is unreinforced. A second response
is then made in which the person attends to the difference between the
stimuli that indicates which is reinforced and which is not. For example,
if colour is the relevant difference then the person attends to this dimension, noticing that one stimulus is red (and reinforced) and the other green
(and not reinforced). In comparison with more able groups, the low profound group took longer to make this 'attending response'. Also, they
tended to forget the correct response to a greater extent than the other
groups even after only one hour. In addition, special teaching procedures
were often required with both profoundly retarded groups.

The authors comment that we cannot conclude on the basis of these
data that there are 'untrainable' individuals among those with extreme
neurological impairment. There may have been teaching techniques that
were not employed that may have led to mastery of the problem. This
consideration begins to move us towards the issue underlying Ellis *et
al.*'s study, i.e. the relation between laboratory learning of the kind we
have discussed and adaptive learning and behaviour in the wider environment.

Reinforcement and Profound Retardation

In defining instrumental learning we noted that an event that is reinforcing is regarded as such because of its effect on behaviour. Thus, we can never say in advance that for a particular person a given kind of event will definitely be reinforcing. We have, however, seen that some kinds of events are likely to be reinforcers for people who are profoundly retarded and multiply impaired. These have included edible reinforcers as in Fuller's study and sensory reinforcers both visual and auditory in Rice's work. A sampling of possible reinforcers for an individual will frequently yield one or more that can be employed to change behaviour. For example, Murphy (1982) reports on an unpublished study by Campbell (1980) in which varying coloured lights, strobe lights, kaleidoscopic images, auditory stimuli including music, as well as heat and vibration, were employed. Campbell found that for two-thirds of children who were profoundly or severely retarded at least one reinforcing stimulus was found. Many children responded to a specific stimulus, for example, one boy to the kaleidoscope but to no other visual stimuli. Others in contrast responded to the whole range.

There is some evidence that the effectiveness of sensory reinforcers is related to the developmental level of the person. Thus, as an infant matures so there is a shift in the modalities through which reinforcement is most likely to be effective. Such a view is based on Schachtel's (1959) suggestion that there is a hierarchy of sensory development that follows a proximal to distal sequence, i.e. from touch and proprioceptive senses through to the distance senses of sight and hearing. Byrne and Stevens (1980) cite an unpublished study by Murphy (1978) in which this view is illustrated through an example of what occurs in infant clinical and neurological testing. It was suggested:

> . . . that auditory response is minimal in the testing of neonates or
> very young infants who are hungry, cold or otherwise distressed,
> because the olfactory (smell) and tactile (touch) dominance of the
> 'normal' newborn may prevent response to visual or auditory inputs
> unless these are so intense as to cause startle or discomfort. (Byrne
> and Stevens 1980 p. 86)

This view is quite consistent with that in Chapter 4 on visual impairment where we discussed Prescott's (1976) account of the primacy of somatosensory development in normal and abnormal functioning.

Evidence for such a view has come from studies on individuals who

Table 9.1: Reinforcement Survey Hierarchy for Severely and Profoundly Mentally Retarded Individuals

Name	Relationship	Intelligence Test Data		
Age	Date of Birth	Name	IQ	MA
Rater	Date Completed	Name of Test		

Please rate each item in regards to how much pleasure you feel the individual being rated receives using the below listed point scale.

1-none 2-some 3-a fair amount 4-much 5-very much N.O.-no opportunity

I. Eating of
    1. potato chips
    2. fruit
    3. dry, sweet cereal
    4. sweet candy
    5. M & M's
    6. cookies
    7. pudding
    8. ice cream
    9. raisins
    10. applesauce
    11. cake
    12. lollipops
    13. pickles
    14. pretzels
    15. chewing gum
    16. popsicles
    17. olives
    18. buttered bread
    19. graham crackers
    20. pastries

II. Drinking of
    21. juice
    22. kool-aid
    23. white milk
    24. chocolate milk
    25. sucking ice
    26. lemonade
    27. coffee
    28. sweet carbonated water
    29. soft drink

III. Listening to
    30. radio
        1. rock 'n roll
        2. country western
        3. show tunes
    31. TV
    32. sing-along
    33. story telling
    34. tape of own voice

    35. music box
    36. tape of student made noise
    37. musical mobile
    38. records
        1. Sesame Street
        2. Movement Records
    39. rhythm instruments
    40. musical instruments
    41. nursery rhymes
    42. noise-maker
    43. bells
    44. clocks or watches

IV. Looking at
    45. view master
    46. catalogs
    47. flashing lights
    48. kaleidoscope
    49. colored cellophane
    50. show n'tell
    51. lights
    52. magazines
    53. looking out window
    54. bright colors
    55. mobiles
    56. shining objects
    57. flashlights
    58. faces
    59. films
        1. cartoon
        2. nature scenes
        3. animal
        4. home movies of children in class
    60. TV
    61. picture book
    62. mirror
    63. picture of self
    64. shadow box

240 *Development and Learning*

Table 9.1 continued

V. Playing with/on/in
65. moon-walk
66. piano
67. puzzles
68. clay/putty
69. water (soap suds)
70. sand box
71. dress-up clothes
72. scotch tape
73. drum
74. wearing jewelry
75. rocking horse
76. flashlights
77. finger puppets
78. stacking towers
79. rhythm instruments
80. water bed
81. swinging in net
82. toys
  1. pop-up
  2. stuffed animals
  3. blocks
  4. rattles
  5. beads, necklaces
  6. slinky
  7. musical
  8. push-up toys
  9. rings and pole
  10. dolls
  11. cars
83. straws
84. balloons
85. crayon and paper

VI. Academic Activities
86. coloring book
87. pasting pictures in scrapbook
88. watering classroom plants
89. running errands
90. taking pictures with camera
91. drawing on blackboard
92. painting with brush
93. drawing
94. scribbling
95. marking attendance on blackboard
96. teacher's helper (holding things)

97. finger painting

VII. Home Living Chore Activities
98. pushing mop across floor
99. sweeping with broom
100. running vacuum cleaner
101. watering plants
102. rearranging furniture
103. dusting with mop
104. dusting with cloth
105. feeding fish
106. wheeling a food cart
107. clearing off carts
108. wiping tables

VIII. Touching/Feeling of
109. pat on back
110. holding hands
111. wet sponges
112. texture boxes
113. clay
114. colored water
115. pet animals
116. wet paint
117. cooking dough
118. fur squares
119. moisture cream
120. Astro turf rug
121. patty cake
122. felt objects
123. squeeze soft toy
124. string
125. towels
126. sheets
127. vibrating objects
128. brushes
129. carpets
130. stroking by person

IX Social
131. verbal praise
132. physical contact
133. medals, ribbons, plaque
134. first in line
135. hug
136. applause
137. being carried piggy-back
138. rough housing
139. tickling
140. hide n' seek

Table 9.1 continued

141. kiss	150. soap
142. sit on lap	151. after shave
143. being held	
144. smiling	XI. High Frequency Behaviors
145. shaking hands	152. rocking in chair
146. pat on back or head	153. crinkling paper
147. laughing	154. flicking lights
	155. mouthing objects
X. Smelling of	156. hand clapping
148. perfume	
149. hand lotion	

Source: Rotatori *et al.* (1979).

are profoundly retarded and has consequences for intervention with them. Ohwaki, Brahlek and Stayton (1973) compared the effectiveness of vibratory and visual stimulation in children with retardation of CA 5–12 years and MA 15–47 months with IQs ranging from 15 to 65. The lowest MA group (16.9 months and IQ 19.1) was found to have a significant preference for vibration over visual stimulation relative to higher-ability non-profoundly retarded groups. In a second study Ohwaki and Stayton (1976) considered Schachtel's theory directly. As described above, this involves a shift from proximal to distal receptors, or in Schachtel's terms, from autocentric to allocentric. Ohwaki and Stayton define the autocentric mode as subject-centred and with a close relation between sensory quality and feelings of pleasure or displeasure. Thus the child is not interested in what is out there producing the felt effect, only in the effect itself. All the children in the study were ambulatory and without marked sensory deficits, though the description given indicates some must have been profoundly retarded. Again, as in the earlier study, MA was positively correlated with preference for visual over vibratory stimulation.

In both of these studies preference for the different types of stimulation was considered rather than the relative reinforcing potential of them. Byrne and Stevens (1980) considered the validity of the sensory hierarchy explanation in a group of children who were sensorily impaired and retarded using a lever pressing response. The potential reinforcers were white noise, vibration to the hand, light, auditory, social reinforcement, and no outcome of the response. Their study confirmed the

242   *Development and Learning*

hypothesis. With increasing adaptive behaviour the children's relative preference for visual or vibratory stimulation was found. The authors point to the value of the sensory hierarchy theory in informing choice of reinforcers to optimise teaching efficiency. While such a view is useful in considering our approach to a given child, it raises the question of how we go about determining possible reinforcers for specific children. While this question takes us directly to the issue of intervention and teaching, we will deal with it in this wider account of learning in people who are profoundly retarded because it underpins so much of the material in the second volume.

A match between an individual's own motivation and appropriate reinforcers is clearly central to behavioural intervention. Rotatori, Fox and Switzky (1979) list 156 possible reinforcers, basing their choice on interviews with teachers, examination of programme information and published studies. Eleven categories are listed: 1. Edible; 2. Drinkable; 3. Auditory; 4. Visual; 5. Manipulative; 6. Academic; 7. Home living chore activities; 8. Tactile; 9. Social; 10. Olfactory; 11. High frequency behaviours. From Table 9.1 it will be clear what these consist of. The survey is administered individually to a teacher or other professional, the respondent rating the reinforcing value of each item on a five-point scale. On the basis of the hierarchy produced, direct sampling of potential reinforcers can be attempted. For example, with a person who is profoundly retarded five or six reinforcers would be presented, e.g.:

hand warmer, vibrator, picture puzzle, which are present in the classroom. The child would be allowed to select and sample the potential reinforcers while the teacher recorded the order of the selection. Repeated testing would be carried out and a rank order of preferences etablished. Systematic observation of behavior consequented by these reinforcers would provide a continual measure of their effectiveness. (p. 1309)

A simpler schedule appears in Kiernan and Jones (1982 p. 63), again eliciting information on preferences for potential reinforcers. It is, however, Rotatori *et al.*'s (1979) last observation that is the key to effective programming. It is only when one of these events is actually shown to increase and maintain behaviour that we can consider it a reinforcer.

Development and Learning

The account of development during infancy and childhood proposed by

Piaget and other cognitive theorists is usually seen as incompatible with views based on the principles of associative learning. The former see such learning as being too narrow a concept to account for the important changes in cognition that we have described earlier, and consider concepts such as 'reinforcement' as having limited value in explaining cognitive change. Similarly, learning theorists argue that it is unnecessary to resort to internal mechanisms such as 'accommodation' and 'assimilation' to explain such a change, and that the kind of learning that accounts for behavioural change in adults is equally applicable to change in infancy and childhood.

There can be no doubt that, as stated, this divergence of views is a real one, and given the general approach of this book, i.e. both developmentally and learning theory based, we must comment a little further on the implications for intervention. One response to the disagreement has been to see developmental theory as the source of content for the application of learning-based techniques. This view was presented some years ago by Bricker (1970) in an important paper with the title 'Identifying and Modifying Behavioral Deficits'. In this he wrote:

> In the existing behavior modification literature, any behavior, such as a word, a walking response, spitting, smiling, hitting, reading, or imitating a speech sound is equivalent as a measurable and manipulable response. The benefits of this viewpoint are numerous in that all behavior is considered potentially operant in structure and therefore subject to direct manipulation. However, the assumption that responses are equally modifiable leads the behavior modifier away from sources of information that may facilitate the development of useful programs of instruction, namely, that body of information contained in the more cognitive approaches to language and thought. The potential benefit of cognitive theory is in providing a more adequate definition of terminal behavior in the form of flexible (rule-like) repertoires and the specific content of learning that will lead to that terminal state. (p. 17)

The work of Bricker and his colleagues did indeed point the way to many of the programmes described in the second part of this book, programmes based on the proposition that the content of developmental observation could be taught through the operations of associative learning.

The feasibility of this approach is partly demonstrated by designing and implementing successful programmes within such a framework. However, it is now possible to go beyond the strategy of linking developmental content and learning operations and to point to a number of common elements between these conflicting accounts of child development. We can approach the problem by considering the relation between Piaget's two functional invariants, adaptation and organisation, and certain aspects of associative learning.

Adaptation. At the heart of both Piagetian and associative learning accounts of behavioural development is the concept of adaptation. In Piagetian theory this is one of the functional invariants that lead to the development of increasingly complex mental structures that permit successful interaction by an individual with the environment. Of this Piaget writes: 'There is adaptation when the organism is transformed by the environment and when this variation results in an increase in the interchanges between the environment and itself which are favourable to its preservation' (Piaget 1953 p. 5). Skinner (1938), too, emphasised the central importance of adaptation, seeing instrumental learning as the main event permitting such adaptation, while underestimating the role of respondent learning.

With respect to the basis of development in early infancy, Piaget and learning theorists both accept the existence of innate reflexes and Piaget also refers explicitly to early respondent learning: '. . . reflex processes are progressively integrated into cortical activity. The new adaptations constitute what are ordinarily called "acquired associations", habits or even conditioned reflexes, to say nothing of intentional movements' (Piaget 1953 p. 47). In his subsequent account of the development of sucking behaviour, Piaget effectively describes the development of instrumental behaviour from respondent learning in a way that directly parallels the example given above. While Piaget goes beyond such an account in invoking the various familiar mental mechanisms, the adaptive outcome is again increased efficiency of interaction with the environment.

Organisation. The process of mental organisation which Piaget attempts to account for leads to generalised adaptive behaviour that goes beyond simple associations between stimuli and responses. It is just such associations that developmental theorists attack as inadequate explanations of development and hence a reason for relegating the contribution of associative learning to child development. Yet recent advances in the study of associative learning have also rejected simple S-R connections as being of use in accounting for all learning. Reviewing these advances, Mackintosh (1983) suggests an alternative to classical reflex theory as being based on S-R connections in the following way: 'Conditioning can be regarded not as the acquisition of new reflexes, but rather as the acquisition of new knowledge about the world' (p. 11), i.e. learning about events in the environment, their probabilities and their relation to behaviour. 'The suggestion, then, is that as a result of conditioning, animals acquire knowledge about events occurring in their environment. The function of conditioning, it has been suggested, is precisely to enable animals to discover the causal structure of the world' (p. 11). In other words, Mackintosh is concerned with the organisation of cognition, Piaget's second invariant function. Both would also agree that behaviour is only an imperfect indication of such knowledge, and care must be taken in exploring behaviour if we are to make inferences about what has been learnt.

It is not suggested that these various parallel quotations, nor the reinterpretation of Piaget's observations in learning principle terms, resolves very real disagreements in a final way. However, it does appear that a closer relation exists between developmental content and learning than Bricker's view suggested. In practical terms, however, his analysis still provides a way forward while we wait upon a more unified account of the nature of development in which cognition and learning are more closely related. One important reason for this is that whatever discrepancies exist in theory, both the Piagetian and learning-based positions emphasise the interaction of an infant or young child with the environment. Child and environment modify each other in turn in a continual active exchange. From this interchange Piaget's functional invariants emerge and from deficits in the interchange Bijou accounts for functional failures in development leading to retardation. It is to amelioration of such failures that we turn in Volume 2, drawing upon developmental *and* learning theory, and where relevant, approaches from various therapies directed to the range of specific impairments that often accompany profound retardation.

References

Bailey, J. and Meyerson, L. (1969) 'Vibration as a Reinforcer with a Profoundly Retarded Child', *Journal of Applied Behavior Analysis, 2*, 135–7
Bijou, S.W. (1966) 'A Functional Analysis of Retarded Development' in N.R. Ellis (ed.), *International Review of Research in Mental Retardation: Vol. 3*, Academic Press, London
Bijou, S.W. (1976) *Child Development: The Basic Stage of Early Childhood*, Prentice-Hall, Englewood Cliffs, N.J.

Bijou, S.W. and Baer, D.M. (1966) 'Operant Procedures and Child Behavior and Development' in W.K. Honig (ed.), *Operant Behavior: Areas of Research and Application*, Appleton-Century-Crofts, New York

Bricker, W.A. (1970) 'Identifying and Modifying Behavioral Deficits', *American Journal of Mental Deficiency, 75,* 16–21

Brownfield, E.D. and Keehn, J.D. (1966) 'Operant Eyelid Conditioning in Trisomy-18', *Journal of Abnormal Psychology, 71,* 413–15

Byrne, D. and Stevens, C. (1980) 'Mentally Handicapped Children's Responses to Vibrotactile and other Stimuli as Evidence for the Existence of a Sensory Hierarchy', *Apex: Journal of the British Institute for Mental Handicap, 8,* 96–8

Campbell, J.H. (1980) personal communication reported in Murphy (1982)

Cyrulik-Jacobs, A., Shapira, Y. and Jones, M. (1975) 'Automatic Operant Response Procedure (Play Test) for the Study of Auditory Perception of Neurologically Impaired Infants', *Developmental Medicine and Child Neurology, 17,* 186–97

Ellis, N.R., Deacon, J.R., Harris, L.A., Poor, A., Angers, D., Dioro, M.S., Watkins, R.S., Boyd, B.D. and Cavalier, A.R. (1982) 'Learning, Memory, and Transfer in Profoundly, Severely, and Moderately Mentally Retarded Persons', *American Journal of Mental Deficiency, 87,* 186–96

Franks, C.M. (1964) 'Individual Differences in Conditioning and Associated Techniques' in J. Wolpe, A. Slater and L.J. Reyna (eds.), *The Conditioning Therapies: The Challenge in Psychotherapy*, Holt, Rinehart and Winston, London

Friedlander, B.Z. (1968) 'The Effect of Speaker Identity, Voice, Inflection, Vocabulary and Message Redundancy on Infants' Selection of Vocal Reinforcement', *Journal of Experimental Child Psychology, 6,* 443

Friedlander, B.Z., McCarthy, J.J. and Soforenko, A.Z. (1967) 'Automated Psychological Evaluation with Severely Retarded Institutionalized Infants', *American Journal of Mental Deficiency, 71,* 909–19

Friedlander, B.Z. and Cyrulik-Jacobs, A. (1970) 'Automated Home Measurement of Infants' Preferential Discrimination of Loudness Level', paper presented at annual meeting of the American Speech and Hearing Association, New York

Friedlander, B.Z., Wetstone, H.S. and McPeek, D.L. (1974) 'Systematic Assessment of Selective Language Listening Deficit in Emotionally Disturbed Pre-School Children', *Journal of Child Psychology and Psychiatry, 15,* 1–12

Fuller, P.R. (1949) 'Operant Conditioning of a Vegetative Human Organism', *American Journal of Psychology, 62,* 587–90

Glenn, S.M. and Cunningham, C.C. (1984) 'Selective Auditory Preferences and the Use of Automated Equipment by Severely, Profoundly and Multiply Handicapped Children', *Journal of Mental Deficiency Research, 28,* 281–96

Hardwick, C. and Lobb, H. (1982) 'Eyelid Conditioning and Intellectual Level: Effects of Contextual Change on Extinction', *American Journal of Mental Deficiency, 87,* 325–31

Haskett, J. and Hollar, W.D. (1978) 'Sensory Reinforcement and Contingency Awareness of Profoundly Retarded Children', *American Journal of Mental Deficiency, 83,* 60–8

Hill, J. (1980) 'Use of an Automated Recreational Device to Facilitate Independent Leisure and Motor Behavior in a Profoundly Retarded Male' in P. Weyman and J. Hills (eds.), *Instructional Programming for Severely Handicapped*

Youth, Virginia Commonwealth University, Richmond, Va.

Hogg, J. (1976) 'The Experimental Analysis of Retarded Behaviour and its Relation to Normal Development' in M.P. Feldman and A. Broadhurst (eds.), *Theoretical and Experimental Bases of the Behaviour Therapies*, Wiley, London

Hogg, J. (1983) 'Sensory and Social Reinforcement of Head-Turning in a Profoundly Retarded Multiply Handicapped Child', *British Journal of Clinical Psychology*, 22, 33–40

Hogg, J., Remington, R.E. and Foxen, T.H. (1979) 'Classical Conditioning of Profoundly Retarded, Multiply Handicapped Children', *Developmental Medicine and Child Neurology*, 21, 779–86

Iwata, B.A., Dorsey, M.F., Slifer, K.J., Bauman, K.E. and Richman, G.S. (1982) 'Towards a Functional Analysis of Self-Injury', *Analysis and Intervention in Developmental Disabilities*, 2, 3–20

Kiernan, C. and Jones, M.C. (1982) *Behaviour Assessment Battery*, 2nd edn, NFER-Nelson, Windsor

Lovett, S. (1986) 'An Experiment to Investigate Discrimination Learning in Multiply Handicapped Children Using an Electromechanical Chair' in P. Sturmey, J. Hogg and A. Crisp (eds.), 'Organizing Environments for People with Mental Handicap', submitted for publication

Mackintosh, N.J. (1983) *Conditioning and Associative Learning*, Clarendon Press, Oxford

Murphy, K.P. (1978) 'The Early Development of Auditory Function', unpublished, Proceedings of the American Speech and Hearing Association, Autumn, San Francisco

Murphy, G. (1982) 'Sensory Reinforcement in Autistic and Mentally Handicapped Children: A Review', *Journal of Autism and Developmental Disorders*, 12, 265–78

Ohwaki, S., Brahlek, J.A. and Stayton, S.E. (1973) 'Preference for Vibratory and Visual Stimulation in Mentally Retarded Children', *American Journal of Mental Deficiency*, 77, 733–7

Ohwaki, S. and Stayton, S.E. (1976) 'Preference by the Retarded for Vibratory and Visual Stimulation as a Function of Mental Age and Psychotic Reaction', *Journal of Abnormal Psychology*, 85, 516–22

Piaget J. (1953) *The Origin of Intelligence in the Child*, Routledge and Kegan Paul, London

Piper, T.J. and MacKinnon, R.C. (1969) 'Operant Conditioning of a Profoundly Retarded Individual Reinforced through a Stomach Fistula', *American Journal of Mental Deficiency*, 73, 627–30

Prescott, J.W. (1976) 'Somatosensory Deprivation and its Relationship to the Blind' in Z.S. Jastrzembska (ed.), *The Effects of Blindness and Other Impairments on Early Development*, American Foundation for the Blind, New York

Remington, R.E., Foxen, R. and Hogg, J. (1977) 'Auditory Reinforcement in Profoundly Retarded, Multiply Handicapped Children', *American Journal of Mental Deficiency*, 82, 299–304

Rice, H.K. (1968) 'Operant Behavior in Vegetative Patients III: Methodological Considerations', *Psychological Record*, 18, 297–302

Rice, H.K. and McDaniel, M.W. (1966) 'Operant Behavior in Vegetative

Patients', *Psychological Record, 16,* 279–81

Rice, H.K., McDaniel, M.W., Stallings, V.D. and Gatz, M.J. (1967) 'Operant Behavior in Vegetative Patients II', *Psychological Record, 17,* 449–60

Rotatori, A.F., Fox, B. and Switzky, H. (1979) 'An Indirect Technique for Establishing Preferences for Categories of Reinforcement for Severely and Profoundly Retarded Individuals', *Perceptual and Motor Skills, 48,* 1307–13

Schachtel, E.G. (1959) *Metamorphosis,* Basic Books, New York

Siqueland, E.R. (1970) 'Basic Learning Processes: I, Classical Conditioning' in H.R. Reese and L.P. Lipsitt (eds.), *Experimental Child Psychology,* Academic Press, London

Skinner, B.F. (1983) *The Behavior of Organisms,* Appleton-Century-Crofts, New York

Woodward, M.W. (1979) 'Piaget's Theory and the Study of Mental Retardation' in N.R. Ellis (ed.), *Handbook of Mental Deficiency, Psychological Theory and Research,* 2nd edn, Lawrence Erlbaum, Hillsdale, N.J.

AUTHOR INDEX

Numbers in italics indicate pages where a full reference is given

254   *Author Index*

Whitaker, H.A. *124*
White, B.L. 68, 69, *87*
Whitmore, K. 121, *126*
Whittacker, C.A. 198, 199, *222*
Wilbur, R. 118, *125*
Wilcox, B. 181, *183*
Wilkins, L.E. 208, *222*
Williams, C. 11, 12, 18
Wills, D.M. 99, *110*
Wing, L. 177, *185*, 199, *222*
Wisniewsky, H.M. *18*
Wohlhueter, M.J. 196, 197, 215, *222*
Wohlwill, J.J. 40, 41, *87*
Wold, D. 10, *18*
Wolf, B. 208, *222*
Woll, B. *85, 125*
Wolpe, J. *246*
Woodford, E.P. *86*

Woods, G.E. 11, *19*
Woodward, W.M. 70, 71, *87,* 150, 162, 163, 165, 166, 167, *185,* 188, 189, 190, 201, 202, 204, 205, 208, 209, 210, 215, 216, *222,* 232, *248*

Yarrow, L.J. 144, *147*
Yeates, S.R. 177, *185*, 199, *222*
Yoder, D. 60, 61, 63, *86*
York, R. 3, *19*
Yule, W. 3, *17,* 148, 165, *183*

Zdzienicka, E. 7, *19*
Zeaman, D. 194, *220*
Zigler, E. 22, 27, 187, 188, 190, *222*
Zinkin, P. 88, *109*
Zubek, J.P. 144, *147*

SUBJECT INDEX

258 *Subject Index*